ONCE A SOLDIER, TWICE A CITIZEN

Escape From France 1940 and Life After Wartime

by

Colonel Leslie W. Wright
O.St.J., T.D., D.L., M.A.

Editor's note

In 2015, the French authorities commemorated the fall of Calais in 1940. This was unlike previous ceremonies in one crucial respect. For when the moment came at which survivors of the battle lay their own wreaths in tribute at the memorial, only one stepped forward. That man was Col. Leslie Wright, literally the last man to escape from Calais – and almost certainly the last still able to tell the tale.

He wrote this book, tracing his life in war and peace, as the new millennium dawned. In his early eighties at the time, it is hard not to be impressed by his factual recall and grip on detail. This account does not cover the intervening decade, but Leslie remains as sharp and active as ever today, a mere 95 years old.

In consultation with the author, the original manuscript has been edited. Any amendments have been carried out with the express intention of preserving the authentic voice of a unique witness to momentous times.

Author's note

Almighty God has been very good to me. To Him I am most grateful
for the rock from which I was hewn; for my beloved wife, Kath,
without whom I could have done very little; for my beloved daughter
Christina and her husband George; for the Howard family, for Colonel
Gerry Underwood, Colonel Richard Grimwood-Taylor, Colonel
Richard Pickford, Major General Christopher Man and Donald
Storrs-Fox; for so many friends in and out of the Armed Services; and
for the Royal Corps of Signals, the University of Sheffield Officer
Training Corps, the Worcestershire and Sherwood Foresters Regiment
and the Royal Green Jackets.

To all these I dedicate this chronicle of my life.

First published in Great Britain in 2015 by RMC Books
RMC Books – www.rmcbooks.co.uk
6 Broadfield Court, Sheffield, S8 0XF
Tel: 0114 250 6300

Editors: John Hawthorne, Adam Kay and Martin Edwards
Design: Richard Abbey and Dan Wray

Printed and bound in Great Britain by CPI Colour Ltd.

A CIP catalogue record for this book is available from the British Library.

ISBN: 978-1-907998-21-8

Contents

In a broadcast in 1951, the Chief of the Imperial General Staff, the late Field Marshal Viscount Slim of Burma, appealed for more people to join the Territorial Army. He described every Territorial Soldier as being "twice a citizen" in doing two jobs – and how right he was!

Chapter I

My Early Life

When Robert Louis Stevenson returned to the Island of Samoa, he became very friendly with the governor and his family. One of the governor's daughters was born on Christmas Day, and Stevenson, feeling that she might receive only one present a year rather than two, bequeathed his own birthday to her. Many, many years ago, I heard the very old lady concerned recount this story and she announced that she, in turn, had bequeathed Stevenson's birthday to another Christmas Day birthday child. Long may this custom continue.

I was born precisely halfway between Christmas Days on 26th June 1920 at 19 Norfolk Street in the town of Glossop in Derbyshire, at the meeting point of Derbyshire, Cheshire, Lancashire and the old West Riding. Old Glossop, where I spent most of my youth, is a charming part of the town, set in the spectacular scenery of the Peak District, and the seat of Baron Howard of Glossop, whose descendant is the present Duke of Norfolk of the Fitzalan-Howards. I was the third of four sons: the others were Kenneth, George and Colin.

My father, Leonard, like so many of his tragic generation, joined the Officer Training Corps of Owen's College, the Victoria University of Manchester, and was commissioned into the King's Own Yorkshire Light Infantry. He came of good Lancashire stock, the Wrights and Atkinsons of Southport.

My mother, Gertrude, was the seventh child of William and Elizabeth Wain of Glossop. Her mother could just remember the last cow being slaughtered on their Galway farm, before emigrating to England in 1854, in the aftermath of the Irish Potato Famine. Elizabeth Wain came of a highly respectable family of Galway, of which she was very conscious, and was generally referred to as "Lady Galway".

Of my paternal grandparents who lived at Woolley Bridge, near Glossop, I was very fond. As did so many parents of that time, they put most of their resources into the education of their son, Leonard, rather than their splendid daughters, Muriel and Irene.

| The author, around 17 years old | The author's father in uniform |

Following his being commissioned my father went with the 8th Battalion of the K.O.Y.L.I. to France to the bloodbath of the Western Front. He suffered wounds and severe gassing. My eldest brother Kenneth had been born on 16th February 1916; my father, on the eve of the dreadful Battle of the Somme, wrote a letter to his baby son to be read by him in due season, should my father not recover. The Battle of the Somme was a dreadful battle of attrition. The object of the offensive was to take the pressure off the French in the Verdun sector, and to make a break through the German lines through which the British 5th Army Corps would deluge to end the stalemate. For seven days before the onslaught on 1st July, the German lines had been bombarded every moment of the day, with the intention of killing the German defenders.

On 1st October 1916, my father, now acting Company-Commander after showing great initiative recorded in the history of the 20th Division, was severely wounded; seven machine gun bullets went through his neck. He and his batman, Pte William Hall of the King's Own Scottish Borderers, fought from a shell hole. I quote from a letter of my father to the mother of his batman, who was awarded the Military Medal for saving my father's life.

The author's father, Leonard Wright | The author's mother, Gertrude Wain

"On 1st October our battalion made an advance in the afternoon. Our job was to take a second-line German trench. The shelling was frightful and one Krupp buried us. When we got going they riddled my neck with machine gun fire."

"Your son was hit in the back with shrapnel and was suffering from shell shock. We were both lying wounded in a shell hole when we were told the Germans were outflanking us."

"Your son got to the edge of shell hole and pulled me up. We fired at point blank range. Your son got seven and I got two. I was finished then and Private Hall carried me on his back through the German barrage of fire to our own lines whilst himself wounded. He is a hero and you will be proud of your son."

"Personally I am his lifelong debtor and probably owe my life to him. Please excuse this scrawl as I have to write this laying on my back."

My father was no longer fit for active service and was eventually invalided out of the services, only to catch the dreadful Spanish 'Flu of 1917-18 which killed more people than all the bombs, shells and bullets of that dreadful Great War.

My elder brother, George, was born on 10th July 1917 and my younger brother, Colin, of great intellectual ability, on 22nd November 1922.

Things were not easy for the ex-servicemen, following the end of the War on 11th November 1918, and this would have been worse had not Field Marshal Earl Haig founded the British Legion in 1920. It was, too, very hard for the ex-servicemen to settle down following the horrors and the great comradeship they had experienced, and many took refuge in drink, as they do after most wars.

My father returned to his occupation as a Sanitary Engineer and Draughtsman in Manchester, and about 1924 we moved to Romiley in Cheshire. I clearly remember being in my pram, being pushed up with pride, by my father, and visiting him in his office in Manchester. But more clearly do I remember the day of his death, 22nd May 1925, five days after his 31st birthday. The cause of his death was stated as pneumonia. There was no reference to his being severely gassed, nor to his wounds which certainly aggravated the condition that caused his death. The consequence was that my brave mother received no war-widow's pension, which would then have been £4 per week, plus £2 for the four children, £6 in all, what was then a considerable amount. Neither did she receive the ordinary Widow's pension, because my father, being a non-manual worker, was not insured. Despite efforts by the Officers' Association, the British Legion and her Member of Parliament, my mother received nothing. She had inherited a mortgaged house, and several unpaid-up shares in a textile company that went into liquidation the year after my father's death. How she brought us up until her untimely death from cancer on 21st December 1938, 21 days after her 46th birthday, I know not.

Fortunately my father was a Freemason, and his Lodge, the Lodge of Hadfield, very generously paid for the boarding education of my two elder brothers at Thornleigh College in Bolton, staffed by the Silesian Order. It is to the everlasting credit of the Freemasons that they paid for a Catholic education of my brothers. My own education started in the Romiley Council School where my acute short-sightedness was discovered. It was staffed by a great headmaster, Mr Heathcote, and fine teachers, two of whom I maintained contact with until the Second World War.

One of my memories following my father's death was falling into the canal at Romiley. It was good to watch the horse-drawn barges and the splendid bargees. I had been 'fishing' in the canal and in the process of pulling moss from the side of the towpath, I fell into the canal. I can still experience the blackness of the water, rising to the surface, sinking again and after breathing in the canal water, resurfacing to be grabbed by my six-year old brother George, who was leaning over the towpath with his arms outstretched. To him I owe my life. We ran home and I had a bath. What treatment I would have received in these more enlightened days! I remember, too, the General Strike of 1926; there were soldiers in Romiley.

In 1928 we moved to Sycamore Cottage in Old Glossop, adjacent to the entrance to Manor Park, formerly the grounds of Glossop Hall, later Kingsmore School. My mother had taken in boarders to eke out a living following my father's death, and this she continued to do in Old Glossop. Sycamore Cottage belonged to the Presentation Nuns, whose convent was only a few yards from the cottage, which had a delightful garden. I recollect so clearly Mother Angela, Sister Dominic and Sister Aloysius, teaching nuns, and Sister Rose who ran the kitchen. Mother Angela was very kind to us. The rent was 15 shillings a week, but there were frequent occasions when my mother could not raise this sum and the nuns were very tolerant of the situation. We had living with us as a boarder at 30 shillings a week, Miss Johnston, a strong Loyalist, from Lurgan, N. Ireland, who worked in the Glossop Labour Exchange. That was my mother's sole source of income. I remember her having to attend court because she could not pay the rates, and the gas being cut-off for non-payment of the bills. These were hard times for the widow and the orphans, and especially for those, to the nation's shame, who received no compensation nor indeed solace. The winters were hard and cold, and I vividly remember a large tree falling, during a dreadful gale, on Christmas Eve 1933, on Sycamore Cottage and bursting in the front door.

We were part of the Parish of All Saints Catholic Church, Old Glossop. The parish priest was the Reverend Father J. Ketels, a Belgian, who had been Personal Chaplain to King Albert of the Belgians during the Great War, and was decorated with the Croix-de-Guerre. In every way he was a splendid pastor and was most highly regarded throughout the town of Glossop. I recollect his marching in his military uniform in the town procession commemorating the centenary of the Catholic Emancipation Act of 1829. He was stricken with cancer and died whilst on leave in his native city of Antwerp in 1937. The town felt as though the world had come to its end, so highly was he esteemed!

From All Saints' School, Old Glossop, where I had been well taught by the nuns, I won a scholarship to Glossop Grammar School, where I continued my education from September 1931. Of this school I cannot speak too highly. It had a splendid headmaster in Mr C.L. Chambers, a perfect gentleman who looked every inch the part. The Senior Master was Mr S. Holt, a brilliant mathematician and disciplinarian. The Senior Mistress was Miss Newton who imbued me with a great love for the Latin language. The French department, consisting of Miss Wanklin, Miss Haxby, and Mr Prellburgh, a White Russian refugee, gave us a good grounding in French. The science department, consisting of Mr Casey, Mr Hodges, and Mr Hall, was very advanced for its time; we were raised on the metric system. Mr Brown was our physical training teacher; Miss Greenwood, a very able geography teacher; Miss Williams, versed in history; and Mr Fairclough supervised our musical studies. All the female teachers were spinsters or widows, because marriage precluded employment. Most of the men had served with distinction in the Great War. They took a keen interest in their pupils. The Headmaster arranged clothes grants for me and my younger brother Colin, who gained a County Major Scholarship in 1933. Following the Second World War, I attended the funerals of Miss Newton and Miss Wanklin, both of whom I held in particular affection.

We were made to work very hard at school and home. I matriculated in 1936 and pressure was brought on my mother to enrol me at the University of Manchester, but this we could not afford. These were the days of the Great Depression. There was high unemployment in the cotton industry on which Glossop so greatly depended, and long 'dole' queues. Any man earning a pound per week was fortunate; two pounds per week approached wealth.

My eldest brother Kenneth, who had matriculated well from Thurnleigh College, had to take on a labourer's job in an engineering works, Jacksons in Old Glossop, to which he returned after several years' war service in the Far East, and rose to the management ranks. My older brother George, on leaving Thurnleigh College, went into the retail trade in Glossop.

There was little of the social security we enjoy today. Times were hard as indeed were the winters of those days. Freezing blizzards were no excuse for not walking to work or school. Dental treatment was very poor. You waited until a tooth ached and then went to the dentist and paid half-a-crown (12½p) to have it pulled out. And it was hard to find the money to pay the doctor's bills. But we had a happy childhood, well looked after by a splendid mother.

The convent sold Sycamore Cottage and in 1937 we moved to a rented house in Jordan Street, Glossop. My mother's health then began to fail and on 21st December 1938, only just 46 years old, she died in Wood's Hospital, Glossop, her funeral being on Christmas Eve. She was a wonderful and brave woman.

By this time I had been working for about 18 months in the city treasurer's department, Manchester. The Treasurer was John E. Bray, his deputy James Lythgoe who was eventually knighted, and another senior officer, Harry Page who was also knighted. High standards were expected and I attended evening classes in accountancy, economics and French at the Manchester Municipal High School of Commerce with a view to going part-time to the University in 1939 to read for the degree of B.Sc.(Econ.). But Herr Adolf Hitler, the Fuehrer of Germany, stopped all that!

Chapter II

The Second World War, 1939-1942

At the conclusion of the Versailles Peace Treaty of 1920, following the end of the first World War in which some 8 million servicemen and some 6 million civilians had been slaughtered and 21 million servicemen maimed, that great and gallant French soldier and Allied Commander Marshal Foch said of the treaty: *"Ce n'est pas la Paix; c'est l'armistice de vingt ans"* – "This is not peace; it is armistice for 20 years".

A clause in the treaty put therein at the instigation of President Woodrow Wilson created the League of Nations in the hope of maintaining world peace. Unfortunately President Wilson lost the 1920 election, the U.S.A. went isolationist, and so the founding father of the League never joined it.

By 1920 the Bolshevik victory in Russia was complete. Germany and Italy later nearly succumbed to communism. From communism there sprang Fascism in Italy under Mussolini and from communism in Germany there sprang Nazism under Hitler.

In 1933 Germany withdrew from the MacDonald Disarmament Conference and from the League of Nations. Japan, too, withdrew from the League following its refusal to recognise Manchukuo after Japan's aggression of Manchuria. We buried our heads in the sand!

In 1935 Italy attacked Abyssinia. In 1936 Germany re-occupied the Rhineland and we and the U.S.A., who were committed to maintain the demilitarisation of the Rhineland, did nothing about it.

In 1938 on 12th March, Hitler, without shedding a drop of blood, annexed the whole of Austria. In September 1938 the UK, France and Italy agreed to Hitler's taking over the whole of the Sudetenland of the new state of Czechoslovakia. On 15th March 1939 Hitler occupied the rest of Czechoslovakia. We introduced conscription for the first time in peace-time, and the Territorial Army was doubled in size.

In August 1939, a non-aggression pact was signed between Germany and USSR, under Stalin, and on Friday 1st September, Hitler invaded Poland from the West. We mobilised, and on Sunday 3rd September declared war against Germany, closely followed by France and every member of the British Empire and Commonwealth.

Marshal Foch had been proved right!

On the preceding 8th May 1939, there was an appeal by the Mayor of Glossop, the redoubtable Alderman 'Dick' Sellors, consisting of the words: "We have got the guns: We have got the money. All we need now is the men!" He got his men. Colonel G.J. (Gerry) Underwood raised in that one night the 2nd (North Midland) Corps of Signals. Two companies were raised in Glossop, and a third in Chesterfield. The second-in-command of the unit was Major Rex Stephenson, the Adjutant Captain Arthur Haslehouse, and amongst the Regimental Officers were Captains 'Shorty' Woods, John Harrison, Robin Turner and Lieutenants Andrew Goodman and Richard Pickford, all of whom achieved fame during the war. The enthusiasm of the recruits was tremendous!

Colonel Underwood had an enormous influence on me. Later I followed exactly in his footsteps and I buried him in 1973 at Shalden near Alton, Hants, in the presence of Major Andrew Goodman, Colonel Richard Pickford, Colonel Robin Turner, Major Stanley Brown, Colonel Richard Grimwood-Taylor, and many more high-ranking officers of the Royal Corps of Signals, together with Gerry's devoted sister, Ilene.

We trained very hard on two nights a week until we went to the annual camp at Skegness in August 1939, during which time the Ribbentrop-Molotov Non-Aggression Pact was signed. I remember so clearly Colonel Underwood addressing the unit to the effect that war was now inevitable. The morale in the unit was tremendously high. We worked and trained hard to become good soldiers and signallers. Most of my contemporaries from Glossop Grammar School were in the unit and I made so many more strong friends from Glossop and Chesterfield.

We had been home only a few days after annual camp when we were mobilised on Friday 1st September 1939. I said farewell to the City Treasurer of Manchester, Mr John E. Bray and many very kind colleagues and made my way home to Glossop, where that night we were all medically examined by Doctor Hadfield in the main square of the town. I vividly remember his putting his stethoscope to my chest and saying "Can you see that barrage balloon?" I replied yes. He said "Obviously you can hear me. You are A1." The examination had taken two minutes!

For the next ten days we put everything we had into our training, and then on Monday 11th September we received orders to collect all our kit to entrain for Bakewell. I said goodbye to my dear grandmother and grandfather Wright, who were very upset by memories of my father, and left that afternoon. We detrained at Bakewell, and with girls from the knitting factory near the station waving at us from the bridge, we marched into Bakewell to Haddon House and Burton Closes Hall, a mansion designed by the famous architect Pugin.

On arrival at Burton Closes Hall, we were issued with a bowl for eating and drinking purposes, and two blankets and a groundsheet for sleeping. In my room there were about 30 of us. We slept sardine-like on the hard floor in our groundsheet and blankets. My room was nicknamed 'The Bounty', owing to the attitude of the newly-promoted Captain-Bligh-like corporal in charge.

On the morning after our arrival, Colonel Underwood addressed the unit: "Gentlemen, we had a lot of trouble from lice in the last war. Although we have only one water source – and I promise you that this will be rectified – I want each one of you, every day, to wash up as far as possible and to wash down as far as possible, but – as the old Irish lady said – whatever you do, do not forget poor old possible!" Within a week, following the help of the Bakewell Urban District Surveyor, Mr Tom Baker, the water shortage had been rectified. We had no greatcoats and no paillasses to fill with straw until November. Both Burton Closes Hall and Haddon House were densely populated by soldiers.

The latrine consisted of white-washed telegraph poles over open trenches some three feet deep where soil and chloride of lime were thrown over the excrement. When gastritis broke out those latrines worked hard, day and night, in all weathers.

Now many reservists joined us, several from Scotland. The officers' mess which had initially been at the Rutland Arms Hotel moved to Stanton Woodhouse on the Duke of Rutland's estate, and every inn in Bakewell, the Parochial Church Hall, the room beneath the Congregational Chapel, now the Catholic Church in Buxton Road, the Co-operative Hall and the rooms over Carrington's Tobacco Shop were all requisitioned.

We were now re-designated 4 Corps Signals, i.e. the Signal Regiment to the 4th Army Corps under command of General Sir Claude Auchinleck. The overcrowding in Burton Closes Hall and Haddon House resulted in an outbreak of spinal meningitis and a very serious influenza epidemic. The Co-operative Hall in King's School became a hospital manned by V.A.Ds. In particular I remember the late Miss Catherine Cockerton, who nursed so many of us. I fell victim myself and was moved into the Co-operative Hall and from there to the Union, now

Newholme Hospital. Everything is a matter of degree, and to have a bed in the Union – or Workhouse – was paradise compared with the conditions at Burton Closes Hall and Haddon House. I hasten to add that none of this was the result of poor command. We had a splendid commanding officer and very good regimental officers. It was the result of trying to achieve defence on the cheap, as we are still doing to the nation's shame.

Then in January 1940, the district became snowbound and there were 40 degrees of frost on the Fahrenheit scale. We were given the task of digging out the high villages. I vividly remember freeing the access to the Bull-i-th'thorn Inn: the reward to many thirsty soldiers was nothing. I doubt if the inn had any beer to give us!

Despite these local treats, we worked hard at developing our skills as soldiers and signallers, subject to stern but sensible discipline.

In April 1940, Hitler invaded Norway and Denmark and 4 Corps became the North-Western Expeditionary Force (NWEF) under General Sir Claude Auchinleck. We became NWEF Signals. Vaccinations consisted of being scraped by what appeared to be a rusty pen-knife, and we had our Tetanus and TAB (Typhoid) injections before moving to a tented camp at Minley Manor, near Aldershot.

Here I must pay tribute to the people of Bakewell who were so kind to us. The Reverend Canon Kidson, the Reverend Father Hunter, the Reverend Mr Williams-Boot, Mr J W Raine, headmaster of the Methodist School and Mr Dick Alcock, headmaster of the C. of E. School, were all particularly good to me. The Society of Friends turned their meeting house into a splendid canteen, manned largely by the British Legion. Bloomers, who ran the Bakewell Pudding Shop in Matlock Street, were a great draw to us in the evenings, to eat poached egg on toast followed by hot milk. They were a great family. To me, the Howards who owned the boot and shoe shop in Matlock Street were especially kind.

I met Kathleen Howard, together with her sister Mary, at a W.E.A. class in the Methodist School Rooms. The subject was psychology, taught by Professor Sumner who referred specifically to Francis Thompson's splendid lyric 'The Hound of Heaven' which is the love of God and no matter how you try to evade it, it will catch you up. I fell in love with Kath, a very beautiful and graceful girl, a talented actress, elocutionist and playwright. We were married on 30th August 1941 and lived happily ever after until her death, so bravely borne, on 28th September 1996. However, owing to the exigencies of war, we saw very little of each other until my release from war service in mid-1946. She was a splendid and brave wife and mother, and a great homebuilder, utterly loyal and a source of great succour to all in any form of illness or distress. Not only was she a great actress, with a particular love for Shakespeare and a memorable performance as Lady Macbeth to her credit, but she also wrote a play, 'Thank you, Mr Pepys', which won first prize at the Buxton Festival in 1939, and was produced in the theatre at Chatsworth.

In April of 1940, before leaving Bakewell to proceed to Minley Manor, near Aldershot, I walked through the woods overlooking Bakewell, which had meant and still means so much to me, I was a member of the Advance Party which prepared the camp for the arrival of the main body of the Unit, redesignated N.W.E.F. (North-Western Expeditionary Force) Signals. We were to provide the command signals for General Sir Claude Auchinleck.

However, the force was ill-prepared for this campaign, and Norway and Denmark fell to the Germans within a few weeks. We continued our signals training and at last, our Number 9 wireless sets arrived, but we had little time to train on them before I found myself in action with Number 12 Wireless Section. Fortunately, we had all fired 50 rounds of .303 ammunition.

Here I can do no better than to include my personal account of the fighting at Calais, copies of which are now in the Imperial War Museum, King's College, London and the Universities of Sheffield and Leeds.

The author in the summer of 1940,
soon after his return from Calais

Personal Experiences
May 1940 by Lieutenant-Colonel L.W.Wright, T.D., R Signals (T.A.)
Later Colonel L.W.Wright T.D., D.L.

Calais 1940

In early May 1940, No. 12 Wireless Section was standing with its parent unit N.W.E.F. Signals to move to Norway after the German invasion, during the previous month of April. N.W.E.F. Signals was the redesignated 4 Corps Signals, previously 2nd North Midland Corps Signals, Territorial Army. 4 Corps Signals was thus redesignated because it had been chosen as the major signal unit to join the North Western Expeditionary Force in Norway.

On Monday 20th May 1940, No.12 Wireless section took part in a practice move-off with its parent unit. The section was completely mobilised in all respects, and it therefore came as no great surprise to its members when the section was ordered to stand by, after return to camp from practice move-off. Popular rumour had it that we were to proceed as an advance party to N.W.E.F. It came as a very great surprise to us, when we were eventually briefed that evening, to find that we were leaving our parent unit and proceeding to France as an independent section, moving off from camp at Minley Manor, near Aldershot, very soon after midnight. We hurriedly despatched home our surplus personal kit and bade farewell to our comrades whom we were leaving.

At approximately 0100 hours on Tuesday 21st May 1940, we paraded in full marching order, and having said goodbye to our C.O., Colonel G.J. Underwood, TD, and others of our officers, we moved off in our wireless vans to Dover.

Shortly after sunrise our small convoy arrived at Dover. There had been a slight accident en route between our 3-ton stores lorry and one of our two motorcycles; fortunately nobody was hurt.

We had breakfast in Dover, and afterwards paraded on the quay. Here we were briefed by our O.C., Lieut Evitts. The section had been chosen to effect wireless communications between Dover and the three channel ports, Dunkirk, Calais and Boulogne, guarding against the event of the submarine cable being damaged by the enemy. In technical language, we were to 'superimpose' the trans-channel submarine cable. We were given frequencies and call signs by the O.C. section, Lieut Evitts, and we 'netted' our four wireless sets, there and then on the quay at Dover. Lance Corporal Glew and detachment were detailed to stay at Dover as control set.

The three detachments intended for the channel ports and the H.Q. Section embarked at Dover early in the afternoon. A seaman confided to me that we were Calais-bound. The defence of the ship was partly our responsibility and we were each issued with ammunition.

The troops on board a ship returning from France gave us a tremendous cheer as their ship passed ours at sea. They had some idea of what we were going to; we did not.

We watched England disappear into the distance and beheld France looming over the horizon. There was a deal of sea-sickness amongst us, but nothing of importance occurred until we entered Calais harbour at about 1700 hrs.

As our ship approached the jetty, three aeroplanes appeared out of the clouds and I asked an R.A.F. Sergeant whether they were British or French. Before he had time to answer me, the aeroplanes dropped their bombs! So we had our baptism of bombing, but fortunately the ship was not hit.

Thereafter the vessel was tied up at the jetty, but there were no stevedores to be seen. It seems that they were either frightened or on strike. Just after the personnel of 12 Wireless Section had disembarked, we were again bombed. The captain of the ship would not accept responsibility for his vessel to remain in the harbour subject to the bombing, and so the ship untied and made her way out to sea; on board her were our wireless sets, all our vehicles, all our stores and much of our personal equipment. We were left with our arms, ammunition and small kit, dodging the flying masonry in the bombed 'Gare Maritime'. The 'Gare Martime' from then was subjected to very heavy, almost incessant bombing.

Lieut Evitts arranged sleeping accommodation for us at G.H.Q. in La Clinique up La Rue Leon Gambetta. We eventually marched there, finding our way through the well-nigh deserted streets of Calais.

Here we had our first meal on the continent – bully beef and biscuits served from a discarded German helmet by Lcpl Clarke. That night, as we were, we slept on the stone floor of La Clinique. Throughout the night there was bombing of Calais, and the Fifth Columnists were at work, flashing lights to the German aeroplanes.

WEDNESDAY 22nd May 1940
Early in the morning of Wednesday 22nd May 1940, we left H.Q. at La Clinique and made our way to the docks, but the ship carrying our vehicles and wireless sets had not returned to Calais. Lieut Evitts had arranged accommodation for us at the rest camp in Calais, and we marched there from the docks. In the meantime, since all our transport was still on board the ship, an abandoned civil vehicle, a War Graves

Registration Commission truck, had been requisitioned for the section use, and from what I remember, it indeed proved very useful.

At the rest camp we received news of the very close proximity of the advancing German armoured units. Boulogne was taken that day and R.A.F. airmen who had retired from Boulogne under very exciting conditions, joined us at the rest camp. Here there were three German prisoners, who adopted an arrogant attitude, and a French Fifth Columnist who had, I believe, been shot in the leg by one of our Military Police during the previous night whilst flashing lights to the German aeroplanes. Groaning and looking very sorry for himself, he lay in straw.

One of our section had lost, or had stolen, his rifle, and thereafter we took very particular care of "our best friends", our rifles.

During the Wednesday afternoon, a battalion of Queen Victoria's Rifles (Q.V.R.) and a battalion of tanks arrived from England, but alas, our wireless vehicles were not with them. I well remember a soldier, I believe it was one of our section, being reprimanded by a Major of the Tanks for failing to salute him. This was indicative of the high state of discipline. Great difficulty was experienced in unloading the Q.V.Rs and the tanks, owing to the stevedores not working. The sappers came to the rescue.

As the evening wore on, we began to hear sounds of gunfire from the direction of Boulogne. I wrote a letter to my wife, then my fiancée, unable to tell her where I was or what was happening, owing to censorship regulations. This did not matter, because the letter never reached her. I made my will, as did most of us.

We had a meal of tinned pineapple, rolled ourselves in borrowed blankets, tied our rifles to our bodies, and slept for a few hours.

THURSDAY 23rd May 1940
Very soon after daybreak of the next morning, Thursday 23rd May 1940, we were out of our blankets, and we marched down to the docks. Still our wireless vehicles had not arrived!

The docks and dock area were crowded with thousands of refugees; they were like a swarm of locusts, everywhere. It was a pitiful sight! Men and women, old and young, and children, even babies at their mothers' breasts, families with their entire belongings loaded on hand carts and perambulators, all of them crowded the dock area and hampered the military. And then the German bombers started the day's bombing, and the airmen did not hesitate to machine-gun us from the sky. Many of the refugees must have been casualties.

So difficult did the refugees make the situation that many of us were put on police duty. A Naval Officer, who will be mentioned later in this account, ordered me to keep back the refugees from a certain part of the dock area. It was a hot business on a hot day controlling this swarming mob of humanity, subject all the time to attack from the air.

That day the 60th Rifles and a battalion of the Rifle Brigade arrived at Calais and with them, in the afternoon, arrived our wireless sets (No.9), vehicles and stores. As soon as the wireless vans had been landed, we tried to contact control station at Dover. After a time, we were successful. I believe the operators at Dover had been calling us unsuccessfully for 48 hours, not knowing that we had been denuded of our equipment.

By this time, it was, of course, impracticable to send detachments to Dunkirk and Boulogne; the Port of Boulogne had been captured the previous day by the German Panzers and Dunkirk could not be reached.

O.C. No.12 Wireless Section selected a good site from which to operate, in a small wood bordering a cemetery on the outskirts of Calais. Groups of disorganised continental soldiery passed us as we proceeded to the station site.

There was attached to us a naval signaller or cipher operator, to monitor our wireless messages; we were using naval cipher.

As evening approached, the Germans advanced on Calais and fighting began on the outskirts. The Section H.Q. and the two wireless detachments not actually operating were ordered to proceed to the park opposite L'Hotel de Ville. This area was also being used as a harbour for tanks. At nightfall the Germans started a terrific bombardment on it and we crouched under our vehicles to protect ourselves from the flying shrapnel. The shelling lasted all night; it was very concentrated. There were a number of underground air raid shelters here and they were filled to overflowing with French soldiers. I well remember being reprimanded by military policemen for walking about the park in the early hours of the morning during the shelling. He told us in no uncertain tone that I was taking a great risk. Further encouraged by the shelling, my comrade and I hastily took refuge in a ditch. I heard cries from the tankmen for the Medical Officer. They, apparently, had sustained casualties. The shelling continued with the same intensity throughout the night.

FRIDAY 24th May 1940

Sometime after sunrise the third wireless detachment joined us. They reported that during the shelling, the naval signaller had left the wireless van, presumably for purposes of nature, and had not been seen since. The neighbouring cemetery had been very heavily shelled and we concluded that he had been killed. We were now in a difficult situation; we had been ordered under no circumstances to use 'clear' language and now we lacked the means of enciphering and deciphering messages.

The tanks had now been in action for several hours, and had done a splendid job of work. Such tanks – and I understand they were obsolete – as suffered casualties returned to harbour to effect repairs where possible, and went back into battle. The morale of the tankmen was magnificent.

At about 1000 hrs, the fighting stopped. We understood a truce had been declared for an hour. During this lull we were ordered to immobilise all vehicles other than wireless and anti-aircraft vehicles. I remember how very loath was Driver Bond, in charge of our stores lorry, to immobilise that huge vehicle. The immobilisation was carried out.

At the end of an hour, the fighting recommenced with increased fury. It was quite apparent that we were outnumbered and outgunned. It was later stated that we were outnumbered 10-1 and outgunned 100-1!

Very shortly after the lull ceased, we Signals personnel drove in our Wireless vans to H.Q. at La Clinique. By this time, the enemy had penetrated well into the town and was very close to H.Q. The civilian population had started looting and a French heavy tank was patrolling La Rue Léon Gambetta, outside La Clinique. Owing to technical difficulties, at one stage, we had to transmit from a set on the right-hand side of the road and receive on a set on the left-hand side of the road; the enemy was machine gunning from a position near the bridge where La Rue Léon Gambetta crosses the railway and the fire was directed down the road. We had to run from one set to the other across the enemy's line of fire in order to pass directions between the operators.

When the enemy had penetrated very close to H.Q. at La Clinique, I asked a British officer what he thought about the German chances. His morale was excellent, for he replied, "I will bet you £5 that the Germans don't capture Calais within ten years". About this time we received an O.U. (i.e. Most Immediate) message from Dover. Unfortunately it could not be decoded as we had lost our naval signalman. We had, of course, to use clear language, and I remember Lance Corporal Glew asking me on 'speech' from Dover "where is the naval signalman?" I believe Lieut Evitts overcame the difficulty by borrowing a cipher operator from the marine contingent which had landed. The O.U. message, when deciphered was, I understand, that famous message from the War Minister: "The eyes of the Empire are on you".

The Germans were now well into Calais and only 100 yards or so from H.Q. Lieut Evitts collected all our protected documents with a view to destroying them.

At about three o'clock in the afternoon, we had to evacuate H.Q. under very heavy fire, on Brigadier Nicholson's orders. H.Q. was re-established in the Dock area near La Gare Maritime. The docks were an inferno. Vehicles and oil tanks were blazing away, and the area was being bombed, shelled and machine gunned, all at the same time.

A destroyer was in harbour, and on the quayside was a Naval Officer, Admiral Sir James Somerville. He gave a radio commentary some weeks later about what he saw at Calais.

Soldiers were busily unloading ammunition. I saw a heroic Padre encouraging the troops.

At this stage, Lieut Evitts detailed one wireless detachment under Lance Corporal Jordan, an ex-regular, to stand by to move to the Citadel where the Brigadier was going to move his H.Q. The two wireless sets not being used were destroyed. The remainder of us were attached to Queen Victoria's Rifles and formed into a platoon. We were now to operate as infantry.

The Germans were very close to La Gare Maritime. We were ordered to prepare against the possibility of gas. Respirators were worn in the 'alert' position, and gas capes donned. We then marched up the railway line into defence positions around a lake bordering the docks, amongst the sand dunes. Whilst marching to these positions, I fell and damaged my hands rather painfully. Popular rumour had it that Calais was to be evacuated during the night and that we were to be amongst the rearguard. The fighting was very heavy and the enemy did not seem to value the lives of his own soldiers. Consequently, his casualties were heavy, in proportion.

As night wore on, it became very cold. We expected to be relieved at 0300 hrs. But as the hours passed we realised Calais was not to be evacuated, and it was about 0800 hrs when we were relieved and returned to La Gare Maritime for a respite. We had had no sleep or proper food for a long time. We had learned the wisdom of not standing on the skyline.

SATURDAY 25th May 1940
The station (La Gare Maritime) was being very heavily bombed and shelled. In fact the whole dock area had become a shambles. The M.Ps were enforcing passive air defence and after we returned to the station, we were continually seeking shelter in the basement, for La Gare Maritime suffered many direct hits. The bombing was beyond description. As soon as one squadron of dive-bombers had dropped their load, and machine-gunned us, they were followed up by another squadron, and then by another squadron; and so it continued; it practically rained bombs.

There was a medical officer at the station and he was so overworked that he was tottering on his feet; he worked beyond the limits of human endurance.

The cooks in the station, despite the intense bombardment and under the worst possible conditions, produced a wonderful hot stew.

Early in the afternoon, we went back into the line amongst the sand dunes by the lake. We had to make staggered, spasmodic dashes from the station to avoid the enemy rifle and machine-gun fire. This advance was well controlled by a Q.V.R. Officer. The weather was so hot, and we had to move with such speed, that I had to discard my greatcoat. I threw it over the wall into the station yard; unfortunately it contained several packets of cigarettes and bars of chocolate.

Here in the dunes, we were incessantly shelled and bombed and subjected to machine-gun and small arms fire. I well remember seeing a soldier walking on the skyline on the sea side of us, and a shell bursting against him. He was spread-eagled like a cross in the air, and then just disappeared!

Fire control became very difficult. It was hard at a distance to tell friend from foe, and the matter was aggravated by fifth-columnists. Three times that afternoon, the order 'cease fire' was passed round to prevent firing against our own men. On one occasion a few French tanks began to shell the Citadel where H.Q. was. How they came to shell the Citadel is difficult to say.

The Germans had a spy in the lighthouse which commanded a complete view of the battle scene. Driver Bond, en route to our positions in the line, fired at a window from which we thought we were being sniped at; there was no more sniping from that window.

In the course of that afternoon, two of the German dive-bombers were shot down by a Bren Gunner of the Q.V.Rs. That was a remarkable feat! On another occasion, three R.A.F. fighters attacked a squadron of about 14 dive-bombers; immediately two of the fighters and two dive-bombers came down, having apparently accounted for each other. The remarkable thing is that the remainder of the German bombers turned tail and fled from the one remaining British plane. A great tribute was this to the R.A.F.

At about 1800 hrs, a German biplane came over and dropped leaflets written in French and English. This plane also machine-gunned us and the rim of my helmet stopped one of the bullets, which must have ricocheted over my shoulder for I was not wounded; with any other type of helmet, I should have been. This demonstrated the advantage of the wide rim of the British helmet.

The leaflets that were dropped read to the effect that we were to march to the north end of the town, lay down our arms and surrender, otherwise we would be obliterated by the German onslaught. For all the effect they had, they might as well have never been printed.

As dusk descended, I saw a small boat beach and out of this charged a detachment of Royal Marines who went straight into action. They had been seen by the Germans, though, and as they crossed the skyline they were shelled very heavily, but many of them got through.

We were now ordered to prepare for the even greater onslaught that was expected and to construct small shelters by digging into the sand bank of the lake and building boulders round the outside of the pits. Sig Harrop and I were lifting one of the boulders when there was a heavy bombing raid and unfortunately the boulder fell on my right foot and severely contused it. The pain was most intense, but in the excitement I forgot about it.

A number of us were ordered to rest in the dug-outs, but I was amongst those ordered into the line for night defence. We were all very, very tired, hungry and thirsty. It was now dark and the Germans were using rocket signals and tracer bullets. The tracer bullets were very helpful to us as we were able to avoid their line of fire. So tired was I that I mistook the chimney pots of the station for Germans mounting a machine gun on the roof, and raised the alarm!

The Officers and a particular Sergeant Major of the Q.V.Rs acted splendidly in leadership; they were very, very inspiring. Apart from patrolling, the hours of darkness were fairly quiet. Sometime after midnight, I regretfully and reluctantly took a last sip of the drop of water left in my water bottle. I think the smoke of the explosives made us much thirstier than we otherwise would have been.

SUNDAY 26th May 1940

At about 0300 hrs in the morning, I was relieved and ordered to hand over my rifle to the relief, who had no rifle owing to the shortage of them. I then went to the small dug-out and in a very crouched position fell to sleep.

I awoke after sunrise in the midst of a renewed, terrific bombardment of bombing, shelling and machine-gun fire, to find that about four of us were isolated from the rest; I now had no rifle which did not improve matters. There was at hand a quantity of .303 ammunition in Bren gun magazines. I spent my time extracting the bullets and fitting them into rifle clips for the other three to fire at the Germans. Our fire power was hopeless against that of the enemy.

Eventually an opportunity occurred for us to move, and we crawled about two hundred yards under the cover of a wide sewage pipe bounding the lake. En route, I picked up a discarded rifle, but it was a French pattern and useless for my ammunition. Near the dock station, we found an abandoned army car into which we jumped and drove under heavy fire to a fort above the Northern breakwater which was holding out against the Germans.

Here I found some of our section – Bond, Newmarsh, Harrop and Kirkham so far as I now remember. There were a number of refugees in the fort and one, a pregnant French Jewess, calmly handed to me a British rifle and asked me to get her to England with her husband, as she was expecting her child any time! Nothing could of course be done for her.

A very small launch, marked with the Red Cross, had entered the harbour against the Northern breakwater, and a number of us were ordered to take wounded from the fort across the beach to the breakwater on foot. This was done, and the small launch was so full of wounded that it was very low indeed in the water. At the last moment, a wounded man dashed up under his own power, blood squirting from his leg. Just as the launch was about to move off, a naked Frenchman swam across from the Southern breakwater and tried to board it. Force had to be used to remove him, and a Naval Officer told him very forcibly that there was not room for the British wounded, let alone a perfectly fit Frenchman. I noticed one British Tommy slap his naked rear portions to help him on his way. We handed over our pocket field dressings for use on the launch, and it moved off into the channel. Despite the Red Cross markings, the Germans shelled it, without success.

We then started to make our way back to the fort, adjacent to the jetty at the end of the breakwater, but before we reached it, the Germans captured it. We saw the German troops penetrate and surround it, and the senior officer present was obliged to surrender the position; a white handkerchief was raised on a rifle. The Germans forced our men to double down the beach with arms raised above their heads. The refugees, including the woman who had asked me to get her to England, were rounded up.

We few who had not been captured were not in a good position. The breakwater was being sprayed by small arms fire and attacked by mortars; the land-end at the jetty was in German hands and the Southern breakwater was lined with German soldiers. We sought protection from their fire by crouching in the piles of the breakwater. The tide was rising meaning this form of protection would not last very long; soon we would have to rise with it. About an hour later, our small party began to surrender. I had heard false reports from several sources that the Germans were shooting their prisoners and I was in a frame of mind which caused me to decide it would be as well to be shot on that pier as to surrender and then be shot. I therefore stayed where I was, although the remainder of our party surrendered. For about a further half-hour I stayed there by myself, but an acute sense of loneliness and helplessness came over me and I decided to join the other prisoners by going up to the jetty. I threw my rifle, which was jammed with sand when given to me and now useless, into the sea, to prevent the enemy having it; I did likewise with my respirator and made my way to the Germans.

The Germans had hoisted their swastika flag above the fort they had captured, and this had apparently been seen by two British destroyers in the Channel, for just as I reached the jetty our destroyers began to shell the jetty and fort area.

This put new hope into me and although the enemy were standing directly over me on the jetty, and I was within their grasp, I decided in an instant to try to escape. Turning back from the jetty, I dashed spasmodically from pile to pile of the pier to evade the enemy fire. Unintentionally, at the place where the pier had been cut in two by mortar fire, I fell into the sea. It seemed a long time before I broke surface again, but I swam the short distance to the further end of the break in the pier, and with difficulty got back onto the piles.

I do not think the enemy saw me emerge from sea, for not a shot was fired at me after I clambered back onto the piles of the pier. I ran on to the sea end of the breakwater, where I was overjoyed to see a small group of khaki-clad men. To my surprise I saw their rifles pointed at me and they were about to shoot, when I was recognised by Driver Bond of 12 Wireless Section who was with the party. The immersion in the sea had turned my khaki a grey colour and my water filled respirator container looked like a bomb-bag; consequently our own troops thought I was a German "death or glory boy" trying to attack them. It was very fortunate for me that they held their fire. There were 42 in the party and I made 43. Of 12 Wireless Section, there were Bond, Newmarsh (our cook) and myself. Two of the party were RA 2nd Lieutenants, and one was a captain of marines who was up in the port room above our heads.

It was very cold and I began to suffer from exposure owing to my immersion in the water; I was stripped of my clothing and the others crowded round me to keep me warm. One of the Artillery subalterns literally hugged me to counteract the cold. On two occasions, my knees gave way from fatigue, and as a consequence our helmets clanged together making a noise which nearly attracted attention.

The destroyers continued to shell the dock area, and we saw the Germans line up our prisoners and the refugees, on the beach, in face of the navy's shelling. This was observed by the naval gunners, and they fired over the heads of the British into the hinterland.

There was a grounded ship in the harbour and a plan was made to swim across to it in the darkness, to find if there were any small boats or a raft on board which could be used by us. We were told that in the case of attack it would be "every man for himself" and just too bad for the non-swimmers.

As the tide rose and fell, we had to rise and fall with it, amongst the pier beams. The Citadel fell at about 1800 hrs that night, I understand.

At about 2100 hrs, when darkness had fallen, we climbed up the iron ladder at the end of the pier and joined the captain of marines in the port room. Calais was lit by the burning oil tanks and we took off our helmets whilst climbing, lest their gleam betray us. The port room was blacked out, and the captain of marines had some hot coffee prepared. We were so intensely thirsty that it was most welcome and delicious out of all proportion.

In my condition of nakedness, I found an infantry signaller outside the port room flashing out to sea an S.O.S. message that we were British, hoping it would be seen by the navy. In my weary state, I once thought that a light, which may have been Dover Light or a light buoy, to be an answer. My injured foot had now become very blue, swollen and painful. The captain of marines ordered me to be wrapped in a blanket inside the port room. I remember Driver Bond wrapping me in the blanket and rolling me under a table. This occurred at about 2300 hrs.

MONDAY 27th May 1940

At about 0200 hrs in the morning, I was roused by a cry of "They are coming!" I immediately thought the Germans were upon us, which would have been awkward for me in my state of nakedness. But it was a British launch which had entered the harbour, missing us on the pier end. It drew up by the jetty, tried to tie up, was machine-gunned by the Germans and immediately set out back to sea. The captain of marines ordered us to shout with all our might and flash signals as soon as the boat approached. The boat went past us out of the harbour, but on seeing and hearing our signals, turned alongside the pier end, and under heavy machine-gun fire we jumped down on to its deck. In an instant, the boat was out in the channel, not a casualty having been sustained.

When I got on the boat, I found I couldn't walk owing to the condition of my right foot. We were a very sorry sight, with faces blackened by cordite, and several days' growth of beard. A naval medical officer gave first aid to my foot, and I was given a sea vest, pullover and old grey trousers and sea stockings with which to clothe myself.

The commanding officer of the vessel was the same Naval Officer who a few days earlier had ordered me to police the refugees. To my astonishment, the coxswain was one Jack Woodhead, who was the brother of Dick Woodhead in my parent unit, and lived at Matlock, only 8 miles from my home.

We were given coffee and food, the best meal I have ever had in my life, and we fell into an intense sleep. It was daylight when we entered Dover harbour.

Bond and Newmarsh had to carry me at Dover as I could not walk. We had a meal, the captain of marines paraded us, shook our hands and said goodbye to each one of us. I never knew his name. He was responsible for our escape. He acted splendidly and did an excellent job of work.

The captain of the unarmed boat which rescued us was awarded the D.S.C. His name was Victor Brammall; the boat was H.M.S. Gulzar. His coxswain Jack Woodhead was awarded the D.S.M.

After proceeding to Fleet, and from there to London en route for Saltburn, the officer in charge of my party telephoned for an ambulance as my foot had become worse, and that evening I finished up in Queen Alexandra's Military Hospital, Millbank, London.

**HM Yacht Gulzar, the little ship on
which the author escaped from Calais**

Addenda to the Account:

1) Lieutenant Austin Evitts, commanding 12 Wireless Section, led the first ten men out of the fortress of the Citadel to surrender to the German X Panzer Division. The German commander accused the British of having used 'dum-dum' bullets contrary to the laws and usages of war, and set up execution squads. It turned out that they were French bullets of poor quality and the execution squads were called down.

2) The survivors of the battle marched into captivity for five years. Early in the march, four prisoners escaped and managed to steal a boat in which they set sail for England, eventually being rescued by the Royal Navy. Two of them eventually became Major-General Williams and Major-General Talbot.

3) The late Airey Neave, after escaping and being recaptured, was eventually the first prisoner to escape from Colditz and reach England. After the war, Austin Evitts and I helped him with his book 'The Flames of Calais'. We attended the publication party in 1972 and drank more champagne than we had had water to drink during the battle! Here I met again Lt Commander Victor Brammall D.S.C. with whom I kept in contact for the remainder of his life. A heroic man, he died in sheltered accommodation in Hungerford. Present, too, were the major commanders of the Rifle Brigade, the 60th Rifles, the Queen Victoria's Rifles and the 3rd Royal Tank Regiment. My dear friend Austin Evitts died some ten years later in Bakewell War Memorial Cottage Hospital.

4) Many times I have returned to the scene of the battle: on the 50th anniversary in May 1990; on 20th May 1998, amongst 38 survivors of the battle at the re-dedication of the war memorial to the Royal Green Jackets who now embrace those famous Rifle Regiments; and on 6th June 2000 when, as President of the Sheffield & District Branch of the 1940 Dunkirk Veterans Association, I laid the wreath and conducted a short service at the war memorial and found it very emotional. On the first two occasions the Band and Bugle of the Light Division sounded the Retreat in La Place des Armes, the scene of such dreadful fighting.

5) My own narrative is embraced in 'The Miracle of Dunkirk' by Walter Lord and 'The Flames of Calais' by Airey Neave.

6) In contrast to the treatment meted out to the prisoners in the Citadel, let me tell you of my late friend John Penman, who as a 2nd Lieutenant commanding a platoon of the Argyll and Sutherland Highlanders held up the VII Panzer Division at Sainte Valéry for one and a half hours, a little later than the Calais action. On being taken prisoner he was hauled before the German commander who spoke reasonably good English. This is what he said with a smile to John: "You are a very brave but a very foolish young man, to try and hold up my division on your own!" His name was Erwin Rommel, that great and good German soldier who later commanded the Afrika Korps and as the Field Marshal commanding the German forces in Western Europe was forced by Hitler to commit suicide, following the attempted assassination of Hitler on 20th July 1944. John was awarded the Military Cross; perhaps Rommel had something to do with that!

Home Forces

I spent three days in Queen Alexandra's Military Hospital where I was very well looked after. After a bath, on my admission, I fell into a very heavy sleep. But just before wakening, I found myself back in the noise of the fighting at Calais. This was caused by a pneumatic drill in the road outside my window!

Having been equipped by the hospital with a new uniform and a civilian 'gas mask', I was despatched by rail to Saltburn-by-the-Sea. Here I rejoined my friends Jack Bond and Teddy Newmarsh, the cook. We stood to from an hour before dawn to an hour after dawn, and the same at sunset, in case of aerial invasion. Every day we built pyramids of stones on the beach to prevent landings by glider, and the tide systematically demolished them! We took a dislike to a Sergeant-Major who said he was gong to make soldiers of us; after all, most of the members of the Saltburn holding unit had been evacuated from Dunkirk and were soldiers! Here I was found by my life-long friend, Tom Wragg, who had come out of Dunkirk. One of the senior officers was Major Rex Stevenson of Chesterfield who had been second-in command of our T.A. Unit. He gave Bond, Newmarsh, Tom Wragg and myself four days leave which I spent at Bakewell with my dearest Kath and her family. One day I went over to Glossop to see my brothers Ken and Colin, George now being in the Royal Artillery. Colin returned with me to Bakewell, and being only 17 years old, was quite emotional when Kath and I bade him farewell at Bakewell Station. Those few days with Kath I will never forget; we were indeed in love! Mary, Kath's sister, was in a distraught state because Dick Wragg, to whom she was then engaged, Tom's brother who had been separated from him at Dunkirk, had not returned. Fortunately he came back a day or so later. I returned to Saltburn where I received great kindness from the Kelly family.

Mr Kelly, a stockbroker, was chairman of Middlesbrough Football Club. Their son, William, was in the Signals in France and had not yet returned home. Apparently we bore a strong likeness to each other and when they first saw me at Mass in Saltburn, they thought I was their son! William eventually arrived home from Dunkirk. The Kellys were tremendously kind to me.

At stand-to one summer morning I met Major R.A. Waldrow, an Ashbourne solicitor who was later my post-war commanding officer, and became a very firm friend.

Eventually Bond, Newmarsh, and I were returned to 4 Corps Signals where we were most graciously received by Colonel Gerry Underwood and immediately given four days leave, which I spent mostly with Kath at Bakewell. A few days later

Signalmen Lambert and Dyson arrived from the Holding Battalion, having escaped from Calais via Dunkirk.

Now the Battle of Britain was about to begin. In July our unit, 4 Corps Signals, moved into Buckinghamshire, my own No. 2 Company under command of Major Deyermond being billeted in Misbourne House, Chalfont St Giles, the home of the great poet Milton. Britain was in a state of alert. At all times we had to carry our rifles and respirators, and the L.D.V., Local Defence Volunteers (later to be called the Home Guard) was formed, originally armed with pitch-forks and the like, for the British Army had lost almost everything at Dunkirk.

The 4th Corps was now given the task of defending London and South-East England against the possibility of invasion. Hitler had in fact drawn up a plan, code-named 'Sea Lion' for the purpose. Now the Battle of Britain began, the Germans trying to destroy our air-fields.

When the Battle of Britain was at its height we were moved to a large park at Royston near Bury St Edmunds. Here I saw many a fight between British and German planes, and many brave airmen, both friend and foe, descending by parachute. On 8th September 1940, the code word 'Cromwell' came through on our wireless sets, meaning that invasion had occurred. The church bells rang in some districts warning of invasion, but this was an error in communication. There had in fact been a practice German invasion which had gone wrong. A week later on 15th September, the code word 'Ironside' came through, indicating that the invasion scare had passed. That was the day when Churchill, having visited Fighter Command H.Q. at Biggin Hill, uttered those memorable words: "Never in the field of human conflict has so much been owed by so many to so few." How great a tribute to those splendid young airmen, so many of whom had been recruited from the University Air Squadrons.

Church bells had been silenced and were to be rung only in the event of invasion. All signposts and all place names were removed from villages, towns and railway stations, to hinder any airborne invasion. Possible landing grounds for gliders were obstructed with stakes. The blackout was enforced most vigorously. In retrospect, I think that many of the moves did greater damage to ourselves than they would have done to the enemy!

Shortly after this we returned to Buckinghamshire, and Bond, Newmarsh and I together with 12-14 Wireless Section went to the Wireless Camp at Lodge Farm near Amersham where we provided wireless communication by remote control to Corps Headquarters at Chalfont Latimer. Here we lived at first in pigsties, cooked by primitive method and slept on paillasses filled with straw on mattresses made from signal cable. Later, as autumn turned into winter, Nissen huts were built for us and a good cookhouse established. We worked very long shifts on our wireless sets, trying to read enciphered messages through heavy atmospheric interference and interference from other wireless channels, day and night. At one time I could receive and transmit 25 groups per minute!

Of that 1940 winter, I have two vivid memories. One night in early November, I saw a huge red ball in the northern sky. It was Coventry on fire, amongst the casualties being its splendid cathedral. Then on 29th December, I had been by train to London, returning in the evening. Early that evening the sirens wailed and the entire city of London was engulfed in flames, St Paul's being miraculously saved by the skill of the fire-watchers and fire services. This was, I think, the first time that the Luftwaffe had used those deadly incendiary bombs which had great powers of penetration and tremendous heat. One bomber could carry 300 of these. Only a few days earlier, both Manchester and Sheffield had been bombed, Sheffield on two consecutive nights. In Manchester, the office on Mosley Street where I had worked was completely destroyed. This was bombing in earnest. In London during the blitz, 30,000 were killed and in the remainder of the country another 11,000. The police, fire services, workers, ambulances and hospitals were all magnificent in those dreadful times. Some four and five years later, the Germans were to get a taste of their own medicine: Hamburg, and Dresden, where some 120,000 were killed on one February night in 1945.

On the last day of 1940, several of my wireless section were attending a party in Amersham given by girls from an evacuated insurance company when we received the dramatic news that we were leaving the district at midnight, when 1940 merged into 1941. During the hours of darkness we drove down into Sussex. Both wireless sections, Numbers 12 and 14, were billeted at Kingscote, between East Grinstead and Crawley Down where Company H.Q. was located. Unit H.Q. was at Handcross and H.Q. 4 Corps was at Worth Priory. We were now part of South Eastern Command under General Bernard Law Montgomery who exercised us in no uncertain manner for the defence of the realm.

Near to the Wireless Corps was a camp for conscientious objectors who did agricultural work and we liked them very much. When my brother George, now in the Royal Artillary, visited me, he was very kindly accommodated by the conscientious objectors, because he was not on our ration strength!

The Blitz continued, and I well remember 10th May 1941, when London and district was severely firebombed, the House of Commons was destroyed, incendiary bombs rained on us at Kingscote, and Rudolf Hess, the Deputy Fuehrer, flew and parachuted into Scotland!

I remember two British Army exercises, Bumper and Percy. Montgomery was splendid in his direction. I remember so clearly, too, the many guards I did, apart from wireless operation; the dawn chorus of the birds, the stimulus of the hour preceding and succeeding dawn.

By now there was a strong Canadian army presence in the south, and my wireless detachment was sent to 2nd Canadian Division Signals to provide the rear link to H.Q. 4 Corps, under whose command they were. For this purpose in July/August 1941 we were sent to Heathfield and were well looked after by those splendid Canadians, so many of whom were killed or captured in the tragic raid on Dieppe in August 1942.

My dear Kath and I had now been engaged for several months and had made arrangements to be married at Hassop on Saturday 30th August. The rules on marriage between Catholics and Anglicans were then very hard. They ought not to have been, and were altered by the Second Vatican Council some years later. It must have been hard for the girl with whom I was so deeply in love, not to have been married in her own Bakewell parish church. The Canadian signal regiment commander generously gave me leave to make the wedding arrangements. Shortly afterwards, we returned to our own unit at Kingscote and it was from there that I was given ten days leave from 28th August until 8th September. My comrades gave me a lovely tobacco bowl as a present. We were married by the Reverend Father Louis Drury, who came over from Glossop, bringing with him my brother Kenneth, best man; my younger brother Colin; and my comrade George Colclough, my groomsman. My dearest Kath went to Hassop with her mother and father and sister Mary, and I joined them with Kath's brother Jack to whom I was greatly attached. It was the happiest day of my life and I still thank God every day for my escape from Calais to marry the sweetest girl on earth.

Following a reception at Kath's home, Thorncliffe in Parsonage Croft, we were taken in Arnold Hall's taxi to the New Inns Hotel near Milldale, Dovedale and Ashbourne for our honeymoon; there was a glorious harvest moon. We hired horses from Ashbourne, we walked through Milldale and Dovedale before returning to Bakewell on Thursday 4th September, being collected by Kath's father and mother, who were always so good to me. In the course of my leave we had the tremendous pleasure of seeing the Anglo-Polish Ballet at the Lyceum Theatre, Sheffield, in 'Les Sylphides', 'The Spectre of the Rose' and other ballets much influenced by the music of Chopin. It was with a heavy heart that I had to leave my darling Kath on her 27th birthday on Monday 8th September to return to Kingscote.

I returned to the Wireless Corps at Kingscote sometimes operating from the No.

9 set, sometimes from the remote control in the cellar of Corps H.Q. at Worth Priory. In between my duties I read poetry, having been inspired to do so by Kath whose love of verse and drama I greatly admired. At home she continued to produce and act in plays, as a founder member of The Peacock Players.

In November 1941, we received the momentous news that our unit was to become 'Q' Armoured Divisional Signals, later 11th Armoured Divisional Signals. Colonel Gerry Underwood, who was destined to be promoted Chief Signal Officer of 4 Corps, saw us off in the dark in the early hours of the morning from Three Bridges Railway station, whence we were bound for Scarborough. As I said goodbye to Gerry, I was saddened, but little realised what a tremendous part he was to play in my life.

Scarborough was cold and the winter was harsh. Unit H.Q. was in a hotel overlooking the South Bay, and most of us were billeted in the old boarding houses. The 11th Armoured Division was commanded by Major General Sir Peter Hobart, the first man to have put a wireless set into a tank, and brother-in-law of General Montgomery. He exposed us to the art and science of armoured warfare. Our new commanding officer was Lt. Colonel Horniman with Major Arthur Haslehurst as his second-in-command. We had most intensive training into the signals procedure of an armoured division, based on the splendid No 19 Set, which was threefold in communications from H.Q. to Higher H.Q., between tanks; and within the tanks, which were mostly Matildas and Valentines. The armoured brigades and their parent division had armoured command vehicles. It was a Major Wat Tyler who trained us in armoured warfare signals procedure. I next met him in Athens in 1946!

In Scarborough I became friendly with Mr & Mrs Raine, the uncle of Mr J.W. Raine, headmaster of Bakewell Methodist School; they were very kind to me.

Here I received my first promotion to Lance Corporal. One of my duties on nights when invasion was considered practicable was to speed with five soldiers to a pillbox on the southern jetty, armed only with rifle and ammunition to hold the enemy at bay! It was indeed a hard winter.

Very vividly do I recollect on 7th December 1941 the news that the Far Eastern fleet of the U.S.A. had been decimated by Japanese planes at Pearl Harbour. The U.S.A. declared war on Japan, and a few days later Germany declared war on the U.S.A. Churchill recorded that "when I heard that the entire Far Eastern fleet of the U.S.A. had been destroyed at Pearl Harbour, despite the gravity of the news, my heart leapt with joy for now I knew that the New World with all its might and industrial capacity must come to the help of the Old, and that we were assured of ultimate victory!"

In February 1942, I moved with the support group of the 11th Armoured Division to Malton, where our signal office was in the Talbot Hotel. It was here that I applied for a commission. Shortly afterwards, I was promoted to Corporal. My commanding officer, Lt Colonel Horniman, recommended me to go before the commissioning board, telling me in no uncertain terms not to let him down! I was interviewed by the board at Catterick Camp and recommended for training at the Royal Signals Officer Cadet Training Unit (O.C.T.U.) at Catterick Camp, commanded by a great soldier, Lt Colonel Dent, whose Regimental Sergeant Major was another fine man, Mr Gay.

In April the Division moved south to the Guildford area, and hardly had we got there than I received my posting orders to report to the Increment Company of the O.C.T.U. at Catterick for two months preparatory training before admission to the O.C.T.U. itself.

I was sorry to leave so many of my old comrades, especially Sergeant Howarth who had been very good to me. The 11th Armoured Division two years later covered itself in glory in the invasion of Normandy. I have always valued the training I received in armoured warfare. The training in the Increment Company was hard physically and mentally: mostly infantry training, physical training, mathematics and physics. The officers and cadre staff were splendid.

The author in his lieutenant's uniform

Chapter III

The Second World War, 1942-1946

In July 1942 I joined No. 45 course at 152 O.C.T.U., later re-designated the Royal Signals O.C.T.U. Never have I worked so hard in my life. From Reveillé until 'lights-out' every moment of our time was filled physically, mentally and spiritually. There was daily physical training; a weekly cross-country run of at least five miles; forced marches of at least ten miles in battle order, sometimes wearing our respirators, followed by an assault course; team games; infantry tactics; signal tactics; daily parades with the most thorough inspections; mathematics; physics; map-reading; military law; organisation and administration; and intense floor-polishing and polishing of our equipment. On one occasion, the entire O.C.T.U. was loaded into lorries, not knowing where, and dropped miles away without food, and ordered to get back to H.Q. without crossing any bridges. I recalled being so weary and tired that evening that I lay down in the pouring rain in the rain-soaked gutter of Richmond to rest, resisting the impulse to sleep. When we got back, we were all in a sorry state! The Commandant, Lt Colonel Dent deprived some of the officers of their privilege leave, because they had used transport to get back!

In the middle of the six-month course we were sent to the battle camp at Martindale off the east coast of Lake Ullswater. It was late October. We slept in tents, washed and bathed in the gill, Ramsgill, and were subjected to the most rigorous infantry platoon training. Our faces we blackened with cow muck. At the conclusion of the week's course, the Commandant arrived to watch us carry out an attack under live fire. He accused us of being "gutless" and ordered us to repeat the attack. This was all part of the doctrine of making life very hard for us. The great lesson I learned was of "ground, bullets and speed". It was splendid training.

On return from battle camp we were given 10 days privilege leave, when Kath and I were once again united. It was bliss.

It was during this first part of the O.C.T.U. training that the disastrous raid was made on Dieppe by the 2nd Canadian Division, with whom I had been the previous year. They were killed, wounded and taken prisoner. It should never have happened, and to this day responsibility for the action is still debated. The finger points mostly at Lord Louis Mountbatten, the recently appointed Chief of Combined Operations.

Commissioned: 77 Divisional Signals

On return to O.C.T.U. from leave, my course continued its hard training, towards the end of which we were measured for our service dress – tunic, trousers, greatcoats and trenchcoats – and opened professional bank accounts. We were also prepared for the change to officers' mess customs. Eventually on a very cold 27th January, clad in our new uniforms, and myself wearing my father's Sam Browne belt still scarred with the wounds he received in the Battle of the Somme, having been commissioned as Second-Lieutenants in the Royal Corps of Signals on 26th January, we marched from the parade ground of Somme Barracks to the sound of martial music, the remainder of the O.C.T.U. presenting arms to us. It was a proud moment after so many months of incredibly hard training in so many aspects of the life military. With all my equipment, including my valise camp bed, I made my way to Bakewell for ten days' leave with my dear wife Kath and her parents.

For ten days it was bliss to be alive. From Bakewell at the expiry of my leave, I left for Cottingham near Hull on being posted to 77 Divisional Signals under commend of Lt Colonel F.H. Bury, a direct descendant of Flora MacDonald who helped Prince Charles Edward to escape after the 1745 rebellion to Skye. Our divisional headquarters was at Dalton Hall, under command of Major General Michelmore, a great soldier and ecclesiastical lawyer. The 77th Divisional symbol was the sword Excalibur, since it was the Devon division. Both General Michelmore and Lt Colonel Bury were sticklers for discipline.

Initially, I was given command of a wireless section, but after a short time I was transferred to divisional headquarters at Dalton Hall as commander of the divisional signal section, and I was a member of the mess. This was a tremendous experience, for I was able to study more from the top, being at divisional headquarters, and I consequently learned the ways of the divisional staff all of whom were tremendously kind to me. Within my section were a few very good A.T.S. girls who manned the divisional switchboard and performed other signal duties. I was given personal responsibility for the provision of G.P.O. lines to many formations and units, including R.A.F. Leeming, R.A.F. Pocklington, R.A.F. Catterick and, if my memory fail me not, R.A.F. Finningley.

Dalton Hall being near Beverley, I had the pleasure of visiting Beverley Minster and the beautiful church of St. Mary's where my friend Major Oliver of the London Rifle Brigade, GSO II to the General, was married to a Senior Commander of the A.T.S. on the staff, and I was a guest. I remember clearly another GSO II, Major K.A.N. Thwaites, a splendid leader. He was a great philosopher and told the story of a Catholic friend of his who repeatedly confessed in the Sacrament of Penance, to hating a man; after several confessions, he no longer harboured hate. From Major Thwaite I learned so much.

In the spring of 1943, we were replaced by my old division, 11th Armoured Division, and I handed over the signal office to 11th Armoured Divisional Signals. I remember so clearly my old company commander Major Deyermond.

H.Q. 77 Division now moved up to Scotch Corner. On a motorcycle I led one of the convoys. I shall never forget, where the Railway line crossed the Great North Road (A1) at Leeming Bar, being held up as a train, packed with Italian prisoners of war, rattled over the level crossing. This inspired me! At Scotch Corner Hotel my Signal Office was in what is now the cocktail bar. My responsibilities increased. I made two new friends in the Divisional Staff, Captain John Freeman, Staff Captain 'A', and Major Rose the Deputy Assistant Director of Medical Services. I was already very friendly with Major "Archie" Rose, of the A.S.H. (Argyll and Sutherland Highlanders), the Deputy Assistant Adjutant-General, whom I later visited in hospital in Italy, and a Captain Rodney Maxwell-Le-Froy whom I also met in Italy.

At home, things were not easy for Kath. She was pregnant, her mother was seriously ill, her brother Jack was in hospital following a cycling accident, and her sister Mary was in the W.R.N.S. Kath carried the burden without complaint. Sadly on 3rd July 1943, her wonderful mother died in a Sheffield nursing home, following an operation on her thyroid gland. When I got the news, I travelled through the night by train and bus to Bakewell, where I arrived before the family had risen. For Kath in particular, it was a dreadful time. Owing to her pregnancy, she was advised not to attend the funeral. Her father was grief-stricken, as were Mary and Jack who was soon to be invalided out of the Royal Air Force. Kath now had the burden of managing the home, and helping her father to manage the shoe shop in Matlock Street. All this she did most heroically.

Some weeks before this sad event, I had my first flight in a Halifax bomber from R.A.F. Catterick in Leeming, up over Scotland and back. That indeed was an experience.

A few weeks later, I reluctantly bade farewell to Divisional H.Q. and its signal section to take up the post of Administrative Lieutenant at my Company H.Q., under command of Captain Galbraith, at Gilling Castle, a few miles from Scotch Corner, the officers' mess being in Gilling Grange. I was there when Italy surrendered to the Allies on 3rd September 1943. This followed the to-ing and fro-ing in the Western Desert followed by the surrender of the Italian army and the surrender in May 1943 of the Afrika Korps, after the Battle of Alamein in October 1942.

About this time, the decision was taken by the War Office to disband 77 Divisional Signals, and I felt so proud when at the final dinner in our regimental officers' mess, the commanding officer Lt Colonel F.H. Bury referred very kindly to the manner in which I had organised the telephone system provision for so many units and headquarters, in conjunction with a Mr Lally the Post Office liaison officer.

The officers of 77 Divisional Signals went their different ways on posting. I was posted to 76 Divisional Signals, a drafting unit headquartered in Norwich, and I found that I was due to be drafted to India on 7th October 1943.

Kath's condition was not good, and during my short embarkation leave it worsened so much that her doctor, Doctor Bagot, wrote to the War Office saying that he could not accept responsibility for her well-being unless I were immediately available as the time approached for her confinement in late October. Captain John Freeman, my friend from H.Q. 77 Division, helped very much in the administration of Doctor Bagot's letter. As 7th October approached nothing had been heard, and both Kath and I, so far apart, were on tenterhooks. Finally on 6th October, a signal was received from the War Office that I was to be taken off the draft until Kath's confinement was over and her condition had improved to the extent that I could be posted overseas. The officer commanding the draft, a Major Chalke, was very kind to me, though he was soon to lose me. This restored my confidence in the basic decency of the British Army.

On 29th October in Willersley Maternity Home, Hardwick Square, Buxton at about 6.30pm after a forceps delivery, Kath gave birth to a splendid baby girl, Christina Mary.

It took 24 hours for the news to reach me. In accordance with the War Office's signal, I was granted 10 days leave and, to the best of my memory, I travelled by train through the night from Norwich to Buxton, where a bed was provided for me in Kath's room and I was able to stay with her and Christina throughout my leave. This was good, because Kath was quite weak and I was able to help in her care. Her father, despite having to run the house and the shop, assisted by Jack who had now been invalided from the Royal Air Force, visited us as often as he could. I well remember going to register Christina's birth at the Buxton Registry Office.

The days went by and I had to return to my unit. I can still see Kath, waving to me from the window of her room as, encumbered with my kit, I made my way to the Buxton railway station.

On return, I was posted to my company H.Q. in a park in Worstead and was immediately thrown into the training of the soldiers awaiting draft. The days were getting shorter and the weather colder and wetter, but we worked and trained very hard. Amongst the officers I still remember were Colonel W.S. Ashley, a great friend of Colonel Gerry Underwood, Major Terry Huddle who had taken part in the Berlin Olympic Games supervised by Hitler, Major Philip King, and Lieutenant Richard Crawston who became very famous after the war in television productions, and made the first TV presentation of the Royal Family making arrangements for Christmas.

Whenever it was possible, I took weekend leave, twice I think, to visit Kath, Christina and Kath's father. Then my new posting order arrived for January 1944. I was given a few days embarkation leave and we had such great confidence in Christina's grandfather to care for Christina that Kath returned with me to Worstead to spend about four days staying in a little cottage occupied by a charming couple, Mr & Mrs E.W. Dagless. It was a very cold journey from Bakewell to Norwich and then onwards by taxi, I think, to Worstead. The train, occupied mostly by American troops, was unheated and we spent three hours motionless in March station. Eventually I was able to accommodate Kath, and I spent as much time as I possibly could with her. We visited Norwich, North Walsham and, I think, Cromer.

It was a very poignant occasion when, as embarkation day approached, I took her by train to London, where we met her dear old friend, Mrs "Nanna" Roberts, who was almost completely deaf, with whom Kath was going to spend the night at her home in Ashford, Middlesex. Kath bought me a pair of leather gloves, which I still treasure. It was with a heavy heart that we bade each other farewell at Waterloo station, not knowing what the future held for us, and I waved goodbye to Kath as the train steamed from the platform en route to Ashford. I thank God that she was in the splendid care of Mrs Roberts.

To Italy

About two days later, as officer in charge of the draft with Lieutenant Frank Turner, an officer considerably older than I was, we departed by rail for King George V Dock at Glasgow, travelling mostly through the night. I remember that General Sir Bernard

Montgomery was on Doncaster station as we went through; he was visiting Doncaster to encourage the workers to put their back into industry to aid the invasion of Europe – 'The Second Front', as it was known. At Glasgow we embarked on R.M.S. Almanzora, a very pleasant ship whose timbers and irons creaked so much. The officer in charge of troops was Colonel Boyle of Leeds, an old friend of Colonel Gerry Underwood. Conspicuous amongst the officers was Major Goschen, later Lord Goschen, of the Grenadier Guards. In the course of the voyage, whence we knew not, on Leap Year day he organised a racecourse in which he played the part of the great Tipster 'Prince Monolulu' of "I got a horse" fame. Amongst the passengers was Geoffrey Wincott, a great actor, and the comedian Sandy Powell and his wife. Alcohol was not allowed on the voyage, we were required to remain dressed throughout, and we conformed to a schedule of watch from the upper decks. Down the Clyde we steamed, across the tip of Northern Ireland and halfway across the Atlantic Ocean, in a destroyer-escorted convoy. The sky was grey all the time and the weather very cold. We zigzagged down the Atlantic Ocean and made our way to the straits of Gibraltar. As we approached the straits one of our soldiers had to be operated on for peritonitis. The ship steadied, paravanes were put out and a destroyer circled us, dropping depth charges. The soldier's life was saved. In the course of that voyage of ten days or so, I gave a few lectures, on military and morale matters.

The ship coursed through the Mediterranean and we knew that we were heading for Naples. The night before we docked, the O.C. troops, Colonel Boyle wished us over the ship's loud-speaker system "A happy landing". Hardly had he concluded his message, than the ship's guns went into action against an overhead aeroplane. With greater alacrity than ever did we dash to our action stations, which we had practised to so often. The aeroplanes disappeared! The next morning we sailed past the Isle of Capri into the Bay of Naples, and we disembarked by passenger boats from the Almanzora which I had grown to love. Here I must pay tribute to the splendid men of the Mercantile Marine, who considered that we soldiers were in greater danger on land than we were at sea.

I remember the awful conduct of a padre, who was hurling abuse at the Italian sailors who were disembarking us. He was a disgrace to the splendid clergy of the Royal Army Chaplains' Department whom I hold in the highest esteem.

The Port of Naples which had suffered such devastation from the retreating Germans the previous October was encumbered with sunken ships which General Robertson, the Quartermaster General, had transformed into quays. Within three days of the devastation, Naples had become the busiest port in the world!

From Naples we were taken by truck to Nola, a town of great antiquity that had

The author (seated, front centre) with troops in Italy

suffered heavily from bombardment. The G.R.T.D. (General Re-enforcement Training Depot) was located in an Italian cavalry barracks. In a large garage, I put up my camp bed amongst about 100 others and made myself as comfortable as possible. Here we awaited our postings. It was about 16th February 1944. Shortly after our arrival in Nola, the volcano Vesuvius erupted with a thunderous roar. Dust and boulders were hurled into the air, and streams of molten lava poured down the slopes, destroying villages and a small airfield. At night, there was enough light from the volcano to read a newspaper. The dust covered ports in North Africa, the isles of Capri and Ischia and most of Southern Italy. The eruption lasted for several days, but for long afterwards when it rained, the rain brought the dust down with it, creating a yellowish mud.

It was Vesuvius that in AD79 deluged the towns of Pompeii and Herculaneum. After the eruption I had the great experience of visiting Pompeii still being excavated and showing what life was like when it came to an end there in AD79.

Whenever we could we went by over-crowded train, many Italians sitting on top of the carriage, to Naples where at the San Carlo Theatre, sitting in the Royal Box, I had my first experience of opera, 'Cavalleria Rusticana' and 'I Pagliacci', and I fell

ABOVE LEFT: Overseeing the elections in Crete, March 1946
ABOVE RIGHT: Interviewing the electoral committe of AYIOS CONSTANTINOS near Iraklion, Crete. L–R: parish clerk, interpreter, Leslie and parish priest, March 1946

in love with it. The theatre was under military direction. Bordering it, the royal palace had been converted into a N.A.A.F.I. store and canteen for the troops. Adjacent to the theatre was the officers' club. These facilities gave great respite to troops on leave from the front, and to troops awaiting posting.

The roads and villages running north, south and east of Naples were in appalling condition, and there was hardly a building left standing in some villages. Nola had been badly battered, there was no electricity for the civilians and I remember so clearly the Italian peasants huddled round their charcoal fires.

Within a few days I was put in charge of a draft, travelling by train from Nola to Barletta on the Eastern coast. My superior on the train was a South African captain and in the course of the journey an Italian signorina was hauled before him, suspected of plying her wares on the train. She certainly had no right to be on a troop train and to the best of my memory, she was put off at the first stop, denying that she had done any wrong.

We entered a long tunnel through the Apennines when suddenly the train came to an abrupt halt and all the baggage on the racks fell on us. We had run into a stationary train in the tunnel. Fortunately, before the situation became critical we moved on and out of the tunnel. Only a few days before, a train had broken down in that same long tunnel and many passengers had died owing to asphyxiation.

Having arrived in early morning at Barletta I handed over my draft, saw to my ablutions on the very cold platform and made my way to the signal office in the town. The signal master, Ben Burns, who remained my friend until his death, took me to the Line of Communication Signals Officers' Mess and gave me lunch. In the course of two days or so, I was back at Nola.

My front tooth, on which an apexectomy had been carried out in England, was troubling me and I had to go to Naples to have it extracted. Since it was a crucial tooth for eating and speaking, I had to have an upper plate made and a lower one to balance it. Whilst I was waiting for these dentures I was posted to 4th Indian Divisional Signals but since I could not masticate properly, my posting was cancelled for better or worse. The 4th Indian Division – one-third British, two-thirds Indian – was a famous division and I would have been on Indian army rates of pay, higher than the British.

II L. of C. Signals

Within a few days in March I was posted to II L. of C. (Line of Communications) Signals, with its Headquarters at Castellamare, south of Naples, on the Sorrento peninsula. I was interviewed by the commanding officer, Lt Colonel Harry Kirkaldy, and posted to 42 Line Section, as second-in-command to Captain Walter Lamb, a very experienced lines officer and a post office engineer in civil life.

Many of Walter's second-in-commands had not lasted long, but I got on very well with him and learned as much as I could as quickly as I could. The soldiers of 4th Line Section were billeted in the school rooms of a convent in Vico Equense, and Walter and I were billeted on the Savarese family, opposite the convent. Cavaliere Savarese had lost an arm in the First World War at the Battle of Caporetta in Northern Italy/Austria. Signora Savarese was charming and so were her children Luisa, Olga, Fernando, Sylvarna, Maria, Laetitia and Lydia the baby. The Savareses, whose house commanded a splendid view of the Bay of Naples, were most kind to Walter and me. Sometimes in the evening we would sit round the dining room table, listening to the records of the great operatic singers, Gigli in particular. Kath and I visited them three times after the war.

The nuns, especially the Madre Superiore Maria Pasquale Monti, were very good to Walter and me. Through the medium of French, the Madre Superiore taught me Italian in the course of a week. The cook, Suor Concella, established marvellous relations with our cooks. I remember clearly, too, Suor Agostino who lived to the ripe age of 96; Suor Elmerinda, the portress, a most charming lady who made a beautiful frock adorned with butterflies for Christina Maria; a student who became Suor Alcesta; and the Madre Superiore's sister from Sorrento, Suor Angela. I have a particularly vivid memory of serving Mass in my services dress to the delight of the nuns.

Whilst stationed at Vico Equense, Walter Lamb and I went to Sorrento to see the San Carlo Opera Company put on La Boheme, and here I met my friend of H.Q. 77 Division, Captain Rodney Maxwell-le-Froy who was recuperating in R.A.M.C. convalescence with our friend Major Archie Rose of the Argyll and Sutherland Highlanders, whom I immediately visited the next day. I greatly admired him and was sorry to see him bedridden from wounds or illness. His home was in Oban.

The main task of 42 Line Section was to maintain the copper wire telephone route round the Sorrento Peninsula as far as Salerno, and I learned quickly the art and science of this. I learned, too, that it was always better to give written instructions in this task. The soldiers of 42 Line Section were splendid and had covered themselves in glory in North Africa.

The Germans were now holding the 'Gustav' line across rivers Liri and Sangro on the Italian Peninsula from Gaeta in the west to Ortona in the east through Cassino with its splendid Abbey founded by Saint Benedict himself, overlooking the town and countryside from Monte Cassino – the scene of so much fighting, especially after the destruction of the abbey by the Allied Air Forces. Here the 36 (Texan) and 34 Divisions of the U.S. Army, the New Zealand Corps, and the Indian Divisions had failed to dislodge the Germans from the ruined monastery. In my mind's eye, I can still see the air full of American and British aircraft, on the way to bomb the monastery in mid-February, and I have some memory of another aerial attack possibly on the Feast of Saint Benedict himself, 21st March 1944. In retrospect we should know that the Germans never entered the monastery until after the bombardment and then the splendid young soldiers of the Herman Goering division did indeed take some winkling out. It was General Freyberg, the New Zealand commander, who pleaded with General Alexander, the 15 Army group commander, to destroy the monastery. From my own experience I know that you always felt you were being observed and likely to be shot at from the heights of Monte Cassino. Now a last big effort was to be made by the Eighth Army under General Sir Oliver Reese to dislodge the German defenders.

And so it was that we of 42 Line Section received our marching orders to come under command, for all purposes, of 8 Army Signals, then commanded by Lt. Colonel W. Peachell. We said goodbye to the nuns and the Savareses, and drove north to Venafro, just south of Cassino, via the ruins of Capua, Cancello and Mignano. We drove north in two convoys, owing to the exigencies of movement control on those battered roads, myself leading the first convoy. There was hardly a building left standing on what was known as Route 6. How the Italian peasants survived was a mystery.

Venafro was a base of the 2nd Polish Corps under General Anders. These Poles were tremendous fighters, well disciplined and deeply religious. I remember so clearly attending Mass with them just before the final battle.

Our task now was to provide and maintain the line communication of the 8th Army. Mostly I used a motorcycle to get round the units for which we were providing communications. Always as I rode at speed along the devastated road – if such it could be called – overlooked by the ruined abbey of Monte Cassino, I felt rather insecure. I liaised with the 2nd New Zealand Corps Field Hospital, amongst other units, and vividly I recall having a tooth filled in a field in a very basic foot-operated dental chair courtesy of the Royal Army Dental Corps.

On 11th May, having regrouped to bring the weight of the 15th Army Group into his main effort, Alexander launched a full-scale assault on the 20 mile zone between Cassino and the sea. French, Polish, British, New Zealand, Canadian and American units smashed through the German lines, Cassino finally falling to the Poles on May 17th/18th. Cassino town itself was now mere rubble. At Anzio, where my brother George was in the beach-head, the re-enforced U.S. VI Corps attacked, 23rd May, toward the Alban hills, and two days later contact was established between the British 8th Army and the U.S. 5th Army, under General Mark Clark. The artillery bombardment of 11th May was ferocious and intense. For me who had had my baptism of fire at Calais four years earlier, it was easy to bear – I was now on the winning side, not the losing – but even in North Africa, the bulk of 42 Line Section had never experienced so intensive a bombardment, and thus marvelled.

All the battles of Cassino were nasty. Even in this final battle, with so strong a preparedness of force on the Allied side, the Germans never relinquished their foothold in the ruined monastery until the Poles captured Monte Cairo, overlooking Monte Cassino. Looking back, I have a great admiration, as a soldier, for the German defenders, who were commanded by General Von Senger und Etterlin, a tertiary member of the Benedictine Order, later to be one of Marshal Kesselring's plenipotentiaries at the Armistice proceedings at Caserta in May of 1945. His nephew eventually became Deputy Supreme Allied Commander of NATO, after the war! The slaughter at Cassino had been terrible on both sides. Throughout its history, the Abbey, commanding the routes as it did, had been the scene of at least four great conflicts.

The organisation, logistics, planning and courage of the 8th Army was marvellous and reflected the greatest credit on all concerned. I can still see General Sir Oliver Reese, in his staff car, with his military police outriders speeding up Route 6 near Cassino. After the war, he described it to me thus: "didn't we dash up that road!"

In the course of the next few days my replacement as second-in-command of 42 Line Section arrived and I was summoned by the commanding officer, Lt Colonel H.M. Kirkaldy to return to become signalmaster at H.Q. 56 Area, Naples, under my very great lifelong friend Wilfred Saunders, who eventually became Professor W.L. Saunders C.B.E. of the University of Sheffield and President of the Library Association. It was with a feeling of deep regret that I left 42 Line Section, for I had become very fond of the Linemen and especially of Walter Lamb from whom I had learned so much and whom I greatly admired. Walter eventually became a Lieutenant Colonel and commanded 43 Signal Regiment T.A. after the war. He was a great man.

On my way south, I called at A.F.H.Q. (Allied Force Headquarters) at the Royal Palace, Caserta to visit my friend Tom Wragg who was Wireless Officer in 15 H.Q. Signals. I was given a great welcome and it was a tremendous experience to go round this immense palace.

On arrival in Naples I was accommodated in the officers' mess in Via Aniello Falcone in the Vomero area of Naples and H.Q. 88 Operating Section, of which I was now the commander, was situated not far away. Already I was an experienced signalmaster and I took easily to my new command. I was fortunate in having a splendid section sergeant in Sergeant Rimmer and an excellent section clerk in George H. Whiffin with whom I remained friendly for the rest of his life.

One day at my section H.Q. I was visited by a young United States Signal Corps Lieutenant, Joseph H. Waldron, with whom I established an immediate lifelong friendship. Joe was a very skilled technical officer and he worked in close liaison with our unit, mostly on long lines and telephone exchanges, especially with Alastair Robson and was closely associated with Brigadier Buchanan, the Chief Signal Officer. He received an honorary M.B.E., which was no small distinction. Unfortunately, after the war, he was called up for the Korean War in 1951 and having taken a regular commission in the U.S. Signal Corps, he contracted polio. Ever after, he was in a wheelchair, never complaining, splendidly supported by his wife Trudy and his daughters Debbie and Janet. In post-war years, they visited Kath, Christina and me eight times, Kath and I visited him once, and since the death of my dearest Kath, I have thrice visited him and Trudy at Air Force Village West, a retirement complex for retired officers from the United States Navy, Army and Air Force, near Riverside, California. Here I am always treated as an honoured guest, especially by my namesake Lt. General Jack Wright who was director of infantry. He was a prisoner of war of the Japanese, and later commanded an airborne division in Korea and introduced the Air Cavalry Divisions. He was, too, in his retirement Director of the Boy Scouts Association of the U.S.A.

On another occasion, Sergeant Rimmer announced that there were two nuns to visit me: the Madre Superiore and Suor Almerinda from Vico Equense, who had located my whereabouts. I recalled driving Suor Almerinda in my 15cwt Guy Antelope truck on the occasion of a visit from Naples to Vico Equense. She never forgot it. Nor will I ever forget the tremendous welcome she gave to Kath on our first visit to the Convent in 1951. Suor Almerinda was the portress of the convent and shortly after our visit, she made her flight to paradise.

The officers' mess in the Via Aniello Falcone was populated by fascinating characters: Leslie Robson; Wilfred Saunders; Richard Buchanan-Dunlop, who became an eminent Q.C.; Alastair Robson; John Jacques; Bill Wyse; Bill Malcolm, a tough Scottish Lines Officer whom I greatly admired and still do; Barclay Hankin; Geoffrey Bates; and so many more. The mess had a gorgeous view right over the Bay of Naples. There was a tremendous esprit de corps amongst us.

Shortly after my arrival, Rome fell to the Allies on 5th June 1944. We felt very proud of ourselves, but our glory disappeared in the events of the next day, 6th June 1944: D-Day, when the Allies under Eisenhower, and Montgomery as Land Forces Commander, successfully invaded Normandy. From day to day we marked their progress in the maps as the news came on the American Broadcasting System.

On 26th June, the mess celebrated my 24th birthday in no uncertain manner. We had been entertaining ourselves at the Allied Officers' Club in the Orange Grove in the Vomero and returned to the mess to continue our celebrations. An American infantry officer, Freddie, broke his back whilst swinging on a heavy picture from the wall. He was returned to the U.S.A. in a plaster cast concealing a revolver with which he intended to shoot the man who had broken his marriage! In the course of the evening, Bill Malcolm kept asking me to put on my steel helmet which I refused to do. In desperation he crowned me with an oil painting framed in glass, which went over my head, the shattering glass cutting the face of a U.S. army nurse. Looking back one can only consider that we were mad, but one must remember the context of the times: there was a war on, we were high-spirited and had little or no sense of danger. But it was wrong to treat requisitioned property in that manner.

On 12th August 1944 a conference was held in Naples at the Villa Emma, once the home of Lady Hamilton, mistress of Nelson, and now the naval commander-in-chief's guest house, the communications for which I was responsible. The conference was between Churchill and Tito, the Yugoslav dictator, and Randolph Churchill who worked with the Yugoslav partisans was there too. They became high-spirited in the evening, despite a suspected German bombing raid, causing the Americans to cloud the port with smoke.

Shortly after the liberation of Rome on 5th June 1944 I was sent there on a signal mission, up Route 6 through the remains of Cassino and I shall never forget my first glimpse of the Eternal City, especially of the Basilica of Saint John at the Lateran gate. In the course of my mission I succeeded in finding my brother George, a Bombardier in 56 Light Anti-Aircraft Regiment, who had fought at El Alamein and taken part in the invasions of Salerno and Anzio. I found him at Ostia where the River Tiber joins the sea. It was a great reunion as we had not seen each other for four years. His entire was record was splendid and he never sought the power and the glory. That evening I, then a mere Lieutenant, was accommodated in the senior officer transit hotel, the Hotel Eden, sharing a room with a Padre. When I went down to breakfast I was aghast to find that most of the occupants were colonels and above. To my joy, I was glad to find a civilian which made me feel at ease. Later I discovered that he was the Right Honourable Harold MacMillan, H.M. Minister Resident at Allied Force Headquarters, the biggest brass of all. He was able to relieve General Alexander of all political responsibility.

My brother George joined me from Ostia and we had the great joy of being received in general audience by Pope Pius XII. The splendid hall in the Vatican was crowded with troops of various nationalities: British, American, Canadians, Poles, French, Brazilians. The Pope, a majestic figure, spoke in so many languages. In English he expressed himself in a manner that brought consolation to us all. In post-war years he has quite wrongly been vilified because of a novel by Hockruth called 'The Representative' implying that he could have helped the Jews more than he did. We who fought for the liberation of Rome know that he gave shelter to thousands of Jews, in various ways. It was wonderful, together with my brother, to receive the Papal Blessing. George and I were very fortunate to visit Saint Peter's which took my breath away, and the majestic halls of the Vatican.

Shortly after my return to Naples, I was transferred, together with 88 Operating Section, to headquarters III District near the Riviera di Chiaia, and became signalmaster of III District under my friend Wilfred Saunders. My operations section was retrained as 176 Tele-Operating Section, using teleprinters. I presume that the higher authority merely doubled 88 to 176. We now joined No. 2 Company under command of Major Frank Stoneman, the officers' mess being in the Riviera di Chiaia. All of us – officers, NCO, operators, linesmen, despatch riders and signal clerks – worked very hard under great pressure to maintain communication. We worked on a shift system over three days which meant working through every third night which our bodily systems did not like. Apart from the signals pressure we had, of course, all the usual military pressures and responsibilities.

The immediate cause of the signal pressure was the invasion of Southern France on 15th August 1944, the invasion fleet being berthed in the bays of Salerno, Naples and Baia. It was known as Operation Anvil. Apart from the British the invasion force consisted largely of the First French Army and the Seventh U.S. Army. It relieved the pressure on our invasion forces in Normandy but it considerably depleted the Allied Forces in Italy, producing a state of stalemate through the autumn.

On 18th August my dear wife Kath received a telegram: "Army Council regret to inform you that Lieutenant L. W. Wright is seriously wounded". The next day, a Sunday, the telegraph boy again ascended the path to the house bearing another telegram. You may guess what her fears were! Fortunately her Aunt Ida and Uncle Hubert, who had gained the Military Cross in the First World War, were staying with her. Ida opened the telegram to read: "Army Council regret previous telegram erroneous"! What a dreadful experience, but what relief, thank God!

As officer commanding 176 Tele Op Section, I was responsible for various outposts at Capua, Vairano and Cancello amongst other places, and these were dependent on overhead copper wire routes. The Italian peasants lacked copper sulphate to cultivate their vines and so they made frequent raids to steal the copper wire which broke the communications. I did everything possible to trap them, but never succeeded. All we could do was to continually fill in the breaks with new copper wire.

In the middle of this very busy time, whenever I had the chance, I visited the Teatro San Carlo, Naples' famous opera house which received tremendous support from the area commander, Brigadier BUS Cripps. I was filled with admiration for the Italian classics: Cavalleria Rusticana, I Pagliacci, La Traviata, La Boheme, Il Trovatore, Rigoletto, The Barber of Seville, Faust, Aida, Norma, Lohengrin, Manon Lescaut. Amongst the great performers I remember Ettore Ponno, Benvenuto Franci, Maria di Caniglia, Ugo Savarese, Italo Tajo, Tito Gobbi, Luigi Infantino and Beniamino Gigli and his daughter Rina. On two occasions, together with other officers, when the Italian chorus went on strike, I became a soldier in Faust and Aida!

That winter was a hard winter, especially for the infantry, both Allied and German up in the stalemate condition north of Rome. Snow fell heavily in the mountains and even on the Sorrento peninsula and the weather impeded our means of communication.

Early in December I was sent on a mission up to Rome again, and managed to incorporate with it a few days leave. I met an old friend, Lieutenant Mitchell, and together we visited the great sights of Rome. Again I visited Keats' home, at the bottom of the Spanish Steps, where Keats and Shelley lived, and Keats died at the age of 26. He is buried in a nameless grave in the Protestant cemetery near Saint Paul's

Outside the Walls, and his epitaph is "Here lies one whose name was writ in water". Not far away is buried the heart of Shelley, snatched from his funeral pyre on the beach near Livorno (Leghorn), and his epitaph is: "Nothing of him that doth fade but doth suffer a sea-change into something new and strange" from Shakespeare's 'The Tempest'. We visited, too, the great basilicas of St Peter, St John Lateran, St Mary Major and St Paul's Outside the Walls; the catacomb of St Callistus on the Appian Way; La Scala Santa from Pilate's Hall; the Vatican; and Tivoli. At the Vatican I joined a general audience and at the end of the audience was fortunate enough to be personally addressed by His Holiness, who asked me where I lived and narrowed Bakewell down to being between Manchester and Sheffield. His Holiness gave me His blessing and a medal which I still treasure.

On the way back to Naples, I gave a lift to two Sisters of Queen Alexandra's Imperial Nursing Corps (QAINC) in appalling weather. I relieved my driver/batman, Driver Clements, for an hour or so. It was pitch dark, the road was flooded and it was raining torrentially. I drove rather too quickly on to a narrow temporary bridge over a deep ravine – the original bridge had been destroyed in battle – and very nearly took us all into the ravine from which I doubt that we would have emerged alive. It was a salutary experience!

About this time, coincidental with Field Marshal Von Runstedt's Battle of the Bulge, Field Marshal Kesselring made an offensive in the north from the German Gothic line. In the melée the 92 U.S. All Black Division attacked the Brazilian Division, thinking they were Germans. The 8th Indian Division had to be rapidly transported from the Eastern end of the line on the Adriatic to the Western end in the Tyrrhenian to plug the gap. Tim Hillyard who came from Bakewell was Adjutant to the 8th Indian Divisional Signals and received the M.B.E. for his sterling effort in the transition.

The Allies not only had Von Runstedt's and Kesselring's offensives to deal with, but also civil war in Greece between the nationalists and the communists. The 4th British Division was sent out from Italy to try to quell the fighting. So serious was the situation that Churchill, Eden (the Foreign Secretary), Macmillan and General Alexander went to Athens over Christmastide. Churchill appointed Archbishop Damaskinos as Regent of Greece.

In all these affairs and in those at Force J133 in Yugoslavia we played our part in the provision of good communications.

On Christmas Day, as is the Army custom, the officers took tea to the soldiers before Reveille and served Christmas dinner to them. A vivid memory I retain is of going to the outpost at Capua to serve the detachment there. Every Christmas, my friend George Whiffin and I recall the events. About this time, we were closely involved in the transfer of the 2nd Canadian Division from Italy to North West Europe, further depleting the Allied Forces in Italy.

As winter turned into spring the momentum of the offensive increased and the Germans were pushed back over the basin of the River Po and eventually into Austria. Mussolini and his mistress Clara Petacci were executed by the Partisans and their bodies hung upside down in a garage near Milan.

In April I was moved to take charge of signals affairs in Capua. I lived in the mess of the town mayor, a delightful, elderly, very competent officer, with a great affinity for whisky. Sharing the mess were the R.T.O. (Rail Transport Officers) with whom I struck up a close friendship. In the same complex, a military barracks which had served as a P.O.W. camp for captured British before the Italian surrender, was Lt James (Jack) Stewart, a Scot of my own unit, II L. of C. Signals. In Capua I met an old school-friend, Teddy Greenwood of Glossop, then an officer in the Royal Army Medical Corps.

During this time negotiations were being conducted between plenipotentiaries from Field Marshal Kesselring's Headquarters and General Alexander at Allied Force Headquarters at Caserta. Amongst the German plenipotentiaries was General Von Senger und Etterlin, who in his book 'Neither Fear Nor Hope' refers to the tremendous kindness shown to him by a Lieutenant-Colonel Jack Profumo, a staff officer at AFHQ. Profumo was later to become Secretary of State for War and to resign over the Christine Keeler affair, taking up splendid charity work. For him I have a great admiration. During these negotiations the room of the German Plenipotentiaries was 'bugged' and my post-war friend at the University of Sheffield, Professor Maurice Bruce, then an intelligence officer on Alexander's staff and fluent in German, translated the results.

Vividly do I remember on 2nd May the old Italian lady who had a flat above my billet opening the window and crying to me: "La guerra e finita". The war in Italy was indeed finished, Armistice having been signed. It was a moment that I shall relish forever. Six days later, on 8th May (V.E. Day) the war in Europe, generally, had finished. The Germans were very keen to surrender to the British and Americans rather than the Russians!

Just before V.E. (Victory in Europe) Day, I was posted back to Naples as chief signalmaster in the place of Wilfred Saunders who had become Adjutant.

Every precaution was taken to ensure that spirits did not ride too high on V.E. Day; for example the military police discarded their pistols for the day. I recollect the words of Major General Clowes, the district commander at a parade to commemorate V.E. Day in Naples: "Human memory is very fickle". How right he has been proved!

The pressure on signals was as great as ever and I found my duties as chief signalmaster, apart from my normal regimental company and section duties, very pressing and stressing.

By this time Naples signal office had a large proportion of A.T.S. girls who were very remarkably efficient as teleprinter and switchboard operators. They had various officers, the best of whom, in my opinion, was Subaltern Joan Rand, a very young widow whose husband had been drowned at sea. I was amazed to discover that Joan had worked for my great friend, Colonel "Gerry" Underwood, who had gone out to Burma as chief signal officer, 4th Corps. After giving very distinguished service, his health broke down, and he was repatriated to the U.K., to become chief signal officer, London district. He told me later that he had fallen in love with Joan, but there was of course, a great disparity in age. Joan had now fallen in love with a Major James Watson of the Royal Artillery, who had been decorated with the Military Cross by General Sir Harold Alexander himself. I met Jimmy Watson and liked him very much, and I was very generous in granting leave of absence to Joan whenever Jimmy was in the vicinity.

The arrival of the A.T.S. caused some difficulties. They were very attractive to both American and British soldiers, but the Americans were better paid and had better transport and this did not incur the pleasure of our British soldiers. But all worked out well in the end and two marriages occurred between the A.T.S. and soldiers of our unit, before the troops started to be repatriated.

We were still at war in the Far East and I was very likely to be posted to that region, but the dropping of the atomic bombs on Hiroshima and Nagasaki stopped all that and victory over Japan came on V.J. Day 15th August, 1945. Had it not been for the atomic bomb I would surely have been sent to the Far East and I might not have survived.

Again, there were great celebrations on V.J. Day – but not for me! I did an unbroken 48 hour shift in the signal office so that my subordinates might enjoy themselves.

At home a general election had been held following the defeat of Germany. The national government had resigned in preparation for the election and the Prime Minister, Winston Churchill, had formed a caretaker government, pending the election. There were so many votes to be counted from our servicemen and women overseas that the results of the election did not come through until the time of the Potsdam Conference, attended by President Harry S. Truman (President Roosevelt having died on 12th April); Winston Churchill and Clement Attlee; Joseph Stalin; General Charles de Gaulle; and General Chiang Kai-Shek. The result of the general election came through just before the main meeting. Churchill and the Conservatives had been decisively defeated, and the Labour Party under Attlee had been returned with a tremendous majority. Both Churchill and Attlee had returned to London for the result of the election. Attlee returned as Prime Minister and the decision was taken at the conference to drop the dreadful new weapon on Japan, unless they surrendered. Churchill recounts that the British people had given their verdict so overwhelmingly that, much as he would have liked to stay in office – which he could have done until the dropping of the atomic bomb on Japan – he felt that he did not wish to serve the people one moment longer. He therefore went to the King to tender his resignation and to advise His Majesty to send for Mr Attlee!

In the course of that conference, mention was made of the Pope. Stalin said, "The Pope, how many divisions has he got?" Later, on the death of Stalin in 1953, the Pope, Pius XII remarked, "Mr Stalin will now know how many divisions I have got."

In many places the peace was fragile. General Alexander issued a special order informing all under his command that he had warned Marshall Tito of Yugoslavia that if he did not vacate the area of Venezia Giulia he, Alexander, would eject him. At about the same time the Chetniks who had fought with us in Italy under Mihalailovich were returned to Yugoslavia and, probably, to death.

The war in Greece had certainly not ended because the Nationalists were fighting the Communists, and the civil war lasted long after the Second World War.

The pressure on the signals became even greater as arrangements were made for the disbandment of units and the return of personnel to the U.K. either on leave or for release. It had been the policy to grant 28 days leave to those who had not been home for five years. This procedure was known as Python. L.I.A.P., or "leave in advance of Python", was now established, granting 28 days leave to those who had been abroad for two years or so. Many of our own personnel received this and I soon found myself not only as chief signalmaster, Naples, but also as M.T.O. (Mechanical Transport Officer), and in several other functions without the means or personnel to properly execute these functions. It was very hard, taxing and trying work and occasionally one would seek solace in alcohol when spirits became very high. About this time, too, we moved our mess from the Riviera di Chiaia to the Via Francesco Crispi. Changes in command were being made, too. Our commanding officer, Lt Colonel Harry Kirkaldy on release to the United Kingdom, was replaced by Lt Colonel L.C. (Inky) Udell, a professional soldier who had risen from the ranks and exuded leadership. At first we held him in awe, but grew to love him. Our company commander Major Frank Stoneham had been replaced by Major Harry Betts who proved to be a splendid commander.

In the past months I had twice seen my brother George, who visited me in Naples when he had been sent down on a mission, and again in Capua where he had been at Cancello awaiting conversion from Light Anti-Aircraft to Infantry – in his case, the Cheshire Regiment, which he joined in the Trieste-Udine area.

Throughout my days overseas I wrote usually every day to my dear wife, Kath, who kept me posted with the progress of our daughter Christina and events in Bakewell. My father-in-law was now chairman of the Bakewell Urban District Council and a magistrate. My sister-in-law Mary was serving in the W.R.N.S. (the Wrens) in the Tilbury area, and my brother-in-law Jack following his accident, had been invalided from the R.A.F.

Shortly after V.E. Day I was fortunate enough to be granted 7 days leave which I spent on the Isle of Capri with Alan Mitchell, and Gordon Sayers and "Titch" Govier of the chief signal officer's staff. This was all very relaxing but I was foolish enough not to wear my beret and I think that this may possibly have encouraged my on-coming baldness. Nonetheless, it was wonderful to have the island practically to ourselves. We made many distinguished friends and became very good swimmers. I vividly remember swimming round the Faraglioni, the little islets of Capri. We stayed at the Villa Eudesandra just below Capri en route to the Marina Grande.

On visiting the town of Anacapri we were fortunate enough to be taken round the Villa of San Michele, built by the great Swedish Doctor Axel Munthë by his cousin, a German baroness, both of whose sons were officers in the German army. 'The Story of San Michele' by Axel Munthë has remained one of my favourite books.

Earlier in the year, some months before the armistice in Italy, my unit had been joined by Lieutenant Robert J. Wilkins R.A. who wanted to gain signals experience since, in civil life, he was employed by G.E.C. in his home town of Coventry. Bob had commanded a battery of guns on the Isle of Capri, protecting the Straits of Ischia against enemy intervention, and it was through his contacts that we enjoyed our delightful leave on Capri. On joining II L. of C. Signals, Bob was put under my care in the signal office. He was a rapid learner, very popular in the mess, and soon commanded a line section. On his first night of leave from the Army, he had endured the dreadful blitz on Coventry in the winter of 1940. He became, and with his wife Madge has remained, a very dear friend of Kath, myself and our daughter Christina and her husband, George. It is a friendship I value most highly.

In the summer of 1945, Bob Wilkins, Bill Malcolm and I were promoted to the rank of captain on the same day and I shall treasure the photograph taken in our khaki drill on that day. To this day, Bob, Bill and I are in constant touch.

As the winter of 1945 drew on in November I became anxious about being granted 28 days leave. It seemed to me that my chances were non-existent and I recounted the words of Job: "The Lord hath given; the Lord hath taken away. Blessed be the name of the Lord". Within a very short time I received a call from the Adjutant, my dear friend Captain Wilfred Saunders, that an allocation had been made to me from our No. 3 Company in Rome for 28 days leave terminating in the U.K. on 26th December, Boxing Day.

It was a remarkable journey through war-devastated Europe and it took me some 10 days to reach home via Rome, Milan, Domodossola, Lausanne (how sweet and beautiful and peaceful was Switzerland!), Strasbourg, Calais (so reminiscent of the dreadful battle of 1940 with the mortar break still in the Eastern jetty where I had had to swim for it), a very rough sea journey to Dover, and eventually, arriving in the early morning, in Bakewell!

I cannot describe my joy at being back with my darling Kath and Christina who had been only a few weeks old when I last saw her and was now more than two years old and very beautiful with fair curly hair, and my father-in-law. It was a wonderful reunion. Kath had worked so hard in maintaining the family home and caring for her father who was now known as "Garg", a name bestowed on him by Christina. Jack was working in the shop and Mary came home on Christmas leave. It was good to meet so many of my friends in Bakewell. Kath and I paid a visit to Glossop but my three brothers were now all overseas: Ken in India, George in Italy and Colin at Supreme Headquarter Allied Expeditionary Force at Versailles.

Kath and I had the great pleasure of going to Sheffield to see the late Sir Donald Wolfit play in 'King Lear'. England, despite the winter, seemed very green compared with Italy. We were joined for Christmastide by Kath's Uncle Hubert and Aunt Ida of whom I became very fond. I got on very well indeed with Hubert Howard who had been awarded the M.C. in October 1918 whilst a company commander in the Sherwood Foresters; I found it easy to communicate with him. Kath's brother Jack was always very kind to me, but I was saddened to see that his marriage to Betty was floundering. My leave went all too quickly and Christmas Day was saddened by the knowledge that on Boxing Day, the Feast of Saint Stephen, I must return to my unit in Italy. Never can I thank Kath adequately for the joy of those 28 days leave.

In the afternoon of 26th December 1945, I was seen off at Matlock station by my dearest Kath and Christina, Garg, Uncle Hubert and Aunt Ida. In precisely five days, after reversing my tracks through war-torn Europe, I arrived back in Naples on New

Year's Eve. Despite my tiredness I was soon revelling, with the Scots in particular, in welcoming the first year of peace since 1938. I have a memory of walking down the Via Nazionale clad in battle dress and a bowler hat, but it was, I think, excusable. On New Year's Day I was back in the signal office coping with maintaining the ever-pressing means of communication.

Early in February I was telephoned by my commanding officer, Lt Colonel "Inky" Udell. He instructed me that I was to proceed to Allied Force Headquarters to be interviewed by Major General "Mungy" Morrison with a view to my being his representative on the Allied Mission for observing the Greek elections to be held on 31st May 1946. I passed the test! I had in fact been recommended by my friend Wilfred Saunders who was now staff captain at Allied Force Headquarters. Two or three days later I was attached to 15 H.Q. Signals for all purposes and attended a few days' indoctrination course on Greece at Lammie Camp, Naples. It was a wonderful course carried out with typical military precision.

The night before my departure from Naples I was given a tremendous send-off by my colleagues in the officers' mess, including the district medical officer Captain "Doc" Lanyon. My dear friend Joe Waldron, who had been awarded an honorary M.B.E., came to bid me farewell too.

On Sunday 24th February 1946 I embarked at Naples on U.S.S. Daniel Hulger – a U.S.A. Liberty ship – that is, all welded. The conditions were congested, the sea was very rough, but I avoided sickness. The British, American and French Officers – the constituent nationalities of the mission – were all very good and pleasant.

The next day, we sailed through the Messina straits, having a splendid view of the snow-covered volcano, Mount Etna, and of Taormina and Reggio. On the 26th we sailed through the Ionian islands of the Gulf of Patras, passing Missolonghi to the North where Lord Byron died from Malaria in 1821 during the Great War of Independence. The terrain consisted of lovely, rugged country with snow-capped mountains. We docked at noon, but were not allowed off the ship. It was very hot and I sunbathed. The next day we were allowed to walk round Patras – where St Andrew was crucified – overlooked by a very old castle.

The next morning we sailed from Patras in a very rough gale which continued throughout the following day, and we docked at Iraklion (Heraklion) in Crete at 0800 hours. I supervised the unloading of our jeeps before being taken to our base at the American 18 A.T.C. Camp, which is now Iraklion airport, but then had only a short landing strip. This was Saturday 2nd March and the following Wednesday being Ash Wednesday, the Cretans, who observe Lent very fervently, had organised a dance in the beautiful Mediaeval Hall of Saint Mark, to which we British, American and French officers went and established a strong camaraderie. The town and port of Iraklion were in a very battered condition from the effect of the German invasion and subsequent fighting of May 1941; the roads were nothing but pot-holed dirt tracks. Indeed it was sometimes easier to drive along the dried-up riverbeds in the hot season.

On Sunday 3rd March 1946, having located the Catholic Church in Iraklion, served by a charming Greek Franciscan, I attended Mass with Commandant Pinon and Captain Guy de Sagonzac, the French Element of A.M.F.O.G.E. in Crete. In the afternoon, together with Major Irwin and Captain Roger Halliwell, I was fortunate enough to fly west to Maleme air strip in an Avro Anson. This was most enjoyable and thrilling. We flew over Suda Bay, a graveyard of ships with H.M.S. York beached and towering over the waves. At Maleme, before returning, we saw the wrecks of German planes and gliders from 1941.

In the evening, discovering that we had attended a Nationalist celebration the previous evening, we returned to the Hall of Saint Mark, adjacent to the beautiful fountain where we parked our jeep to attend a pre-Lenten evening with the Communists, so as to retain our impartiality. It was a splendid excuse for another convivial evening!

The aim of A.M.F.O.G.E. was "to report on the arrangements for, and the carrying out of the Greek elections". It was basically a political mission, but the military of the three involved nations – the U.S.A., the U.K. and France – were selected for the mission owing to the various hazards for which they were equipped and trained. Of the observers about ten were American, seven of us British, and two French, with the back-up of 18 A.T.C.

On Monday 4th March, we held a conference in readiness for the morrow and waited for our drivers who did not arrive until 1 a.m.

The next day, I set off with my driver to reconnoitre S.E. Crete via Malia, Agios Nikolaos, Kali Khoria, Kati Khoria and Lerepetra, interviewing various mayors and schoolmasters through the medium of a French-speaking Cretan. After travelling 200 miles over atrocious roads and tracks I returned at 2200 hours, when my driver announced that having "got a dose" (i.e. venereal disease), he was to be sent to Athens on the morrow for treatment. I did not see him for several days – but he was a great chap, despite "catching a dose".

Eventually I was given a young interpreter by the name of Candiles, who was very good but somewhat nervous of the political situation.

In between my missions I had the tremendous pleasure of being escorted round the Palace of Knossos, built in 2–3000 B.C. for King Minos, and the labyrinth's scene of the Minotaur, Ariadne and Thesus by Professor Hutchinson, the curator who lived with his mother in the lodge of the Villa Ariadne and had worked as a young archaeologist with Sir Arthur Evans himself. This greatly increased my classical knowledge. The Cretans and the Greeks disputed the burial place of the God Zeus, each claiming a site, and so they went to war. King Minos won and he demanded of King Aegios of Athens that seven young men and maidens should be sacrificed annually to this creature, half-bull and half-man, the Minotaur, borne of his Queen who had become enamoured of a bull, and constructed a wooden cow to enclose her so that she could conceive of the bull; the result was the Minotaur. Theseus, the son of King Aegios, was one of the seven young people condemned to be sacrificed to the Minotaur, kept in the labyrinth. He fell in love with Princess Ariadne who gave him a ball of twine so that, if he succeeded in killing the Minotaur, he could find his way back to her. Theseus got so drunk at the wedding that he forgot to change the sails of his ship from black to red, and when King Aegios saw the black sails, thinking that his son was dead, threw himself into the sea and drowned, since when it became the Aegean Sea!

We were kept busy visiting the towns and villages of Crete, interviewing the village committee consisting usually of the mayor, the priest, the schoolmaster and the doctor, and inspecting the electoral rolls which were all out of date, if not destroyed.

At the village of Krousson after I had interviewed the committee, the village doctor gave me a beautiful Cretan vase which he had dug up in his garden and considered it to be as old as Knossos itself. Having foot-slogged it to Krousson, I returned by mule taking the greatest care of the vase which I still greatly treasure.

In the course of the mission we were visited by Mr Mallory, the American Minister of State on the mission and by Mr Windle, representing H.M. Secretary of State for Foreign Affairs, the Rt. Hon. Ernest Bevin; by Mr O'Grady, the U.S.A. Ambassador to Greece; by General Malony of the U.S. Army; and Major General Dumbreck, our own military head.

At a village near Timbakion, I was entertained by a lovely old man who had been Secretary to the late General Venizelos, a Cretan hero.

On a visit to Agios Nicholaos, then a small fishing village, now another spoiled by British tourism, I visited the school and the children all rose most politely and gave me the Nazi salute! It was kindly meant.

On his visit to Crete, General Dumbreck accompanied me to Agios Constantinos, near Iraklion to visit the parish priest and parish clerk. I was very relieved and delighted when he conveyed his pleasure at the way I had done things. I had the pleasure, too, of observing demonstrative meetings addressed by Kyrios Venizelos, later to be Prime Minister, and General Plasdiros.

The investigation of terrorism was not easy. The Communists (K.K.E. party) were very good at making complaints which I frequently found groundless, and at Rethymnon my interpreter was very nervous when we called at the K.K.E. headquarters and a neighbouring taverna for refreshments. They made it very clear that they did not want their king back!

When I look back, I realise how dangerous were some of the situations, but we had little regard for danger. When I left Naples, my commanding officer, Lt Colonel "Inky" Udell, said: "Leslie, I do not want you to finish up hanging on a lamppost". But in many of the villages I was received with great hospitality and garlands of flowers. On the island at that time was Major Patrick (Paddy) Leigh-Fermour, who with Stanley Moss had kidnapped the German Commander, General Kreipe, during the occupation and taken him to Egypt. The consequence was the burning of two villages and the execution of some Cretans. Paddy, a very great man, was and remains very popular in Crete.

On a spring day I had to fly to Athens for urgent dental treatment and had the thrill of visiting the Acropolis, the Parthenon and other landmarks. Ancient Athens was wonderful, the stones living with history. I had the pleasure, too, of meeting three old friends: Lt Colonel "Wat" Tyler from 11th Armoured Division days; Dan George, a stoic Anglo-Catholic; and Len Chivers from my own unit. On Sunday 24th March I attended Mass with General La Parra, head of the French mission, looking most impressive, at the Catholic cathedral. There were lovely processions in Athens in readiness for the morrow, the "Greek National Day of Independence". I felt very proud of Greece and the Greeks. In the evening, with Len Chivers, I attended a symphony concert conducted by my friend Alastair Royalton-Kisch. In the Grieg Piano Concerto in A Minor, the soloist was Ron Dossor, another friend whose brother served in my unit.

The following day, 25th March 1946, I flew back to Iraklion to investigate more terrorism after consulting the chief of police.

It fell to me to arrange a party for the mission at the British Vice-Consulate, now a museum. The Vice Consul was Kyrios Elliadi, a cousin of Lord Crossfield. Amongst our guests were Professor Hutchinson; an English lady, Mrs Newlyn; and Norma Constantinedes, the daughter of the chief of police who returned to camp to dine with us. I returned to Knossos with Professor Hutchinson to meet his aged mother. It was a great party and dinner and many of us had very thick heads the next morning, when I had to make an abominable journey of 200 miles over very rough roads to Stilos, near Khania and Suda Bay.

Election Day was Sunday 31st March 1946. I rose at 0200 hours and opened my sealed orders, which were that I was to attend the election at Ano Viannos in the south of Crete and that I was to be there before sunrise. Although we were ordered not to show arms, we were advised to have loaded pistols inside our battledress blouses. The journey to Ano Viannos was hard, over dreadful tracks with no sign-posts, but it was wonderful to see dawn break and the sunrise over the mountains.

I spent all day at the polling booth until after the count. My name was inscribed in the minute book as Kyrios L. W. Wright. Out of a voting list of some 573 only 46 people voted, because the villagers were predominantly 'Left' and hoped that the election might be declared invalid. The Royalists and the Nationalists tied. At the end of the proceedings I went with the electoral committee to the village doctor's house. He told me that the Nazis had almost destroyed the village before evacuating it, and that the villagers believed they would get a heaven on earth if they went entirely to the Left, having seen what the Right had done! An old shepherd member of the committee wept when I left the village. I drove back through the darkness taking the Judicial Representative with me to Iraklion and very weary, I got to bed at 0200 hours. Candilis, my young interpreter, had done very well.

I should explain that only men had the vote, which was on a proportional representation basis. After the initial count, the surplus votes went to a second count at regional level, and the surplus votes from that to a third count at national level. It was very fair.

The next few days in Crete were spent in compiling my report, going to Agios Nicholaos to pay off my interpreter and to visit the Nomark or Mayor, and going to Neapolis to visit the Court of First Instance, where the judicial representative who had been at Ano Viannos with me gave me some delightful almonds.

One day, 5th April – a pleasant day, too – I went with three of my British colleagues to Khania as members of a Court of Enquiry convened by Colonel Merritt, the head of the British military mission in Crete, with whom we dined. Again I saw H.M.S. York majestically beached in Suda Bay which was a graveyard of ships.

The next day we embarked on M.S. Quercy, a small French warship, where Commandant Pinon and Captain Bernard de Sagonza entertained us to cocktails, the British Vice-Consul, Norma Constantinedes and others attended. Then, in M.S. Quercy, we sailed to Greece, arriving at the Piraeus at 0730 hours on Sunday 7th April 1946, to be taken to Kifissia, a suburb of Athens, to the Sarimaris Hotel.

On 8th April we viewed the great sights of Athens, and bade farewell to our French colleagues at the officers' club. The following day we met the American observers at 'La Grande Bretagne', and dined with them at 'The Cellar', Athens' best restaurant. We then proceeded to The Argentina, getting home very late.

I suffered a dreadful bout of nose-bleeding on the morrow, but it did not stop me from bidding farewell, at the Piraeus, to our American friends. In the bay was the U.S.S. Missouri, the biggest battleship in the world, on which the Japanese had surrendered to General MacArthur. Despite a very sore throat I dined with my British colleagues at The Cellar again, in the presence of Admiral Hewitt of the U.S. Navy and the French General La Parra.

On Monday 15th April we embarked at the Piraeus on H.M.T. Empire Eddystone, in dreadful accommodation in the forward hold. During the night I again suffered dreadful nose-bleeding which soaked my blankets and blocked my throat; a scream, alone, saved me from suffocating to death. After an unpleasant voyage in bad weather, we disembarked at Naples on Thursday 18th April. I said goodbye to Major Beeby, Major Irwin and to Tony, Bif, Roger and Michael who had proved such splendid friends, and I took myself to dinner at No. 2 Company Mess of my unit.

Next day, I found myself posted back to II L. of C. Signals and made my way to A.F.H.Q. at Caserta to dine with Wilfred Saunders and Subaltern Rand. I saw a good deal of Wilf in the next few days.

Very soon I found myself as Chief Duty Signal Officer again, replacing the incumbent who had gone down with suspected smallpox, as a consequence of which the entire unit was put into quarantine. Fortunately this did not last long, for Mark Dash was declared free of the disease.

I was now very tired and was delighted to spend three days at Ravello in the Hotel Palumbo, with its marvellous views of Amalfi, and its two beautiful villas, the Cimbrone and the Rufolo. Later I was sent to Capua to investigate the signals commitment there, and I recommended the cessation of all teletype communications there. My commanding officers, Lt Colonel L.C. "Inky" Udell M.B.E. and Major Alan Mitchell, did their best to persuade me to defer my release, offering me the post of second-in-command of No. 2 Company. It was all very tempting because I knew little of anything except *la vie militaire*, but my duty now was quite clearly to my dear Kath and Christina.

On Friday 3rd May I deployed a very smart guard at the Fort Del'Ovo, now our unit headquarters. The next day I was asked to give away the bride, Private R.M. Harrison of the A.T.S., at her wedding in Caserta, but I was unable to arrange this in time. However, I had the pleasure of meeting the bride and groom on the steamer which was taking John Gates, Vic Durrant and me to the Isle of Capri for the weekend. We stayed at the Villa Eudesandra and in the evening met my friends Signor and Signora Géros of the Villa Axura. Signor Géros was Greek. His wife had had a rough time in a German concentration camp. Having attended Mass in Capri the next morning, I took John and Vic to the villa of San Michele, Anacapri and down to the Faraglione where we swam in very cold water. Signor and Signora Géros called on us in the evening and we joined them at the Due Palme where I danced with Signora Géros, who had completely lost her hearing during her imprisonment. My diary records: "This has been a lovely weekend. I wish to God that Kath were with us".

On the Monday we caught the 0700 hours boat back to Naples and I spent the day packing and sending my trunk and box to the military forwarding officer for transport to my home.

I had a parting interview with my commanding officer, the splendid Inky Udell, never dreaming that we would soldier together again in the future!

The company officers' mess gave a splendid dinner party, presided over by Alan Mitchell in honour of the Release Group 27 Officers who were departing the next day: Bob Wilkins, Alf Turner, Fred Phillips and myself. There were many guests including "Doc" Lanyon and Tom Russ of Cable and Wireless. It was a splendid party and at 0200 hrs in the morning I inscribed the wall with my signature before going to bed.

On Tuesday 7th May 1946 we were seen off at Garibaldi Station by the commanding officer Alan Mitchell, "Pop" Blyth, Robbie (Athol Robson)… 16 officers altogether. It was a very emotional moment. Nothing breeds comradeship as much as war and like any good regiment, we had become a family linked by hoops of steel. Despite the joy of starting the journey home, it was a very hard parting. The strength of our comradeship is shown in the fact that so many of us have held a reunion every year. But today we are a dwindling number!

That night we had supper in Rome and the next day, the first anniversary of V.E. Day, we had breakfast at Rimini, lunch at Bologna, and dinner at Padua. By way of Verona we passed Venice through Mestre, and arrived at Villach in Austria at 0500 hours, where we de-trained. We had caught up with Peter Whaley whom we had seen off on the Medloc train. We explored Villach, showered and were in bed by 2200 hours.

On Saturday 11th May we entrained at Villach and passing near to Bertchesgaden, of Hitler fame, we steamed up the Drau valley through beautiful Tyrolean scenery and stopped for tea at Traunstein. Thence we passed Mount Glockner, passing through the battered Munich during the night, and through Germany by way of Augsberg, Ulm and Karlsruhe, to enter France at the badly battered but beautiful city of Strasbourg where we crossed the Rhine. On Monday 13th May in the early hours we reached Calais, where I took photographs of the places of activity of May 1940.

We had the worst crossing of the Channel I have ever known. From Dover we went to Aldershot for the release procedure and to receive our "de-mob" clothing. Having bade farewell to Alf, Freddie, and Bob in London, I made my way to St Pancras station, where I gave a porter every bit of English coinage that I had, and he spat in it!

That evening I de-trained at Wellingborough where I was met by Uncle Hubert, and I spent the night with Ida and him before leaving for Matlock on the morrow, 14th May, where I was met by my dearest Kath and Christina and my father-in-law. I was so glad that Mrs Roberts, who had taken care of Kath when I left her at Waterloo station in January 1944, was staying with Kath. It was wonderful to be home. God had been good to me!

I was on leave until 5th August, when I was to be released from active service and transferred to the Regular Army Reserve of Officers.

My first Friday at home I was delighted to find in the Rutland Arms Hotel smoke room Colonel Gerry Underwood, Colonel Arthur Haslehurst, "Shorty" Woods and John Harrison, together with R.S.M. Cutts and Captain G.M. Morley and, to my great joy, Austin Evitts who had gallantly survived the five years as a P.O.W. since commanding us at Calais, and had maintained a clandestine radio set during his imprisonment. He had received a mention in despatches, but did not know whether this was for Calais or for his imprisonment. With all these I maintained a very close friendship until their deaths.

On 25th May at All Saints Catholic Church in Old Glossop, my brother George was married to my schoolfriend Barbara Malkin, who had served in the W.A.A.F., and Kath and I attended. My brother Kenneth, who had by then been released as a sergeant from the Indian Electrical and Mechanical Engineers, was there too. It was a lovely wedding. That same day I met Walter Harrop, six years to the day since we had been separated in the fighting at Calais. He, who had suffered five years as a prisoner of war, thanked me most sincerely for the letter I had written to his parents.

At the end of May, Kath and I went to Stratford-Upon-Avon for a few days' holiday, staying again at the York House Hotel. At the theatre we saw 'As You Like It', 'The Tempest', 'Love's Labour's Lost' and 'Cymbeline'. We were met by Bob Wilkins with whom we went on the river in a rowing boat and rescued two girls in great difficulty in a punt.

We had, too, a delightful holiday, with Ida and Hubert at Wellingborough, including a few days in London where I paid my first visits to the Tower, Westminster Abbey and Cathedral, and Downing Street where we saw the Prime Minister, Clement Attlee. At the theatre we saw 'Merrie England' and Shaw's 'Caesar and

Cleopatra'. I took the opportunity to telephone the Adjutant-General's department at the War Office who would be willing to accept me back up till six months after my release, should I decide to make the army my career.

We took Christina to Southport to stay with my Aunt Muriel. I also had a delightful week at Llandudno where we stayed in the best hotel, the Imperial, for £1 per day! During this week we had the pleasure of calling on my old section clerk, George Whiffin in Anglesey.

Shortly before my release from active military duty on 5th August 1946, and transfer to the Regular Army Reserve of Officers, we were visited by my old cypher officer John Gates and his fiancée. John was to visit us again some 20 years later when he was one of H.M. Inspectors of Planning.

On 5th August, a chapter in my life was concluded. There is no doubt that the army had got into my blood. Memory mercifully had blotted out the worst of the bad times, and much of the anxiety that went with them, and I tended to remember mostly the better times. It was a chapter that had lasted nearly seven years. During the war we were not allowed to keep diaries but I did in Crete, hence an imbalance in my narrative.

But a new chapter with all its post-war difficulties had opened. And above all I had my dearest Kath and Christina.

Chapter IV

Post-War Years, 1947-1951

The Reconstituted Territorial Army

Some months before my release from active military service I had been accepted for emergency training as a teacher, but there would be a delay of at least a year, and so I accepted a temporary teaching post at Bakewell C. of E. Secondary Modern School, under a good headmaster, Mr C.R. (Dick) Alcock, specialising in French. It was poorly paid, about £4 per week, but I did not find it difficult and I enjoyed good relations with both staff and pupils, all of whom are now retired!

My wife Kath and sister-in-law Mary took a very great interest in the Peacock Players of which they were founder-members. Kath was a splendid actress, producer and costumier, and I was given small parts in her plays, the first being 'The Farmer's Wife'. I also helped in the donkey-work involved in any production.

In October 1946, I attended two great reunions: one of II L. of C. Signals in London, where I met so many of my old comrades; and the other of our original T.A. Unit, 2nd (North Midland) Corps Signals, raised by Colonel "Gerry" Underwood, in Glossop. There were about 600 present and Gerry kindly referred to me in his address with reference to the fighting at Calais in May 1940. It was indeed a great reunion and The Glossop and District Royal Signals Old Comrades Association was formed that night.

In the autumn I was elected to the General and Service Committees of the Bakewell and District Branch of the Royal British Legion to which I gave unbroken service as Hon. Secretary, Hon. Treasurer, Chairman and then President for 30 years until 1978.

That autumn was alleviated by radio broadcasts of the great operas by the San Carlo Opera Company which had been brought from Naples by Brigadier BUS Cripps under whom I had served.

My younger brother Colin came home from the Far East, a splendid looking young fellow after the three or more years since I had seen him. He had rendered conspicuous service in the Signals Branch R.A.F. at Supreme Headquarters Allied Expeditionary Force at Versailles and Supreme Headquarters Far Eastern Forces under Admiral Earl Mountbatten in Changi, Singapore.

As did so many of the ex-servicemen, I found it not very easy to settle down to civilian life after seven years' war service, despite all the goodness and love I received. The War Office was willing to have me back in my War Substantive Rank, but after reflection, I decided against it. I hated the thought of leaving dear Kath and Christina for what would be long periods. As it happened H.M. Government reconstituted the Territorial Army and at the request of Colonel Gerry Underwood, Tom Wragg and I were gazetted as captains into the new T.A. in May of 1947.

In December and January of 1947 Kath was very busy producing The Farmer's Wife in which I played a small part as the Doctor. It was a tremendous success for Kath, who immediately started rehearsing for her condensed version of 'The Taming of the Shrew' which she put on most successfully at the Bradshaw Hall in Chesterfield. We were indeed fortunate to get to Chesterfield, for on 3rd February a terrific blizzard heralded several weeks of the country's being snowbound. Schools were closed because no coal could get through from the mines. Indeed, a national fuel emergency was declared. Most of the country's roads were impassable and many of the railways. A locomotive was snowbound in Millersdale for some six weeks. The gas and electrical supplies were haphazard and there were many explosions when occasionally gas supplies were restored because people had forgotten to turn off the gas taps! Little coal was reaching any household. At Parsonage Croft we all lived in the very small kitchen to keep warm and conserve fuel. To return to 'The Taming of the Shrew' we went to Chesterfield on Hulley's bus and several times we had to get out and push it through the snow-drifts. A Lancaster bomber which was dropping supplies to the top country near Hartington crashed. Electricity restrictions were imposed until further notice.

About 18th March a big thaw set in leading to very severe flooding especially in East Anglia, causing another national emergency.

The cold winter was followed by a very warm summer and several times I went to the river to dive into the Big Bend and swim, but river-swimming stirs up too much mud from the riverbed.

Having joined the reconstituted T.A. in the 21st Corps Signal Regiment in the squadron based at Chesterfield, I now became very busy training soldiers and it was splendid to resume my great friendship with the Honorary Colonel, Gerry

Underwood. In the regiment, too, were Richard Pickford and "Wally" Waldron with both of whom I had served in the early days of the war, and both of whom had been at Dunkirk; there was another Dunkirk veteran, too, Richard Grimwood-Taylor. With the three I developed a lifelong friendship and each eventually commanded the regiment, as did I, and in due time I attended all their funerals and wrote their obituaries.

During the summer, we were visited by my old friend Captain Bill Malcolm and his wife Lu, together with their daughter Carole. At Coventry on 26th July I attended the wedding of Captain Bob Wilkins to Madge. Bill, Bob and I had been promoted to captain together and our friendships have remained strong ever since.

In August, Kath and I drove to the home of Bill and Lu in Edinburgh via the Lake District and had a delightful holiday savouring the history of Edinburgh. Later that month I attended a fortnight's course at The School of Military Administration at Colchester, which I found, and still find, invaluable. My mind was still playing with the idea of taking a permanent regular commission, and the War Office was very interested in me. In September I attended a signals tactics course at the School of Signals at Catterick Camp, where I met a brilliant signals officer, Major John Higgins, who had been a war-substantive Lt. Colonel at the age of 22. He later became Training Major to my T.A. regiment and we remained firm friends until his death in 1977.

At the beginning of October, I resigned my post at Bakewell Boys School, to start my degree course at the University of Sheffield. Between my T.A. and R.B.L. duties and my family responsibilities, I fear I had little time for study in the evenings. My principal lecturer in physics was Mr J.R. Clark, who in the First World War, as an Officer of The King's Own Light Infantry, had been certified dead after a head wound. He came to in the mortuary, read his obituary in the Sheffield Telegraph and, not being satisfied with it, wrote another! Some twenty years later, we found ourselves together on the University Military Education Committee and became very firm friends. He died towards his ninetieth year and as Honorary Colonel of the University Officer Training Corps I was represented at his funeral. Kath was particularly fond of his third wife for they frequently stayed at the Milford Hotel near our home.

In the fall of the year I attended two great reunions: one in Glossop of 4 Corps Signals and one in London of North Africa and Italian L. of C. Signals, where I acted as Mr Vice-President amongst so many old friends. One of these, Peter Riley, a very high Anglican, had entered the Society of the Sacred Mission at Kelham Hall and I spent three days with him there. Eventually he was ordained and spent most of his ministry in Jamaica.

I greatly enjoyed the fairly frequent visits of Uncle Hubert and Aunt Ida of whom Kath was very fond. Hubert had been awarded the Military Cross in the Sherwood Foresters in 1918, and with our common military background he and I were very much like brothers despite the disparity in age. At Christmastide we all assembled at Parsonage Croft together with Kath's cousin Kathleen Noton and her companion June. Christina, who had not been very well, was very much the centre of attention.

1948

During 1948 a small group of us began to gather to discuss Christianity. This was initiated by Richard Akeroyd, who had recently resigned his commission in the Royal Navy after war-service in submarines, and included my friend Tom Wragg, Edwin Sellors, a dentist, and later, my great friend Donald Storrs-Fox, recently retired District Commissioner of the Nyere District of Kenya. It had occurred to Richard in Notre Dame Cathedral, Paris, in his own words that he was "committing spiritual suicide by remaining in the Royal Navy". Eventually he became a Professor of Theology in an American University. For Richard I had the greatest admiration.

At the religious level, I myself became Honorary Secretary of the United Christian Council, with Father Hunter as President, and I remained Honorary Secretary for many years. The finest speaker we ever had was Father Agnellus Andrew, a Franciscan who later became a Bishop in charge of communications at the Vatican. I will never forget his address in which he said that "we must bring Christ out of the churches into the fields, the farms and the streets, and that every generation should be to itself what Christ was to his generation".

On 8th May 1948, the third anniversary of V.E. Day, I organised a dinner at the Rutland Arms Hotel, Bakewell, which we resolved to repeat every year. On that and all subsequent occasions I always sent a telegram to Winston Churchill, the Architect of Victory, on behalf of the Bakewell V.E. Club, to which he always very kindly responded.

Later that week, Kathleen (Kennedy), Marchioness of Hartington, was killed in an aeroplane crash in France, on 13th May. Only recently I had knelt with her at Mass in Bakewell. Her husband the Marquess had been killed in France following the invasion of 1944. Her brother John was destined to be assassinated as the president of the U.S.A. on 22nd November 1963.

By now I was very involved in the training of the 21st Corps Signal Regiment T.A. and was frequently in the company of my dear friend Colonel Gerry

Underwood, our Honorary Colonel. Soon after college closed on 10th July 1948, I set off to the Tactical (later re-designated "Senior Officers") School at Earlstoke Park, Devizes. At the Technical School I quickly befriended Lt. Colonel R.H. Lumley-Webb, M.C., known as "Squire", and his Adjutant Captain John Penman, M.C., both of the Argyll and Sutherland Highlanders. "Squire" stood 6 feet 6 inches tall and had just retired from distinguished service in Palestine. John had gained his M.C. at Sainte Valery in June 1940. He was the young man who was complimented for his foolhardy bravery by General Rommel. Later, John gained a bar to his M.C. in Korea, but unfortunately himself fell victim to a trap he had organised against the Chinese insurgents. After discharge, and one week before being ordained into the Church of Scotland, he died from his wounds. During that fortnight's course on tactics I grew devoted to these two splendid officers. The course was very hard but rewarding and I was delighted to receive an 'A+' commendation at the end of it. My military knowledge had been tremendously increased.

My regiment had its first T.A. annual camp at Pickering. We packed a lot into seven days, and were visited by the Rt. Hon. Emanuel Shinwell, Secretary of State for War, whom I found very pleasant, zealous and enthusiastic, a very good minister who eventually became Secretary of State for Defence. During camp in the wireless scheme I assumed the role of divisional commander and received a very good compliment from the chief signal officer, Brigadier J.W. Childs.

Within a few days of returning from camp, Kath, Christina and I sailed from Liverpool to the Isle of Man to spend a fortnight at Port Erin. This was a very pleasant holiday in mixed weather and we met some charming people, but the food rationing was very tight and the hotels rather dated; the Isle of Man had been used as an internment area for enemy nationals during the war.

On our return I was plunged into the selection of a new prospective Conservative candidate following the withdrawal of Mr W. Aitken. Eventually we selected Mr E.B. Wakefield, a Conservative of liberal thinking, late of the Indian Civil Service who had been decorated for services during the Quetta earthquake, and profoundly disagreed with Mr Churchill's views on India's independence. He was, in due course, elected and remained a splendid M.P. until he applied for the Stewardship of the Chiltern Hundreds and later became High Commissioner to Malta.

In September of 1948 Christina started school at the kindergarten on the avenue. Kath and I were now preparing to move to Flat 9 in Haddon House which had been my billet in 1939 and was now converted to flats, having been leased by the Duke of Rutland to the Bakewell Urban District Council for 99 years. Tom and Ida Wragg were allocated to Flat 8. Our flats overlooked the very fertile vegetable garden that we shared by bisecting. Kath always had superb taste and proved herself a great homebuilder. We bought antiques from Tideswell, Sheffield and Buxton: high-back Windsor chairs, a beautiful wardrobe, delightful antique chests of drawers and the like. Otherwise, owing to the ravages of war, the only furniture you could buy was the 'Utility' furniture. Our bed was 'Utility' but it lasted very well for about 30 years! We also spent a lot of time "scrubbing out" at Haddon House and on 27th November 1948 we moved into our new home. The first night the main fuse blew which was remedied by Mr Rawson of the Bakewell Power Station whom I found by travelling on my bicycle, there being no telephone! We had, too, bought a French poodle, "Johnny" but he was very highly strung. Nonetheless, he was a splendid companion for Kath during my long days in Sheffield.

Ever since my arrival in Bakewell on 11th September 1939, Mass had been celebrated in a two-skinned 'Tin Chapel' off Granby Road. This was sold or 'compulsorily' purchased, and the R.C. Diocese of Nottingham bought the Congregational Chapel on Buxton Road. This was 'opened' on Wednesday 1st December 1948 at a Mass celebrated by Doctor Edward Ellis, Bishop of Nottingham in the presence of abut 30 priests and, to his great credit, Mr Richard W.P. Cockerton, solicitor, of Bakewell who was to take a great part in the lives of Kath, Christina and me in later years. Doctor Ellis I had known when he was Parish Priest of Hadfield before the war, and he had done so much for the unemployed during the years of the depression.

1949

We were having a hard winter with much snow over Christmastide and both Kath and I had suffered bouts of flu. Kath's father, John Howard, began to suffer very painful arthritis and went into Smedley's Hydro, now the County Council Headquarters, at Matlock on 29th January. He went there with great confidence and within six weeks he returned home, completely cured.

Kath and I were both kept busy by the Peacock Players. Kath played very well in Emlyn Williams's 'The Wind of Heaven' in late January 1949. It was a good production. She went on to produce Ibsen's 'Ghosts', a splendid production which she put on at the town hall on 3rd, 4th and 5th March, with a wonderful cast. The following month in 'Arsenic and Old Lace' I played the part of the Brewster brother who thought he was President Theodore (Teddy) Roosevelt.

In the meantime, Kath's sister Mary had become engaged to Bill Flewitt of

Ashford and they were married on 20th April 1949, Bill going to live with her at Parsonage Croft.

Music was one of my main subjects at college and I had the great pleasure of singing in Bach's Mass in B Minor at the Victoria Hall in Sheffield. I still think it is the greatest work of all times; the Sanctus is superb.

Throughout the spring and summer, I played a great part in the training of 21 Corps Signal Regiment. Our Adjutant, Captain Frank Berry, had been replaced by Captain Ken Newell who had worked with the clandestine forces S.O.E. (Special Operations Executive) in Europe towards the end of the war. I was very disappointed that owing to college examinations I could not command in Derby the guard of honour for H.R.H. the Princess Elizabeth on 28th June.

When I look back, I realise that I was virtually doing the work of a regular officer in the regiment. For some time I held the office of Adjutant and was regularly in touch with our Honorary Colonel, Gerry Underwood, the commanding officer, and Lt. Colonel R.A. Waldrow who had succeeded John de C. Barber. From 10th to 24th July we were in annual camp at Marske-by-the-Sea where we worked and played very hard indeed. I was proud to clear 4 feet 11 inches in the high jump and to run in the one-mile race in the regimental sports. We carried out a large Corps exercise in which I functioned as the Corps Commander.

During 1949 a great international event had taken place, largely through the initiative of General George C. Marshall, U.S. Foreign Secretary, and the Rt. Honourable Ernest Bevin, our Foreign Secretary: the creation of the North Atlantic Pact with its military organisation N.A.T.O. (North Atlantic Treaty Organisation), to protect the West against the USSR's threat from the East. N.A.T.O. has kept the peace ever since. In my view Ernest Bevin, who left school at the age of ten to become General Secretary of the Transport and General Workers Union, Minister of Labour in the wartime coalition government, and Foreign Secretary in the post-war government, was the best Foreign Secretary of the twentieth century.

On return from camp I was pleased to learn that I had passed my University of Sheffield Institute of Education examination. During the holidays I worked as a farm labourer for two shillings (10p) an hour at Jex-Blake's Haddon Farm: my back ached from transplanting kale, but it did me good. Kath, Christina and I spent a fortnight staying with my Aunt Muriel at Southport and proceeding from there to Keswick in the Lake District, with which we fell in love. There was little traffic on the roads in 1949 and Keswick was not crowded. It was so good to drink in the beauty and history of those beautiful lakes and fells, and Christina was delighted with our visit to Beatrix Potter's house at Sawrey, having read so many of her Peter Rabbit and other books. Kath was always a splendid organiser of holidays.

On 1st September I was summoned for interview by Mr Watkins in charge of further education at Sheffield Education Office and was offered and accepted a "temporary" post as assistant lecturer in the Department of Commerce and Management of Sheffield College of Commerce and Technology, now Sheffield Hallam University, teaching English and Mathematics to full-time students, and outlines of Central and Local Government to "post-entry trainee students" from the town hall. My students were most charming, erudite and hardworking young ladies in the age range of 16–18 years. My "temporary" appointment was to last with a brief interruption until 1980! Within a few days I was asked to coach civil servants for entry to the clerical, secretarial and executive boards. These were mostly mature students, many ex-service of both sexes. The classes were held in the evening and I was paid extra for them: nineteen shillings (95p) for each two-hour stint, but this more than paid for the weekly bus-ticket between Bakewell and Sheffield of 11s-4d (59p)! The full-time secretarial courses lasted a year and it has been a great pleasure to meet my former students again over the years. One student I vividly remember is Susan Phillips, who was to marry the Honourable Mark Balfour, son of Lord Riverdale. Mark predeceased his father, and Susan died some three months before my dear wife Kath in 1996, to be followed the next year by Lord Riverdale, who with his son Mark was a friend of mine through the Sheffield Defence Studies Dining Club. Another good student was Elspeth Urquhart, daughter of Major-General Roy Urquhart who commanded the 1st Airborne Division at Arnhem in the dreadful battle of September 1944. She is now married to Sir Menzies Campbell Q.C., M.P., a great figure in the Liberal Democrat Party.

In 1950 I was given the task of lecturing junior journalists in English and British constitution. They were very zealous and enthusiastic students and this I did for some years. Amongst my students were Michael Parkinson of television fame, and Jean Rook who was already a Manchester M.A. Jean was a thoroughly charming and sweet girl and rose to great fame in journalism before her death from cancer. Her pen was vitriolic, but her nature delightful. Some time before her death she was mugged by burglars and lost all her jewellery. Many of my journalist students rose to very high positions in the BBC, ITV and as editors of great newspapers and it is gratifying to look back on them.

I must here mention Mr and Mrs Roberts always known as "Nanna" to Kath and Christina, who in 1949 came to live in Over Haddon from Ashford, Middlesex. He, a retired excise officer, was virtually blind and she was completely deaf. Mr Roberts presided over "The Brethren" in Bakewell: he certainly knew the Bible and I enjoyed listening to and conversing with him. Mrs Roberts was a tremendous friend of Kath who was broken-hearted when she died some ten years later. Mrs Roberts was an expert lip-reader and very perceptive. She described Kath as "a great homebuilder" and how gloriously true was that!

Christmas of 1949 ended our first year in Haddon House. We administered the flats through a tenants' committee of which I was chairman, and succeeded in getting a payphone installed which was a great achievement, for the Post Office telephone service was still suffering from the ravages of war. The surrounding woods, fields and orchards were delightful for walking and for the children's play. But we did not enjoy good health in that first year. Both Kath and I suffered frequent feverish colds and poor Christina fell very ill with chickenpox. Doctor Cook was a very conscientious doctor.

1950

As we entered the new decade of the 1950s, we endured very bad weather. There is no doubt that the winters of those days were much more severe than those of today. Kath, Christina and I now developed a lifelong friendship with Eric Cotton-Smith and Desmond and Denise Lloyd of S. Anselm's School. Eric I had met at Mass in the 'Tin Chapel'. He was very erudite. His father was a very sincere Anglican priest. Eric and his mother both became Catholics. Eric, who was a brilliant linguist in modern and ancient languages, had worked on intelligence in India during the war with Gilbert Harding, who was then achieving fame on BBC TV in the programme 'What's My Line?' He now confined himself to prep school teaching. He had been at Stamford School with Sir Michael Tippett, the great composer, and another boy who became Father Woodbridge. Eric would have made a splendid priest – preferably of the Order of St. Benedict – but it was not to be. He had a first-class brain which, I now think, was best used on intelligence in India. He had a great influence on our lives. Kath and I attended his funeral near Lincoln in 1987. He introduced us to his friends, Desmond and Denise Lloyd. Desmond had a very good brain: he was a product of Trinity College, Dublin and I think he would have been better used as a university lecturer than as a prep-school teacher. His wife Denise ran a pre-prep school at Holme Hall. She was delightful, with a strong sense of humour. Having brought four children into the world, she was destined to die from cancer when her youngest son Robert was only four years old. Kath was always the soul of kindness, hospitality and generosity to Eric, Desmond and Denise and their children. She was godmother to Philippa, who drove up from south London to attend Kath's funeral in 1996. Between Eric and Christina there always existed a very strong bond.

Apart from my lecturing, and the tremendous time I devoted to the Territorial Army, I was also Hon. Secretary to the United Nations Association and the United Christian Council, and a hardworking member of the British Legion.

When I look back through my diaries, there is a constant reference to meeting Colonel Gerry Underwood who had so great an influence on my life. Richard Pickford and Richard Grimwood-Taylor, both of whom were my predecessors in commanding the regiment and both lawyers, were also having a great influence on me and became very strong friends.

Another of my heroes, Field Marshal the Earl Wavell of Cyrenaica and Winchester died on 24th May 1950. I immediately ordered his splendid anthology of verse 'Other Men's Flowers', containing all the poems that he could remember by heart; that anthology has been my "Vade Mecum" ever since.

A momentous event occurred on 25th June 1950, whilst we were on a T.A. night exercise: the news came through that North Korea had invaded South Korea. President Harry S. Truman, a very decisive man, immediately called a meeting of the Security Council, which was boycotted by the U.S.S.R., thus depriving themselves of exercising their veto. The Security Council on the motion of the U.S.A. ordered the creation of a United Nations Force to repel the invaders. The U.S.A. provided the bulk of the force and we put in a Commonwealth Division. The supreme commander was the redoubtable General MacArthur. I vividly remember a broadcast by the Prime Minister Clement Attlee to the effect that the fire that had started in Korea might burn down our own house! Following a brilliant landing by the U.N. Forces in North Korea, millions of Chinese volunteers were drafted to the aid of the North Koreans. There was talk on the initiative of MacArthur of the atomic bomb being dropped north of the River Yalu. The Prime Minister flew to Washington to dissuade President Truman, with the encouragement of Winston Churchill who, nonetheless, warned parliament: "Serious as is the situation in the Far East, it is in Europe that the mortal danger lies". The Truman administration decided that it would settle for two Koreas divided by the 38th parallel, to MacArthur's disgust, leaving Truman no choice but to dismiss him and replace him with General Westmoreland.

One of the greatest British operations in the Korean War was the Battle of the Imjin River in which the Glorious Gloucesters played so great a part. Lt. Colonel

Carne VC DSO was subjugated to many months solitary confinement during which time he carved a crucifix. His Adjutant, Anthony Farrar-Hockley escaped five times and was recaptured five times. Eventually he became Lt. General Sir Anthony Farrar-Hockley whom I met and with whom I corresponded in later life. His account is given in 'The Edge of the Sword'. His chaplain the Reverend Sam J. Davies M.B.E. who described his dreadful experiences in 'In Spite of Dungeons', became a friend of mine in a pilgrimage I led to Malta in 1998. Bakewell lost one of its young men, Cecil Clark, in that Korean War. Hostilities eventually ceased in 1958 after President Eisenhower had succeeded Truman. To this day, there is no proper peace between the two Koreas, but the war showed that the United Nations had got teeth.

During the time of the Korean War, I was constantly uneasy lest the T.A. should be embodied to go to war, but it was not to be.

To revert to family life Kath, Christina and I had a delightful holiday in the summer of 1950. We stayed with the Bramwells at Northend, scene of the Battle of Edge Hill, and had delightful days in Stratford-upon-Avon (where we saw Sir John Gielgud play Cassius in 'Julius Caesar'), the Cotswolds, Blenheim Palace and Oxford. Thence we travelled via Burford and Windsor to Olga Roberts, the widow of Philip Roberts, a friend of Kath's. We visited the sights of London – the National Gallery, Hampton Court, Madam Tussauds – and sailed on the River Thames. For Christina and me, these were "first times" under the splendid tutelage of Kath. Kath and I also went to the theatre to see 'Oklahoma!' which was superb.

On return I attended annual camp at Marske-by-the-Sea not far from Saltburn where I had been sent after my escape from Calais in 1947. It was a great delight to see again Mr and Mrs "Bill" Kelly who had been so good to me in 1940, and their children: Helen, who came to our mess functions; Bill, who had been at Dunkirk; and Dennis. We worked and played hard during that 15-day camp, carrying out two regimental exercises, and being visited by General Penney, the representative Colonel Commandant, who had commanded the 1st British Division at Anzio; Brigadier Childs, the Command Chief Signal Officer; and our Honorary Colonel, Gerry Underwood. In the course of camp, it fell to me to organise the sports day, which was ruined by rain, and in which I achieved my high jump feat.

Shortly after camp, I attended a signals tactics course at Catterick at the School of Signals where I met many officers: Louis of the French Army who had been incarcerated in Dachau and Buchenwald, those dreadful concentration camps; an Iraqi officer who unfortunately was sick over my trousers; and Ned Doyle and Frank McNamara of the Éireann Army. A few days afterwards, Frank, a charming officer, was electrocuted whilst alighting from a radio van at Scarborough.

In September 1950, I bought my first motorcar, an Austin Seven Ruby, for £150. This I maintained myself, constantly having to drain water from the carburettor and adjusting the timing. We had great fun with it, but the fun had to be paid for. Every night during the winter I drained the radiator lest there be frost, and every morning before setting off for Sheffield I refilled the radiator with hot water. The roads were seldom salted in those days and I had some hazardous journeys to and from Sheffield. Its advantage over the bus was marginal and I was glad to sell it in the spring of 1951!

On Tuesday 26th September, the dreadful Creswell Colliery disaster occurred, in which 80 miners lost their lives. Some 40 years later I represented the Lieutenancy, at the Lord Lieutenant's request, at the annual dinner of the Creswell Royal British Legion and I referred very delicately but sincerely to the disaster in my address.

Despite illness during the fall of 1950, I worked hard training the T.A. and I was particularly proud of the standing orders for signal officer procedure that I wrote at the request of Lt. Colonel Pickford. Of the Adjutants, I was and remained until his death a great friend and admirer of Captain Ken Newell, who had served in Special Operations Executive during the war – a very dangerous service.

It was a hard winter, starting with heavy snow storms early in December. We bought a Valor stove to help heat our very cold flat. It is worthy of note that on Christmas Eve, Saint Peter's Tomb was irrefutably identified beneath Saint Peter's in Rome.

1951

On the Feast of the Epiphany, 6th January, Father Hunter died. A solemn Requiem Mass, presided over by the Bishop of Nottingham Doctor Edward Ellis, was celebrated at Hassop on 10th January. For some weeks the Parish was cared for by Dom Vincent Fogarty OSB from Alderwasley.

At college I was now given an extra paid job on Thursday evenings, lecturing civil servants and coaching them for the executive class at the civil service. This was to last for some ten years and I met some very interesting and talented students, and was gratified that my results were good.

In my regiment there were changes: Lt. Colonel R. A. Waldron was succeeded as commanding officer by Lt. Colonel Richard Pickford. The three of us had been with the British Expeditionary Force in 1940. My good friend the Adjutant, Captain Ken Newell, who had worked clandestinely with the Special Operations Executive, was succeeded by Captain Peter Ashlin. Wally and Ken were dined out at a weekend camp held at the Peveril of the Peak Hotel, Dovedale on 13th January. It was a splendid occasion, presided over by Colonel Gerry Underwood. Life in the T.A. was taken very seriously for the Cold War had begun. A week later I accompanied the C.O. to H.Q. Derby, where I was amazed to meet my C.O. of the Italian Campaign, Lt. Colonel L.C.U. "Inky" Udell, M.B.E., who now being retired from the regular army had applied to join the T.A. as a captain which was a measure of his tremendous humility and patriotism. He was received with acclaim! Soon he was promoted to major in command of the Wolverhampton Squadron and remained my friend for life. His obituary fell to me to write. The chief of the Imperial General Staff was now Field Marshal Sir William Slim who had commanded the 14th (the "Forgotten") Army in Burma. Eventually he was to be raised to the peerage and succeeded H.R.H. the Duke of Gloucester as Governor General of Australia. He was a great leader and gave many interesting talks over the radio on subjects such as "The Great Soldier", and "Morale". He appealed for more people to join the Territorial Army and he described every Territorial soldier as being "twice a citizen" in doing two jobs – and how right he was! One of his most famous lectures he gave at Sheffield City Hall on 'The Making of an Army'. He had a wry sense of humour. Once, clad in all his insignia as Governor-General, he was travelling through the Australian outback when his car broke down in a remote town. Whilst it was repaired, he was ushered into the local saloon. On seeing him, the bartender called out "Christ", whereupon Slim responded "No – Slim, Governor-General!" He was one of the greatest soldiers of the twentieth century.

The new C.O., Richard Pickford, relied greatly on me in training matters and it fell to me to organise many of our weekend camps and the like. Lecturing was my forte.

On 21st March, my friend Donald Storrs-Fox was received into the Catholic Church at Matlock by Father John Goodwin, a former journalist, and I was his sponsor. Donald had decided to jump over the wall between Canterbury and Rome and to pull down the wall from the Roman side!

Donald, a product of Repton under the headmastership of Doctor William Temple, later to be Archbishop of Canterbury, was very highly intelligent and a natural leader, who had fought in the First World War, been commissioned into the Sherwood Foresters, transferred to the Machine Gun Corps and eventually to the Royal Flying Corps, later the R.A.F. In October 1918 he was shot down, upside down, into the German lines. In the P.O.W. hospital, he contracted Spanish 'Flu and vowed that if he got better, he would escape. This he did and was on the loose for a few days, not knowing that Armistice had been signed on 11th November. He had been declared "missing" to his parents in Bakewell, who dreaded that he had been killed. Donald made his way back to 'Blighty', arrived by train in Bakewell at midnight, walked to S. Anselm's School, where his father was headmaster, climbed the fire-escape into the boys' dormitory, told the boys not to worry and that he was only the headmaster's son and went down to the drawing room where he fell asleep on the sofa, to be found by his delighted parents the next morning!

Two days after Donald's reception into the Catholic Church, we together attended the Good Friday Liturgies at Cressbrook Hall, then a novitiate for the Sisters of the Presentation to whom Father Drury was the Chaplain. The veil of one of the young novices caught fire from the candle she was holding, and she was in terrible danger. Donald, ever a man of action, leaped over the bench and ripped from her the burning veil and other parts of her vestiture that were now on fire. He certainly saved her life. Shortly afterward in the course of the liturgy I heard Donald giggle. The psalm we were saying in Latin contained the line "With burnt offerings, O Lord, Those wilt not be satisfied"! This incident convinced Donald that he had done the right thing in jumping over the wall to Rome. He always referred to it as "the incident of the burning nun". Some 30 years afterward I met that charming nun at the Padley Pilgrimage. She recognised me and thanked me for saving her life. I corrected her and told her that it was Donald. Looking back, after all these years, I suppose that I must have gone to Donald's assistance and she had seen me and thus remembered me.

Meanwhile at Sheffield I continued to make very good friendships amongst the journalists whom I lectured. Kath very kindly had a few of them over to Haddon House and on one occasion we visited Miss Monica Hodgkinson at Hathersage who lived in the house which was the setting of St. John River's home in Charlotte Bronte's 'Jane Eyre', much of which was written at Hathersage.

Just before the end of term in July 1951 I received a request from the International Summer School Society to lead a holiday group to Rome and Sorrento. I, of course, went for nothing and Kath went with me as a student, Christina staying at Parsonage Croft during our absence.

Leaving home on Friday 20th July to collect the documents, we stayed with Olga Roberts at Ashford and before leaving for Rome with my 34 students whom I collected from St. Peter's School, near Victoria Station. Kath and I visited Westminster Abbey and the South Bank 1951 Exhibition which had been opened by the King. We must have had tremendous energy. From Victoria, via Folkestone and Boulogne we arrived in Paris at 5.17pm and after refreshments we departed from La Gare de Lyon at 7.45pm. Twenty-four hours afterward, via Dijon, Lyon, Mondaine, Turin, Genoa, Spiezia, Leghorn and Pisa, we reached Rome. We saw so much from the train. After accommodating my group, Kath and I walked to the Colosseum. I will never forget dear Kath's enthusiasm for everything. It was her first trip abroad. Indeed, I believe we were the first Bakewellians to venture abroad following the war!

We visited all the sights of Rome, ancient, modern and ecclesiastical: the Capitaline; the Palatine; the maritime prison where Sts. Peter and Paul were imprisoned; the English cemetery where the hearts of Keats and Shelley are buried; the four great basilicas and St. Peter's-in-the-Chains which houses Michelangelo's great Moses; the Castel Sant Angelo; and Keats' house by the Spanish steps, where we were to go on subsequent occasions. We had the great pleasure, too, of seeing operas performed at the Baths of Caracalla, going there by horse-drawn carriage.

Kath was a very beautiful girl with great dress sense and I shall never forget how she attracted the admiring gaze of the Romans, especially one great Roman gentleman who bowed most profoundly and sincerely to her in the Corso.

Through the kindness of the director of our pensione, the Pensione Nazional, I was given an introduction to the Papal Chaplain, His Excellency Monsignor Van Lierde, a very impressive Dutch man who arranged for me to visit the British Legation to the Holy See and the Maestro della Camera at the Vatican. The consequence was that a letter was delivered to me by Vatican Despatch Rider notifying me that our group was to be given a special audience at Castel Gandolfo, by His Holiness Pope Pius XII at 9.00am the next morning!

We departed by coach at 8.00am for Castel Gandolfo, the Pope's summer residence by Lake Albano. After notifying the Swiss Guard of our arrival, we were ushered through several rooms until we found another group of English pilgrims. Shortly after 9.00am a little bell tinkled and the Holy Father walked briskly and elegantly into the room. We all genuflected for a moment on his entry. His Holiness presented medals to everyone.

When His Holiness came to me, I explained who we were and that I had been honoured by a few words with him during the war. He then welcomed everybody one by one to Castel Gandolfo and asked if we were enjoying Rome.

The Pope then gave an address, praying that the peace of Christ would descend on us all. He then, in a most impressive, sublime and majestic manner, gave his Apostolic Blessing to us, our families and the religious objects we had with us. His Holiness was obviously glad to meet us. Thereafter, the court photographer Felice took a photograph of us grouped round the Holy Father, dressed in his white clerical apparel with beautiful red velvet shoes, noticed particularly by Kath! He then went out on to the balcony overlooking the beautiful Lake Albano.

It was a very happy occasion, and I felt very gratified when members of my party, one of whom was a detective inspector at Scotland Yard, thanked and congratulated me for arranging this special audience. We returned to a Rome which looked much better than when I saw it battered in 1944, when it had been the headquarters of the German Commander Field Marshal Kesselring.

That evening there was delivered to our pensione a gold ring, which I had had made by a Roman goldsmith for Kath, to house an aquamarine stone from a necklace given to my mother by my father.

The next morning, Sunday 29th July, we departed by train down the coast via Formia to Naples where we were met by a coach that unfortunately broke down on the Autostrada near Torre Del Greca, and had to be replaced. We stopped for drinks at Vico Equense where once I had been stationed, and drove on through farmland country to the Hotel Villa Igea on the Capo di Sorrento commanding a wonderful view of the Bay and of Ischia. After dinner, Kath paid her first visit with me to the lovely town of Sorrento and it was an amazing sight to watch the last bus from Sorrento, carrying about 100 people!

The next day, after a glorious swim in the sea and a siesta, Kath and I went by taxi to Vico Equense to visit the nuns of the Convent where 42 Line Section had been billeted. We received a tremendous reception from the nuns. Never shall I forget the tremendous affection with which Sister Almarinda, the door-keeper, greeted Kath who was delightfully overwhelmed; it was Sister Almarinda who had made Christina's beautiful baby frocks. We were received by the Mother Superior who had succeeded Sister Maria Pasqualina Monti, who had now become Secretary General of the Order and, to my deep disappointment, was away. Nevertheless, she had left a beautiful letter written in French and a box of chocolates for Christina. All the nuns assembled to make us welcome. Kath and I prayed in their beautiful chapel and were then taken round the convent, its gardens, and our old billets now a refuge for poor children. I was so glad to meet again the two ladies who did the menial tasks such as our washing in 1944. I was very close to tears.

We then visited the Savareses, where I myself had been billeted: the Signora, Maria Luctitia, Lydia, Sylvana, Anna, Olga and Louisa. They were ever so kind to us. Cavallerio Savarese who had fought in the Battle of Caporetto had died. To finish the day we went to the opera in the Circolo del Forestieri to hear 'La Traviata'.

The next day we had a glorious tour of Pompeii under a splendid guide Prosperi, to be followed the next day by a sail to the Isle of Capri where we visited both Capri and Anacapri and Axel Munthë's villa San Michele. To revive my personal memories I visited the Villa Eudesandra to pay my respects to the Signora, who clearly remembered Alan Mitchell and me staying there on leave in 1945. I had a swim in the beautiful Blue Grotto.

On Thursday 2nd August, I took a group by boat to Naples. We ought not to have visited the Museo Nazionale; it was much too tiring. Kath and I hired a taxi to visit my friends Signora and Signorina Rosetta Giordano Orsini in the Via Tasso, who entertained us with vermouth. Rosetta and Kath liked each other very much and the Signora was enthusiastic and rapturous about Kath, her personality and her beauty! The Cavaliero was at work at his bank. And so back by boat to Sorrento.

On our last full day we had a dreadful drive along the peninsula to Positano, Amalfi and Ravello where we had lunch. Kath was delighted by the Villa Rufolo, once the residence of Nicholas Breakspear, the only English Pope, as Adrian IV.

On Saturday 4th August, we rose at 3.00am to drive to Naples to catch the Rome train, then from Rome the Paris train, and arrived in Paris at 10.30am on the Sunday. Kath, Bobbie, Maureen and I drove by taxi, down the Champs Élyseés, seeing the Arc de Triomphe, the Eiffel Tower and paying a quick visit to the beautiful Cathedral of Notre Dame. This determined Kath and me to revisit Paris as soon as possible.

Eventually by train and boat, Boulogne to Folkestone, we arrived in London at 11.00pm, to be greeted by Ted and Edie Roberts. After saying goodbye to our splendid party, particularly to Pat and Joey Barnden, who became lifelong friends, we went home with Ted and Edie.

We lunched at St. Pancras with Ted and Edie the next day, and eventually reached home in the early evening to be reunited with dear little Christina, whom it was so splendid to see.

Shortly afterward, Kath, Christina and I had a delightful week's holiday at Scarborough, making sandcastles, visiting museums, seeing new films, visiting Whitby and returning on Kath's birthday by way of York.

On Friday 21st September 1951, Christina started attending the Convent High School as a day-girl. Looking back, I regret that she did not stay at Miss Segrave's school up the avenue, thus averting long journeys to and from Matlock.

On 6th October, my regiment took part in the biggest exercise ever held in the United Kingdom, Exercise Surprise Packet under the direction of the Chief of the Imperial General Staff, Field Marshal Sir William (later Viscount) Slim, and visited by the Deputy Commander of NATO, F.M.Viscount Montgomery. I took the main convoy from Chesterfield to Tilshead on Salisbury Plain. We were a composite unit made up of territorials, regulars and sailors. I had about 25 lorries with trailers, and many of the vehicles had been vandalised by some disgruntled man or men, by cutting through the high tension cables. This I rectified by the use of paperclips which I opened to form an electrical connection between the two parts. I was leading the convoy. We reached Budbrooke Barracks, Warwick to refuel. Here I discovered that the solitary petrol pump attendant had been told that all the convoys had gone through and that he had gone home! It took a long time to find him. Then because the empty tanks of the vehicles were on the opposite side to the pump, we had to detach all the trailers before the lorries could be turned round, and then refuelled. All this took 2-3 hours. As dusk descended I found that few of the lights were working on these "impressed" lorries – and then one of the Land Rovers set on fire of its own accord. Eventually we reached Tilshead at about 2100 hours, very tired, hungry and thirsty, and I felt like casting my belt to the ground and crying "I will soldier no more!"

As a regiment, we were to provide command and control communications and I was to be in the hot spot as chief duty signal officer and signalmaster. The next few days I devoted to establishing as good a signal office as I could with the material, technical and human, with which I was provided and gradually established order out of chaos.

Exercise Surprise Packet started at midnight on Thursday 11th October. In the early morning, unfortunately, some soldiers were killed when they were run over by a tank. I well remember meeting tanks called after the Four Horsemen of the Apocalypse: Death, Famine, Pestilence, Hell. The exercise lasted until Tuesday 16th October, and many hard lessons were learned. Just before the end of the exercise a real message was received to the effect that an entire tank brigade was to be despatched to Egypt without delay, where King Farouk had been overthrown by General Naguib. The brigade was actually on the move and I used every means I had to ensure that this highly important message got through.

In the course of our fifteen days based largely on Tilshead, I was able to visit Stonehenge, Salisbury Cathedral and Devizes, with Tom Wragg and 'Jonah'.

Our 'reinforcements' departed on the Friday, and the next day I had the task of leading my large convoy back to Chesterfield. I rose at 0530 hours and reached home, very tired, at 2100 hours, to return to college on the Monday 22nd October.

Three days later came the general election. The Conservatives were returned to power with an overall majority of 18, and Mr Churchill was again Prime Minister. One of his first actions was to make Mrs Ernest Bevin a Dame of the Order of the British Empire.

Kath in addition to her many duties was attending W.E.A. classes in social history given by a splendid lecturer Mr Thornton from the University of Nottingham, who greatly impressed us.

Christmas was soon upon us, and Donald Storrs-Fox was very kind in transporting us to the various services, Anglican and Roman. We had our Christmas lunch at the Rutland Arms Hotel with "Garg", Bill and Mary. Christina was delighted with her presents.

On New Year's Eve we were saddened to hear that Eric Cotton Smith's post at S. Anselm's had been terminated!

1951 had indeed been a momentous year!

Chapter V

1952–1959

1952

On 6th February 1952, H.M. King George VI died in his sleep at Sandringham in the early hours of the morning. The new young Queen Elizabeth II returned from Kenya, and was proclaimed Queen throughout the country on 8th February. The funeral of His Late Majesty took place on 15th February with great but mournful ceremony. I remember so clearly the three Queens: Elizabeth; Elizabeth the Queen Mother; and Queen Mary; and the Royal Dukes, Windsor and Gloucester. The country was stunned.

As a consequence of the war in Korea H.M. Government called up all reservists to go to annual camp with the T.A. Units. Our Unit, 21st (North Midland) Corps Signal Regiment, was made up to full strength and on 21st June went to annual camp at Strensall, the depot of my father's regiment, the King's Own Yorkshire Light Infantry. Amongst the reservists I met many old friends with whom I had served during the war. In a few days time the regiment was up to war standard and we carried out a large corps exercise, Exercise Red Beetle in Yorkshire. On one occasion in the course of the exercise, I found myself based at Castle Howard, later to become famous in the TV presentation of Evelyn Waugh's 'Brideshead Revisited'. The success of the exercise reflected the greatest credit on the reservists and the T.A. During camp I received the news that I had been awarded the Territorial Decoration.

Kath, Christina, Garg and I had an enjoyable week's holiday at Llandudno in early August.

On 17th August, Kath and I departed from London, where I met my party of twenty International Summer School Society students whom I was leading to Italy, via Folkestone and Boulogne. In Paris Kath and I visited the beautiful cathedral of

Notre Dame and on a lovely Parisian evening, walked down Les Champs Élysées. We left the Gare de Lyon and travelled through the night on the Milan Express. We went through Switzerland as first light broke, through the Simplon tunnel and through the beautiful scenery round Lake Maggiore, and, via Milan and Bologna, reached Florence in the early afternoon, where we were accommodated in the delightful pensione Rigatti, Lungarno Diaz 2, owned by Signora de Benedictis and her lovely daughter, Gabriella, with whom we became lifelong friends.

Florence is the jewel of Europe. How wonderful it was to visit the Palazzo Vecchio, Piazza Republica, the beautiful Duomo and its Baptistry and Campanile, the Camere Medici, Michelangelo's David, Cellini's Perseus and the Rape of the Sabine Women. We visited, too, Pisa with its splendid cathedral and Leaning Tower, its Campanile and Baptistry, and carried on to majestic Lucca. And we visited Fiesole, the delightful little town so near to Florence, with its delightful cloister manned by the charming Franciscans. Never will I forget in Florence the splendour of the Uffizi, especially Botticelli's 'Primavera' and 'Birth of Venus', nor the Ponte Vecchio, the Church of Santa Croce housing the tombs of Michelangelo, Rossini, and Machiavelli, and a monument to Dante. And how fascinating were the churches of San Lorenzo and San Marco with the beautiful frescos by Fra Angelico.

For the second week we took the train to Verona, where we visited the Amphitheatre, the Ponte Castelvecchio, and Juliet's tomb, and whence we were taken by coach to Maderno on the shores of beautiful Lake Garda. One day we went by coach into the Brenta Dolomites to Madonna di Campiglio where Kath and I had the wonderful ear-popping experience of ascending a further 2000 feet by chairlift, giving a gorgeous view of the mountain peaks and glaciers and making one praise God for all the beauty.

I had great fun swimming in the Lake and Kath and I greatly enjoyed the walking.

After six days we returned home by the same route, but having time to visit the beautiful and stately cathedral in Milan before travelling through the night. The next night we stayed with Joey Barnden in his Chelsea home and on 1st September reached Matlock at 5.30pm, where we were met by Garg and Christina, whom it was so good to see again.

During the autumn, apart from my college work and British Legion duties, I worked very hard in the training of the T.A., including the regular weekend camps based in Dovedale.

Wednesday 5th November stands out in my mind: when the Bakewell United Christian Council was addressed by the great Franciscan, Father Agnellus Andrew who gave an address in the packed town hall on 'The Christian – 1952 Edition'. He said that we were to bring Christ out of the church, into the fields, the farms, the factories and the streets; and that each generation should be to itself what Christ was to His generation. Many years later Father Agnellus Andrew became Bishop in charge of communications at the Vatican when, after receiving a letter from Richard Cockerton and me, he said that he clearly remembered his visit to Bakewell.

On 18th November, the family was saddened when Jack's wife Christine gave birth to a baby girl, Jane, who suffered from Down's syndrome. But Janie was a delightfully loving child and it was distressing when she died a few years later.

Nonetheless, we had a very happy Christmas Day when we were all joined by Hubert and Ida for Christmas lunch at the Rutland Arms Hotel. On the 29th, Christina's school report arrived: she was top of her class at the convent. And, typical of the times, the British Legion Club gave a rabbit pie supper on New Year's Eve!

1953

New Year's Day 1953 saw me visiting Regimental H.Q. at Derby and writing a voice exercise for training purposes. This year I was to work very closely with Major Roy Tayler, our training major.

The first week of January heralded atrocious weather. Icy road conditions caused the Sheffield bus to be abandoned between Calver and Hassop, though I managed to get home via Baslow. We then had heavy snowstorms, to be followed on 1st February by disastrous floods down the East coast and in Holland. Hundreds were drowned and tens of thousands rendered homeless. And then more dreadful snowstorms occurred on 10th February, closing all roads from Bakewell except that to Matlock. This coincided with an unpleasant fever which I contracted, but I was well treated by my dear friend Doctor John Emerson, who had given a distinguished wartime medical service in the Royal Navy. I was off work for 15 days.

About this time I heard from my friend the Madre Superiore at Vico Equense that the portress Suor Almerinda had died on 2nd December 1951. She was very fond of Kath and a letter which she had earlier written to Christina was received later.

On 31st January, the day before the disastrous floods, a dreadful gale occurred, sinking the S.S. Princess Victoria between Larne and Stranraer at the cost of 128 lives. The following week I got Michael Parkinson, then a junior journalist and a student of mine, to read Ralph Hodgson's 'Song of Honour' which refers to "ships going down like lead". Even then I was conscious of Michael's great potential.

These were the days of early television. The great thing on Sunday evening was to watch 'The Play', and I remember so clearly Maurois's splendid play 'Asmodée'.

Throughout the spring and early summer I worked hard in the training of the T.A., concentrating on "The Division" and New Procedure.

On 2nd June we heard that Edmund Hilary and Sherpa Tenzing had conquered Everest, which heralded the coronation of our beautiful young Queen on Tuesday 2nd June – unfortunately a very wet day, causing the cancellation of our sports day in Bakewell. My dear friend, Colonel Gerry Underwood, as our honorary colonel was present in Westminster Abbey. At home, in Haddon House, Kath, Christina, Uncle Hubert, Aunt Ida, Desmond Lloyd and I watched the coronation on TV.

Following the end of the academic year, when my students were kind enough to give me presents, Kath, Christina and I entrained for Paris via London, Folkestone and Boulogne. We had two days in London, visiting Buckingham Palace, Trafalgar Square, the Tower (where we saw the crown jewels), and the shops. Poor Christina was sea-sick but was tended by a charming stewardess, and we safely arrived at the Hotel Avenido, 41 Rue da Colisé and immediately visited the Champs Élysées. In the course of our week's stay we visited: La Madeleine with its superb liturgy; Sacré Coeur, St. Denis and Montmartre; Versailles via Malmaison, the home of Napoleon and Josephine, where we were deeply impressed by Le Petit Trianon and the palace in general with its strong connections with the French Revolution and Marie Antoinette; La Conciergerie, prison of so many Royalists and Marie Antoinette; La Sainte Chapelle with its glorious stained glass, built by St. Louis, King and Confessor to house part of the Crown of Thomas; the Louvre where we were enthralled by the Winged Victory, the Venus di Milo, Da Vinci's Mona Lisa, Fra Angelico's 'Coronation of the Virgin' and Rembrandt's splendid 'The Two Disciples at Emmaus'; the Latin Quarter, the Cluny Museum, the Panthéon, Ste. Genévive, St. Etienne du Mont, the Church of Notre Dame where Ste. Catherine Labour had visions of Our Lady; Les Galleries Lafayette, a joy to Kath and Christina who bought a glass bird; Barbizon, where Robert Louis Stevenson met his wife; Fontainebleau; the opera; the Eiffel Tower, l'École Militaire, the Arc de Triomphe and, of course, the superb cathedral of Notre Dame! Not bad for a week! We returned home via London where we visited St. Margaret's Westminster and the Houses of Parliament, where in the Lords I met my old friend Rex Lawson with whom I worked in Manchester treasury department and last saw in Naples, now a captain in an airborne field ambulance! And so home after a magnificent holiday so splendidly organised and planned by dearest Kath.

Within three days I was off by road on the advance party to annual camp at Weymouth where I took over the officers' mess. The main body arrived by train three days later.

We carried out two major exercises in Dorset; one evening I slept near Hardy's monument – I am not sure whether it is a monument to the admiral or the author! In the course of the 14-day camp, we were visited by our honorary colonel, Gerry Underwood, who invested me on regimental parade with the coronation medal, of which I am rightly proud and for which I am deeply grateful.

On my return home, Kath, Christina and I had a pleasant week's holiday in Southport, staying with Aunt Muriel. Kath and I were able to see Sean O'Casey's 'Juno and the Paycock' at the Repertory Theatre.

On 10th September, Mary gave birth to our niece Serena, a lovely child. During Mary's confinement, Garg came to live with us and stayed with few interruptions until his death in 1964.

In October we held our grand Glossop Signals reunion at the Rutland Arms Hotel at which Gerry Underwood presided. This was attended by our old friend Charlie Greene who stayed with Kath and me.

That same month I had the pleasure of having tea with the Lord Mayor of Sheffield and listening to a splendid address on the United Nations Association by the famous Mr Behrens, then the Vice-Chairman of the United Nations Association and a tremendous supporter of U.N.A. In contrast with this, a Prince of the Church, Cardinal Wysinski, the Polish Patriarch, was put under arrest by the Communists and days of atonement were held throughout the Church. It was many years before he regained his freedom.

I was still working hard at college and was delighted when I was informed by Kenneth Van den Toarn, my chief, that I was to be upgraded to Assistant Lecturer Grade B in the New Year. This meant a considerable increase in salary. Of my students, both full-time and part-time, I was very fond. It gave me great delight when Kath and I went to the Sheffield Lyceum to see 'Swan Lake' – a magnificent production – and two of my former students came to us in the interval: Pamela Weston and Margaret Bardgett, whose uncle was conductor of the famous Huddersfield Choral Society. At the end of term my civil service students took me out for a drink on the strength of my promotion. Many of them became lifelong friends.

The autumn was however clouded by the death in a Derby dogs' hospital of our poodle Johnny. But we were able to buy one of his offspring from Mrs Robinson of Youlgreave, a chocolate poodle whom we called Dinah and who brought such pleasure to us all for so long.

Our M.P. at this time was E.B. Wakefield, whose mother had been brought into the world by Doctor Thompson, father of the great poet Francis Thompson, and I was so delighted to discuss this with him at the Chrtistmastide prize-giving at the Conservative Club.

And so, after a happy Christmastide including lunch at the Rutland Arms Hotel, attended by Garg, Kath, Christina, Hubert and Ida, we entered 1954.

1954

On 15th February 1954 the United Christian Council, under my supervision, held a well-attended public meeting addressed by the Venerable Dilworth Harrison, Archdeacon of Chesterfield on 'The Chief End of Man'. The new chairman was Doctor Pye-Smith, uncle of Donald Storrs-Fox, and a few weeks later he asked me to call a special meeting to consider the declining moral standards of current literature. Were he alive today, I dread to think what he would say about the current abysmal standards not only of literature but of TV and the media in general.

In my lectures in Sheffield I did my best to encourage a love of music amongst my students and it was good to find so many attended Sheffield City Hall Concerts to listen to the Hallé and other orchestras, conducted by Sir John Barbirolli and Sir Charles Groves, and recitals by Beniamino Gigli, Tito Gobbi and Paul Robeson.

With the T.A. I worked and trained hard, concentrating on signalling over directional radio beams. The chief signal officer of Northern Command, Brigadier L. De M. Thuillier, a big man of great reputation who went on to finish his career in the Cabinet Office advising on satellite communications, inspected many of our exercises, expressing his pleasure.

Before my attending annual camp at Strensall depot of my father's regiment, the King's Own Yorkshire Light Infantry, we left Haddon House, where we had been so happy, for Woodlands, Baslow Road, Bakewell, a large house with two cellar rooms, two living rooms and kitchen, two large bedrooms and a bathroom, and three small bedrooms in the top storey. For this we paid £1,850. Garg was now living permanently with us and so the move eased the situation. We worked very hard on the new house into which we moved on 14th June 1954. Our first visitor was our dear friend Major Tom Wragg, curator at Chatsworth.

After laying the bathroom linoleum on my 34th birthday I, with Tom, drove to camp via Selby Abbey where we inspected the organ. In the course of camp, we were able to visit the splendid Leeds Tattoo. Camp took the usual course, involving a three-day exercise partly based on the Castle Howard estate, which I had the pleasure of visiting with Tom.

Many years later I watched on TV the dramatised version of Evelyn Waugh's 'Brideshead Revisited', based at Castle Howard. Just as the hero found himself in the grounds of 'Brideswell' so did Tom Wragg, our squadron and me, in precisely the same circumstances!

Just after annual camp, Kath, Christina and I had a delightful London holiday based at Ashford in the home of Olga Roberts. We had the joy of visiting Eton College, Windsor Castle, the British Museum, the National Gallery, the South Kensington museums, the Wallace Collection and Whipsnade Zoo, and of seeing the new musical 'The King and I' at Drury Lane.

On 21st August 1954 I led a party of International Summer School Society students, including Kath, to Italy and Southern France. We flew to Nice in a Vickers Viscount, a four-engined propeller plane. Kath had never flown before. It was a dreadful flight. We hit very bad weather over the Rhône Valley causing the plane to divert. Everything in the galley was spoiled, most of us were very sick and I was needlessly worried about Kath. She was perfectly calm and continued to read Jane Eyre and suffered no ill-effects. She was indeed very brave. It took us 4½ hours to fly to Nice!

We stayed in the Continental Hotel along La Promenade des Anglais, and the next morning travelled in our own coach to Rapallo via Monte Carlo, San Remo and Genoa, where we saw the house of Christopher Columbus. At Rapallo, near the beautiful little port of Portofino, a Requiem Mass was being held for the late Signor de Gasperi, Prime Minister of Italy and one of the founders of European Unity. Thence we proceeded to Florence for a few days and then to Venice via the beautiful city of Padua. In Venice we stayed at a delightful pensione on the Salute. Here we had the great pleasure of visiting Saint Mark's, Murano, the Lido, the Rialto bridge embracing Shylock's shop, the Doge's Palace, the Frari with Titian's glorious 'Assumption'; and of course we drank in the expensive cafés in the 'San Marco Piazza'!

From Venice we proceeded via Padua and Verona, where we visited the Amphitheatre, to Maderno on Lake Garda to the same Hotel Milano where we had stayed two years before. Kath and I received a great reception. We arrived on our 13th wedding anniversary which we celebrated the next day.

On 1st September, three of the party and I took a rowing boat, and after two hours' hard rowing reached the Isola Di Garda where we tethered our boat and walked inland to discover it was private. We met the owner, Princess Borghese, who was most charming and invited us to stay for a while. Napoleon's sister was married to a Borghese, and the Princess was a descendent. And so we rowed back for two hours to Kath at our hotel.

Next day we drove on to San Remo via Milan where we arrived in time to see the large funeral procession for the great Cardinal Alfonso Schuster, and to visit S. Maria della Grazia to see Leonardo da Vinci's famous 'Last Supper'.

San Remo is a beautiful, charming place and we had great fun messing about in boats, swimming, taking chairlifts up Monte Bisogne, resplendent with autumn crocus, and visiting the casino in the evening, where Kath and I had a most enjoyable conversation with a charming, cultured Egyptian gentleman. We stayed in the Albergo Milano.

The next morning I swam a long distance from near the lighthouse to the beach, before bidding farewell to San Remo and driving on to Nice for our 3½-hour flight home. And so to London for the night, where we said goodbye to our friends, and next morning returned to Bakewell where it was so good to be reunited with Christina and Garg.

Now the new academic year started. In those days at the beginning of term we had to put in three-session days and supervise enrolment in the evenings, for no extra pay. In addition at the Melbourne Avenue site I personally kept the college warm by stoking the boiler during my lunchtime.

It was a tremendous pleasure to witness the visit to the University of Sheffield by H.M. the Queen, supported by H.R.H. the Duke of Edinburgh. H.M. looked very beautiful and regal.

In addition to my academic work, I worked hard during the autumn training the Territorial Army mostly in the field of radio beam signalling. I spent a weekend, too, at Wolverhampton taking over command of No. 2 Squadron from my old commanding officer, "Inky" Udell. I was to command this Squadron in the rank of major having been promoted in March. That was on the 11th/12th December and I made some far-reaching decisions in the matter of promotions! Inky said I had done more in two days than he had in two years!

On my return home we celebrated Garg's 80th birthday, attended by all members of the family, and so ably organised by dear hardworking Kath.

And so with the usual Christmas activities to the end of 1954.

1955

On New Year's Day we celebrated at the Friends' Meeting House the Golden Wedding of Uncle Joe Howard and Aunt Amy, who were married in Bakewell Methodist Chapel in 1905. It was a great party with all the Howards present, and I felt very proud when Uncle Tom asked me to say Grace. Of both Joe and Tom I was very fond. Tom, a fervent Freemason, delighted in discussing the Pope with me despite having never been baptised. He died suddenly on 16th February whilst watching a boxing match on TV at Uncle Joe's. As the Methodist minister said at his funeral: he was always on the side of the angels. That same minister, the Rev. R.J. Hall, had once been a prison chaplain and told me that "a mixture of strong drink, fast women and slow horses would put any man into prison".

The early weeks of 1955 saw very bad weather. The road to Sheffield was closed for several days and I had to get to work via Chesterfield on the train. For several days I was again laid up with 'flu.

I continued to work very hard, including several evening classes at college, and to train hard with the Territorial Army, mostly at Wolverhampton.

On Easter Monday, 11th March, in what was then considered to be heavy traffic, I was knocked off my bicycle, outside Newholme Hospital, by a car driven by Mr Frank P. Gale, a senior member of Sheffield City Police Force. My knees were out of my trousers, my coat dirtied, elbows and hands grazed, and my back damaged. I liked him and was most lenient with him, deciding there was no need to report the accident, to his relief. He paid for the repair to my clothing and bike. Later, to my joy, he became Chief Constable of Newcastle-on-Tyne.

On 26th May, the General Election day, the Conservatives were returned under the new Prime Minister, Sir Anthony Eden, who had been so long waiting for the stroke-stricken Churchill to retire, to be followed by a rail strike within 48 hours.

That same day we received news that Christina had won a scholarship and also passed the 11-plus examination. After a good deal of reflection, we decided that she should stay at the convent high school, rather than go free to Lady Manners School. In the context of the times I thought this was the better thing to do, but I now deeply regret it. The academic standard and the resources of Lady Manners School were better than those of the fee-paying Convent High School. Christina would have gained more friends; she would not have had to go to school on Saturday mornings; and her day would have been shorter. Nowadays, I would not have hesitated, for Lady Manners School of which I was to become Governor for several years is a splendid academic institution.

Christina had now taken up riding, mostly at Callow Farm, near Highlow Hall, Abney, under the help of Mr and Mrs Dungworth whom she liked so much and with whom she spent many holidays, often when Kath and I were away leading my International Summer School group. Christina had now become very friendly with the very charming Rosemary Cockerton in her riding ventures. That friendship has lasted throughout life. Kath was very fond of Rosemary and so still am I, for she is a strong pillar of support to me.

Our Annual Regimental Camp was held at Otley and now we had a new Adjutant, Peter Gilham, with whom I established a lifelong friendship.

Our main corps exercise was based on Bramham Park under the ultimate command of General Sir Geoffrey Evans, of Northern Command, lasting four long days, and culminating in the simulated delivery of a nuclear missile from near Wetherby Racecourse, reflective of the times of the Cold War. My Squadron played a major part in the signals command and control of the exercise. I was tremendously impressed by the debriefing we received from the general. It all went very well. We had, of course, the Z-Reservists with us and reached a high point of efficiency. At this I was pleased for it was the last annual camp under the command of Richard Pickford.

Christina went to Mr and Mrs Dungworth for a riding holiday on 14th August, and Kath and I made our way to the Bramwells at Radcliffe Semele, via Lichfield Cathedral. On the morning of the next day, the Feast of the Assumption at St. Peter's Church, Leamington Spa, I was delighted to find Padre Gerard Flint, who had been Chaplain at H.Q. 3 District Naples ten years ago, now the parish priest there! In the afternoon, whilst on the river with Mrs Bramwell, Peggy and Kath, we almost collided with a rowing boat containing Bob and Madge Wilkins, and the Revd. Peter Riley about to depart for Trinidad where he was to be ministering at the Cathedral at Port of Spain. Two remarkable coincidences in the same day. We all shared an enjoyable tea.

Thence Kath and I made our way to the West Country visiting Bath, Wells, Glastonbury and Dunster, and over Exmoor to Lynmouth, still very devastated from the floods of the previous year. Our next move was to the New Forest where we stayed at Lyndhurst. The New Forest impressed Kath and me very much. And what a delight it was to pay my first visit to the splendid Winchester Cathedral and to the college where I paid my respects to my hero Field Marshal Earl Wavell of Cyrenaica at his grave in the Garth. We proceeded to London where I paid my first visit to the Tate Gallery and listened to a splendid lecture on Constable. I am very fortunate in that Kath inculcated in me a great appreciation of art. From London we visited Chartwell, home of Sir Winston Churchill, and birthplace of General Wolfe of Quebec fame, and Biggin Hill Aerodrome where so much of our defence in the Battle of Britain in 1940 had been planned and implemented. It was there that Churchill first uttered those immortal words: "Never in the field of human conflict has so much been owed by so many to so few". We returned home after a delightful holiday and brought Christina back from Callow Farm where she had an equally delightful holiday; she then camped out at home with her friend, Susan Edwards.

And so I come to the beginning of another academic year, with its three-shift day for the first week and my usual throat infection.

On 10th October a family misfortunate occurred, in that my brother-in-law Jack's shoe business in Matlock Street, which he had inherited from his father, got into financial difficulties, and he had to sign a deed of assignment of all his assets to his creditors. This as in so many similar cases was the result of over-expansion in buying an additional shoe business in Macclesfield. I was very fond of Jack, a very generous man, and I did all I could to help him.

That same month, Father Wald Judd left the parish for Barton-on-Humber where he died some years later from a brain tumour. I think it had already started for he had acted in such a manner that my friend Donald Storrs-Fox visited the Vicar General and asked for his posting. He was succeeded by young priest Father William O'Dowd, one of three priestly brothers.

Throughout the autumn I had, as usual, worked hard in training my signals squadron in Wolverhampton.

1956

Early in 1956 I was grieved to learn that, as a result of the Cyprus trouble (Enosis as it was called – that is, reunion with Greece, despite the large proportion of Turks on the island), the British Consulate in Iraklion, Crete, where the Consul was a Turk whom I knew from 1946, had been wrecked in an anti-British riot by students.

By now, 46th (N.M.) Signal Regiment T.A. was absorbing a great number of National Servicemen, amongst whom were Peter Revill, boxing champion of Northern Command, later to command 38th Signal Regiment and to remain a firm friend of mine; Tom Wragg; and Brian Rothwell, a teacher of Latin and Russian who worked hard for the T.A. The Cold War was at its height and Bulganin and Khrushchev were in charge of the U.S.S.R. I recollect that when these two visited the United Kingdom by warship, wireless silence was ordered by the military, to prevent any intelligence leaking to the U.S.S.R. through its very efficient electronic spy system.

The T.A. was training harder than ever. On 29th April a dreadful accident took place in the course of a signals exercise. At Edwinstowe in Sherwood Forest, a wireless truck of the Chesterfield Squadron stopped near to some high-voltage power lines and the power was induced into the aerial and the truck. Sergeant Tonge was killed; S.Q.M.S. Ernest Guttridge of my Wolverhamtpon and Derby Squadron was severely injured, to die within two days' time; Major Basil Fenwick lost an arm and a leg, but never allowed this dreadful disability to affect his zest for life for so many years; and Sergeant Seaward of my squadron lost half his foot. The regiment was now commanded by Richard Grimwood-Taylor, the brilliant Derby lawyer whom I greatly admired, and I shall never forget the marvellous manner in which he dealt with this situation, and so well commanded the regiment. Sergeant Tonge, a very promising N.C.O., was buried at Brimington, and together with the commanding officer and the Padre, I attended the funeral of squadron quartermaster Sergeant Gutteridge at Walsall; a brilliant soldier, he would have gone far. My squadron had a very efficient Permanent Staff Instructor, Sergeant W.I. "Taffy" Williams, whom I had inherited from Inky Udell, and he proved to be as steady as a rock, becoming a firm friend of mine. For several weeks, I was visiting Mansfield General Hospital, where Basil Fenwick and Sgt. Seaward were being so well treated mostly under a Sister Kelly, the sister of Father Kelly who succeeded Father O'Dowd as priest at Hassop and Bakewell.

Annual camp was spent at Hornsea, and we held exercises based on Rise Park and Flamborough Head, and a three-day exercise based in the Pocklington and Leconfield areas. In 1943 I had been responsible for military communications at Pocklington and Leconfield aerodromes, and for me they were full of ghosts of the past! The Chief Signal Officer, Northern Command, Brigadier Desmond St. John Hoysted, a very fervent senior officer with whom I developed a long-standing friendship, closely supervised our exercises, and we were given the usual strong support by our Honorary Colonel, Gerry Underwood.

About this time, at the request of Doctor Francis Thompson, the librarian, I undertook work in the library at Chatsworth, producing a calendar of the papers of the 3rd and 4th Dukes. It involved, in the first instance, removing the papers from biological into date order. They were fascinating: letters from the King, the Prince of Wales, Garrick, Robert Walpole, great statesmen, and great patrons of the arts which made a deep impression on me. The 4th Duke, in particular, was a very powerful man. I will never forget the sagacity of the wedding contract drawn up between him and Charlotte Boyle, daughter of the Earl of Burlington, who died young, leaving the Duke to inherit Burlington House, and Lismore in Ireland, amongst other places.

For our holiday, Kath and I went to Scotland, via the Lake District, whilst Christina went to the Dungworths to spend a riding holiday with them. We visited

Keswick, Gretna Green, Loch Lomond, Oban (where I met my old friend Eric Mowatt of my telegraph operating section in Italy), Fort William, Glen Orchy, and Glen Coe. From Fort William we went by train to Glenfinnan where Bonnie Prince Charlie had rallied the clans in 1745. The stationmaster at Fort William kindly held up the train whilst Kath and I went back to our hotel for our coats. Full of Jacobite feelings, we then drove via Fort Augustus, Loch Ness and Inverness to Culloden and the cemetery of the clans. We returned via Pitlochry, Lochearnhead and Stirling to Edinburgh where we stayed with Bill and Lu Malcom. And so we returned home via Bedale and Harewood House.

During the remainder of my college vacation, at the request of Mr J.F. Kiernnan of the Haddon Estate, I took up guiding visitors at Haddon Hall and had the pleasure of taking round participants from the British Association for the Advancement of Science who were meeting in Sheffield. I felt very honoured when the president congratulated me and asked if I were a member of the Manners family. This occurred on our 15th wedding anniversary and Kath and I had dinner at the Peacock, Rowsley, to find that the British Association were also dining there.

Now it was time to resume the academic year. Rather foolishly, I had bought a B.S.A. Bantam motorcycle, because travel by motorcycle would be quicker than by bus. But it was a great mistake. The journeys through the fog, frost and ice were dreadful; it was false economy.

Internationally, affairs grew very serious during that autumn. Our Prime Minister Sir Anthony Eden was furious with Colonel Nasser for having nationalised the Suez Canal, and he plotted with France and Israel to undo this matter. An Anglo-French invasion force from Malta and Cyprus invaded the Suez area against the will of the U.S.A., which ordered its Sixth Mediterranean Fleet to stand by, and in other ways expressed its displeasure. Nasser, of course, blocked the Suez Canal by sinking ships in it. Eventually, before our troops had reached Ismailia at the Eastern end of the canal, a ceasefire was ordered and, if my memory serves me rightly, a United Nations Force went in. Eden's appreciation of the situation had not been good and consequently in the following January, he resigned as Prime Minister, to be succeeded by Harold MacMillan who was narrowly preferred by the Parliamentary Conservative Party, to R.A. Butler.

Whilst these affairs had been taking place, Hungary had rejected communism for democracy and about 29th October, Christina's birthday, Russian tanks invaded Budapest, overthrowing the newly-elected Government and causing Cardinal Mindszenty to seek sanctuary for many, many years in the U.S. embassy. And the world looked on!

Towards the end of November, we had a general inspection of the Sheffield College of Commerce and Technology. I was inspected whilst giving a lecture on local government to students from the town hall on a Post-entry Training Scheme. In the first few minutes of my lecture I referred to H.M. inspector, Mr Lowe, being financed by the Privy Council to ensure that the country got value for the money it spent on education. He asked if he could say a few words and continued his few words until the end of my 90-minute lecture period, and then announced that he was well satisfied with me and would not bother me again! Inspector Lowe was a perfect gentleman and he knew what he was about, and I feel that the standards of the modern inspectorate are well below his!

The events of that winter were lightened by the annual dinner of the Winster Branch of the Royal British Legion whose President was Doctor Desmond Stoker, my Regimental Medical Officer, of great Burma fame. I attended with my friends Oliver Cockerton and Eddie Carrington. Oliver was the piano accompanist to the rendering by Desmond and me of 'Alouette', a custom that continued for nigh on 50 years!

On Christmas Eve in a snowstorm, on my bicycle I rode into the back of a lorry that suddenly reversed into Buxton Road from Arkwright Square. It shook me and broke my spectacles and watch. Nonetheless, I was able to go by bus to Sheffield Royal Infirmary where my sight was retested and a prescription was issued. I cannot see that being done nowadays! We had a very snowy, very white, and very cold Christmas.

1957

Early in January, I listened to a talk by our M.P., Mr E.B. Wakefield, on the Suez Crisis. I asked a question, implying that due to defence cuts and the abolition of National Service by the Eden government, we could not sustain any military operation above corps level. E.B. Wakefield signified his consent, but said that under the new Prime Minister, Harold MacMillan, matters would be rectified. At this time, one of my students was Elspeth Urquhart, the daughter of General Roy E. Urquhart who commanded 1st British Airborne Division at Arnhem. Her great-uncle was Mr R.A. Butler, and I recollect that as I drove her with me to college I said: "This time tomorrow, Elspeth, your great-uncle will be Prime Minister". But it was not to be, wrongly as his supporters felt. Elspeth eventually married Menzies Campbell, the Olympic athlete, Queen's Council, and strong Liberal Democrat M.P.

There was still a great deal of international tension, and we held several mobilisation exercises. The Chief Signal Officer, Northern Command, held big Signal TEWTs (Tactical Exercises without Troops) every year from then on at Northern Command in York, which were of tremendous value.

In March 1957 I gave one of the first lectures to the newly-formed Bakewell and District Historical Society, at the request of Tom Wragg, on 'The House of Cavendish'. It was very well received and I have repeated it on several occasions.

There was much religious fervour in the country, and in Bakewell we had a week's mission from Father Langton Fox Ph.D., a keen mountaineer who eventually became Bishop of Menevia. I clearly remember an illustrated lecture he gave on the Turin Shroud. But these missions, it now seems to me, were too inwards-looking. The Second Vatican Council to be called by Pope John XXIII was some five years hence with its strong appeal for Ecumenism.

Annual Camp 1957 was based at Black Fell Camp Washington in County Durham. We carried out several exercises in the border country, involving the new radio beam set known as the B.70, and were visited by G.O.C.-in-Chief Northern Command, the great General Younger. We now had a new training major, John Higgins who had been a wartime Lt. Colonel in his early twenties and whom I had met at the School of Signals. He was a splendid decisive officer with whom I remained in contact until his premature death in 1976. In the course of camp, together with the Commanding Officer, Adjutant and Padre I went down Unsworth coal mine where ponies were still used and tended most carefully by the miners. We spent about 45 minutes at the coalface with a few miners whose splendid and cheerful spirit in such dangerous conditions made a deep impression on us all. I recollect that it took three days for the coal dust to get out of my eyes!

In mid-August, I led another group of International Summer School Society students to Tours. Kath and I went up to London where we visited the splendid Wallace Collection before meeting my group on the morning of the 18th and travelling via Folkestone/Boulogne and Paris (Gare du Nord – Gare Austerlitz) to Tours in the valley of the Loire. I immediately arranged a coach trip to Langeais where Richard Coeur de Lion died; Azay Le Rideau; Chemonceau, built for Diane de Poitiers and thereafter handed to Catherine de Medici; and Amboise. All these chateaux and the fortified town of Amboise were exquisite and so good for understanding our history.

The next day, Kath and I returned by bus to Amboise, where we visited the tomb of Leonardo da Vinci in the Chateau Chapelle of St. Hubert, and went round the chateau, scene of a horrible massacre forcibly witnessed by the 10-year-old Mary, Queen of Scots.

In Tours itself we visited the art gallery and watched our first Son et Lumiere. We visited the splendid wine cellar of Vouvray where we drank the delicious wine – and powerful it was, too!

With a few of the more agile students I hired bicycles to cycle to the delightful chateau and gardens of Villandry. We stopped at a little tavern en route, where we were mistaken for Hungarian refugees!

Then I organised another coach trip to Blois where the dreadful murders of the Duke of Guise and his brother the Cardinal were perpetrated; to Chambord, a tremendous chateau saved from destruction by the Germans at the plea of the old Curé; to Cheverny; and to the beautiful Chaumont overlooking the Loire.

On the Sunday Kath and I with others attended High Mass in the beautiful cathedral of Tours. Au pied, Kath and I visited the Chateau Plessis de Tours and the beautiful botanical gardens. Before leaving Tours I had the pleasure of assisting at Mass at the shrine of the soldier Saint Martin de Tours.

From Tours on 28th August, we returned by road to Paris to be accommodated in the good Hotel Atlantic near the Gare St. Lazare.

In Paris, Kath and I visited Notre Dame and climbed the tower to "where the Great Devil grins over Paris"; the beautiful Sainte Chapelle; the Louvre; and walked up the Champs Élysées.

On 30th August, our 16th wedding anniversary, I took my party by train to Versailles where we were admitted for nothing. We went through the chateau in our own time, resting as we wished, and after lunch in the grounds we walked to the delightful Petit Trianon of Marie Antoinette fame, which Christina had so greatly enjoyed in 1953.

On the penultimate day, Bill Potts, who had had a distinguished service from a boy in the Royal Signals and with whom I kept in contact until his death, presented Kath and me with a present of 3000 francs from the group. Kath and I made the most of the remaining time, by visiting the Place des Vosges (Old Paris) and having a river trip on the Seine, dining at the Gare St. Lazare and walking via the Madeleine to the Place de la Concorde.

The next morning, before leaving Paris, we attended a little of the splendid Liturgy at the Madeleine, and so returned to England. The customs arrangements were horrible in those days. It took us two hours to go through the customs at Folkestone with the consequence that we did not reach our London abode until 0045 hours the next morning. We were met at Matlock station by Uncle Hubert and Christina, whom it was so good to see.

A few days later I stayed the weekend at Balliol College, Oxford for an

International Summer School Conference, where I met my friend M. Dupays who had so kindly helped me in Paris some years earlier. It was a great privilege to stay in this splendid college, so greatly loved by Hilaire Belloc.

Now another academic year started. I fell ill with 'flu, to be followed by Christina who was very seriously ill for several days. The good Doctor John Emerson was splendid in his care of her, visiting her at midnight on one occasion. I cannot speak too highly of this great man.

The Glossop Signals Old Comrades Dinner was, as usual, well attended at the Rutland Arms Hotel, and in attendance as Representative Colonel Commandant was General "Slap" White, who had been Chief Signal Officer of 8th Army and with whom I had a most interesting conversation. Amongst those present were, of course, my hero Gerry Underwood and Jack Bond, to whom I owed my life at Calais in 1940.

During the autumn I worked hard at college and trained hard for the T.A., mostly at Derby whence my Squadron H.Q. had been moved from Wolverhampton.

Christmastide was marred when Ida and Hubert had a head-on collision at Kibworth on their way to spend Christmas with us on 23rd December, Hubert sustaining a broken leg, later to be amputated, and Ida two broken legs, all the fractures being compound. It cast a shadow over Christmas Day lunch at the Rutland Arms Hotel and on Friday 27th I went by train to visit them in Leicester Royal Infirmary where I found them very brave. They had intended to deal in antiques during Hubert's retirement; but that was now not to be!

1958

On 6th January the rain pelted down and we were flooded at the back of the house, the water entering the basement kitchen, because the culvert entrance in the garden above us was blocked with leaves and debris. In unblocking the culvert, I fell into the icy waters. Within a week I was ill, voiceless, suffering from pharyngitis and was off work in bed for several days.

The centenary of the apparition of Our Lady to Bernadette at Lourdes occurred on 11th February. That day I was visiting Mademoiselle Vettley who taught French at the college. Mademoiselle had lost her fiancé in the dreadful Battle of Verdun in 1916, and held as it were a grudge against God. That day, she was besought by the hospital chaplain to make her peace with the Lord. She did. I visited her at her home on 18th March and she died a few days later, and together with members of staff I attended her Requiem Mass at Saint Catherine's, Sheffield. She was a lady for whom I had the greatest respect, a great teacher and a French woman who had lost so much through the Great War.

We suffered a great snowstorm on 25th February. The roads to Sheffield and Chesterfield were closed. Those people who normally travelled to Sheffield met at the Rutland Arms Hotel and I had pleasant lunchtime drinks with Doctor John Emerson, "Jonah" and Norman Yardley of Yorkshire cricket fame. Early that evening, Christina was taken ill and visited by Doctor Emerson who suspected appendicitis. Observing the dictum that "appendicitis should always be nursed at the portals of the operating theatre", he arranged admission for Christina into the Derby Kingsway Hospital, because only the road to Derby was open. Kath and I accompanied her in an ambulance car fitted for heavy snow. The next day we made a difficult journey by bus to visit her. I returned to work the following morning by Chesterfield but could not get home and spent the night with the Saunders in Sheffield. The next day, the thaw started and Kath and I drove to Derby to bring Christina home; fortunately, it was not appendicitis.

On 14th March, at the request of Tom Wragg who was temporarily car-less, I brought from Matlock station Sir Stephen Martin, the chairman of Christies, the art auctioneers, and his son William. Tom and I dined with them at the Rutland Arms Hotel and I established a warm friendship with Stephen, an elder of the Church of Scotland, godfather of Sir Edward Heath, M.P. and a great friend of Father Martin Darcy, the well-known Jesuit. Sir Stephen, having left elementary school very young, started work at Christies as the tea and office boy. He was transferred to Paris where he paid for French lessons by washing dishes in a restaurant. On the free afternoons, he invariably visited the Louvre and his favourite painting was Botticelli's 'The Deposition of Christ from the Cross'. It is a wonderful painting and it remained his favourite painting for life. I still have a copy of the lecture he gave on his favourite painting to the Canadian University of Brunswick, which I greatly treasure. The object of Sir Stephen's visit was to give his valuation of the treasures at Chatsworth following the untimely death of the previous Duke. I met and dined with Sir Stephen on several other occasions, and I established friends at Christies largely through Tom Wragg who himself had so much to do with the treasures. Through Tom I virtually had open house to Chatsworth. Through Sir Stephen I also met Fritz Lugt of the Dutch Institute, Paris, a big man in every sense of the word, and Tom and I dined with them at the Peacock, Rowsley.

In May, I felt flattered to receive an invitation from Dick Allcock, headmaster of Bakewell C. of E. Secondary Boys School to teach mathematics and French. It was at less pay than my current job, but it eliminated the daily travel to Sheffield. My mind was on a knife's edge: I accepted, withdrew and then accepted again. When the academic year ended in Sheffield, I realised that I had not done a wise thing. I took up the teaching post in September, but found that it was not to my liking. The staff and children I liked very much but I was more fitted for higher education; and my friend Dick the headmaster retired at the end of my first term. I tried to recover my job but it was too late. Eventually, after an interview with Doctor Lawton in the spring of 1959, I applied for the post in the same College of Commerce and Technology to teach english and maths in the Department of Engineering, under a very dedicated Engineer called Harry Hodson. It was inferior to the post I had left in 1958, but in 1960 I transferred to the Department of Science in a higher grade and two years later, back to the Department of Engineering where I could see greater prospects. Although Harry Hodson objected to my taking off time for the T.A., he never stood in my way and in 1965 he left his bed of sickness to form part of the interviewing board that promoted me to full lecturer. Later I became senior lecturer. In retrospect, it seems that I did a good thing in breaking from the Department of Commerce and Management after some nine years there, to plough fresh fields where I was certainly made very welcome.

Annual camp of 1958 was again held at Washington. This gave me a chance to visit Hadrian's Wall and Chesters Fort, and Penrith. Our major exercise was again held in the Border County. On guest night we entertained the Chief Signal Officer, Brigadier "Tojo" St. John Hoysted; Judge Drabble, a delightful man; and of course Gerry Underwood, for whom we put on the usual ceremonial parade. In the course of camp, I was introduced to General Sir Richard Goodboy of Northern Command, a very great soldier. Richard Grimwood-Taylor was a splendid commanding officer. The Adjutant, Peter Gilham, and the Training Major, John Higgins, had now left us and were replaced by Captain Walter Mitchell and Major Bob Wilson. In addition to my command I had now taken on the portfolio of international affairs.

At Bakewell Show, Christina did very well indeed in the pony class, together with Rosemary Cockerton and Jane Caudwell.

On 16th August I left for London to collect a group of I.S.S.S. students whom I was leading to the Mosel Valley and Heidelberg. We travelled by boat and train via Dover, Ostend, Bruges, Brussels, Aachen, the Ardennes, Cologne, Bonn and Koblenz to Brodenbach in the Mosel Valley. I had little or no mastery of the German language, but I was soon able to get by. I particularly enjoyed a river cruise to Cochem, so picturesque; Trier; "Roma Secunda" with its beautiful Liebe Frankischen; and Paulinus Kirche – its Porta Nigra and Roman baths I found fascinating. From Trier we returned home via the delightful Bernkastel.

After a week we proceeded by train to Heidelberg. On the train I met a charming social science lecturer from Mannheim Technical College, Doctor Walter Herz, who offered to help me in any way. At Heidelberg station I was greeted by my agent, Herr Gunthe Krause, who had served in Russia in the Luftwaffe during the war. Gunthe and his wife were very kind to me, taking me to the great amphitheatre scene of Nazi rallies, St. Michael's Basilica, and to Neckarsteinach. He took me and the group round Heidelberg in the evening on a tour of the students' taverns, the Red Ox and White Horse amongst others.

Doctor Walter Herz very kindly took us round the university where we were invited to the students' dance to which in the Mensa Academica we were publicly welcomed in the evening. I was presented to the dean of the international course, consisting of 42 nationalities.

I led my students by coach to the Black Forest, Freudenstadt and Baden-Baden. The scenery in the Black Forest and the deliciousness of the air at high altitude beggars description. En route from Freudenstadt to Baden-Baden we looked across the Rhine into France and saw a solitary German soldier's grave, the wooden cross with the helmet still on. In Baden-Baden, that beautiful spa town, we visited the lovely hospital chapel, the Spitalkirsche.

Gunthe Krause had hoped to present me to Frau Rommel, widow of the Field-Marshal, but this was not possible, so he took me to a tavern kept by a son of one of Rommel's sergeant majors and the venue of the meetings of the Heidelberg branch of the Afrika Korps Association. Here I had a wonderful time and was made an honorary member of the Association, and given my badge. From my diary, I took the portrait of the Queen and put it with the framed photograph of Erwin Rommel. From there I was taken to the Vater Rhein, and so, after too much wine, to bed.

The next evening I had my last drink with the kind Herr and Frau Krause and the local committee of the Afrika Korps Association, who came to see us off on the 2242 hours train for Ostend. Gunthe Krause had the opinion that so far as Western Europe and the U.S.S.R. were concerned, it was "five minutes to midnight". Thank God his fears were not realised. Of his service in Russia he said to me, "I would not wish my worst enemy to have to fight on those cold Russian steppes!"

I must record that I found the Germans very kind and hospitable, especially their ex-servicemen, and I still treasure my honorary membership of the Afrika Korps Association.

I returned home by the same route to hear from Kath the very sad news of the death of our dear friend Mrs "Nanna" Roberts. Shortly afterwards, Garg had a slight stroke.

On 9th October, His Holiness Pope Pius XII died to be succeeded by Angelo Giuseppe Roncalli, a peasant who after a church diplomatic career had become Archbishop of Venice, as Pope John XXIII. He was 79 years old and considered to be a "transitional" Pope; but how wrong this proved to be after his summons of a General Council of the Church, the Second Vatican Council.

At our Royal Signals Old Comrades Association Dinner in Bakewell, always so well presided over by Colonel Gerry Underwood, I met the famous General Nalder who had been our Chief Signal Officer in 4 Corps and at Allied Forces Headquarters in Italy and was now Representative Colonel Commandant and the Signals Historian. For him I had always had the greatest admiration.

On Remembrance Day parade, I laid the Royal Signals wreath in Derby and the British Legion wreath in Bakewell. In early December, Tom Wragg, Basil Fenwick and I attended the Royal Signals Officers Re-union in London where we were joined by Inky Udell.

Before the year was out I had an interview with Doctor Lawton, my former principal in Sheffield Polytechnic, who asked me if I would be interested in taking up an assistant lecturing appointment in the Department of Engineering, with prospects of promotion. Doctor Lawton died suddenly on 12th February 1959 but on 20th February I was interviewed by Harry Hodson, head of the department, was offered the post and accepted. Thus it was that on 24th March I relinquished my post in Bakewell, and on 6th April started my new job amongst very congenial and appreciative colleagues in Sheffield.

That spring I attended the General's study period at Bestwood Lodge, H.Q. 49th Division, Nottingham, and Exercise Smoke Signal, the Chief Signal Officer's Study Period in York.

Donald Storrs-Fox took Colonel Victor Holland, Tom Wragg and me to Mount St. Bernard's Cistercian Abbey at Charnwood Forest, where we were taken round by the guest master, Dom Robert Hodge, and entertained to a splendid luncheon. Dom Robert was of very good Anglican background, a great scholar much impressed by Newman, and in his youth a great horseman. We all thoroughly enjoyed the visit.

Kath and I spent the last week of May, half-term holiday, in the Lake District, enjoying boating and swimming in lakes Windermere, Derwentwater and Ullswater (the latter so reminiscent of my battle course of 1942), visiting Watendlath, Glenridding, the Langsdale Pikes, Tarn Hows and Hawkshead. I also climbed Skiddaw. And, of course, we followed in the footsteps of 'Mrs Tiggy Winkle' up Catbells and looked down the Newlands Valley.

Annual camp was held at Chickerell Camp, Weymouth. Kath, Christina and Jan

Morgan went to Weymouth with me via Stratford, where we had a punt on the river, and Cirencester. I devoted as much attention as I could to them, but it was not enough to warrant their coming down; nonetheless we had some pleasant outings. In the course of camp I spent a day on H.M. Submarine Spiteful. We were submerged for six hours and I was amazed at what I could hear on the surface. It is the gentlest form of motion that I have experienced. The submarine was about to be transferred to the Israeli navy, and on board was a most charming young Israeli Naval Officer. My friend Tom Wragg was in the submarine Sentinel.

On 16th August I led another International Summer School Society tour to Rome and Marina di Pietra Santa. My group of 28 and I travelled via Dover, Calais, Paris, Lausanne, Milan, Bologna and Viterbo, the journey taking two whole days and the intervening night. We stayed at the lovely Pensione Rubens not far from the Spanish Steps. We did all the usual things in Rome, ancient, modern and educational, and attended a splendid performance of Verdi's 'Aida' in the Baths of Caracalla. Never will I forget the triumphant march with the horses and chariots on the stage. I persuaded my students to rise at 0400 hours to travel by train to Naples where we took the 0915 hours boat to Capri. As usual I swam in the Blue Grotto and conducted my students round that beautiful island. On the train journey back, I burst my finger in the train door; fortunately one of my students was a nurse. On the train there were Italian and Yugoslav sailors and soldiers, and since my students were mostly young, beautiful girls I had to take the greatest care of them! But we had great fun singing with the young sailors and soldiers. It was all well worth the long day's travel.

On 22nd August 1959, I hired a coach and we drove via Frascati, Rocca Di Papa, where the drinking water was so good, through the Alban Hills to Castel Gandolfo where I had secured tickets for a public audience of Pope John XXIII. I saw the Swiss Guard mount and at 1800 hours the Holy Father was borne in on the Sedia Gestatoria to resounding cheers. His Holiness spoke in Italian and French, his words being translated into English, Spanish, Portugese and so on. He exhorted us not to pay too much attention to the material things of this life, but to trust instead in God. That day was the Feast of the Immaculate Heart of Mary. He besought us to have recourse to her, to emulate her. We were to strive to live purely. He spoke especially of the sick and the homeless. He blessed us and our families and our religious objects. I thought of my friends when His Holiness blessed us, especially of Kath and Christina and of Uncle Hubert who was very ill in hospital. It was a great day. We rejoiced and we drank the wine I had bought in Frascati.

The next morning, many of my charming students accompanied me to Mass at

San Rocco before departing by train to Marina Di Pietra Santa. Here, apart from swimming, I led the group to Viareggio; Pisa, visiting the Cathedral and Baptistry and climbing the Leaning Tower; and Florence, where I visited my friends Signora and Gabriella de Benedictes of the Pensione Rigatti. In Florence, in one day, I succeeded in visiting San Lorenzo, San Marco, and most of the galleries.

We visited, too, a delightful mountain village with lots of marble quarries. The villagers made a great fuss of us. Peaceful was the atmosphere.

After a dreadful thunderstorm during the night we entrained for home via Viareggio and Genoa to Milan, and thence through the night via Basle, Lucerne, Lugano, and across the Rhine to Strasbourg, Metz Sedan and Calais, where our boat was full. Consequently we had to travel to Boulogne and did not reach London until 2330 hours.

And so after a splendid tour with mostly young Scottish, Welsh and Irish students, I rejoined Kath and Christina and Garg on 31st August.

Shortly after I resumed college, the moors between Bakewell and Sheffield were on fire everywhere, bellowing thick black smoke into the air. It had been a glorious summer, but we were dreadfully short of rain. In the Ladybower Reservoir, the old bridge of Ashopton and the remains of Derwent Village were visible above the water level.

At work, I received the additional paid duties of lecturing the domestic science students, all of whom were very beautiful, talented girls.

In my military duties I was appointed president of the board to examine the Derbyshire Army Cadets for the Certificate A Part II.

Within the family we received visits from Denise and Desmond Lloyd and Eric Cotton-Smith, but during my time in Italy, Kath's dear friend Mrs Roberts had died, and on 5th December my good friend Oliver Cockerton died very suddenly. I had a requiem said for him in Bakewell Catholic Church.

After the usual Christmas festivities, we entered the New Year of 1960.

Chapter VI

1960–1963

1960

In such spare time as I had, I continued my work in the Chatsworth Library on the papers of the Third and Fourth Dukes, which was fascinating.

Within the regiment we were soon to lose our commanding officer, Richard Grimwood-Taylor, who had a tremendous influence on my life. In every way he was the perfect gentleman, a great commanding officer and a brilliant lawyer. He was to hand over to another very good officer, "Vic" Emery, a Post Office engineer, and Tom Wragg was to become second-in-command. Consequently, I relinquished command of No. 2 Squadron at Derby and assumed command of No. 3 Squadron at Chesterfield, which made life easier from the viewpoint of travel. This occurred on 1st March 1960.

At the annual exercise 'Smoke Signal' held at Northern Command, York, we dined in the Merchant Adventurers' Hall – a great occasion.

In the political sphere I became Vice-Chairman of the Bakewell Conservative and Unionist Party. At work I was offered and accepted promotion within the Department of Science, under Douglas Thacker who became a great friend.

On 6th June, a great Scout Rally was held at Chatsworth: the Chief Scout, Sir Charles Fitzroy MacLean, and the son of Lord Baden-Powell were present. Unfortunately, I sustained sunstroke on that very hot day which put me in bed for 48 hours, before the departure of Kath and me to Dolgellau, which with its Welsh-speaking people was like a delightful foreign town. From there we continued our journey to Harlech Castle, and Aberystwyth; Chepstow and the Wye Valley and Monmouth; Symonds Yat and Hereford Cathedral. In Hereford, we called on my old friend Frank G.L. Phillips who had been a course below me in the Royal Signals Officer Cadet Training Unit and whom I had not seen for 17 years.

That July I was refused leave of absence to attend annual camp with my regiment at Beckingham, but I went over for two weekends, giving Kath the chance to stay with our good friends Denise and Desmond Lloyd en route.

Kath was very good indeed in organising our holidays. On 19th July we travelled to Amsterdam by train and boat via Sheffield, Harwich/Hook of Holland overnight on S.S. Duke of York. Amsterdam delighted us. We visited the Rijksmuseum, seeing Rembrandt's wonderful 'Nachtwatch'. By waterbus we went round the Herrengracht and the Harbours.

At Haarlem we visited the splendid Franz Hals Museum. We went to the Cheese Auction at Alkmaar, being given liberal helpings of cheese by charming costumed Dutch girls. We visited the beautiful Knights' Hall, and the Mauritshuis Museum, where we saw Vermeer's exquisite 'View of Delft', at Den Haag. Thence to the House in the Wood and the little model village of Madurodam. Despite several attempts we failed to find open the house of Anne Frank of diary fame; what dreadful memories of the Jewish holocaust! However, we succeeded in taking the train to Arnhem and visiting the Airborne Cemetery at Oosterbeek, so beautifully kept and creating such an impact on the memory and mind. Both Kath and I had to stem our tears. Then we traced the course of the airborne battle, before visiting the delightful open air museum near Arnhem, showing the development of costume, farming and housing in various parts of Holland.

Back in Amsterdam we visited Rembrandt's house and proceeded by bus and boat to the Isle of Marken, inhabited by a small community in their old-fashioned costumes who had kept themselves very much to themselves with considerable intermarriage and inbreeding. By now, it has probably been joined to the mainland. How different was Volendam. Here too the people wore their traditional costume. The people of this fishing port were as delightful as those of Marken were melancholy, as Catholic as their counterparts were Protestant.

We visited, too, the old university town of Leiden and its castle, circumnavigating the town by waterbus. Thence we proceeded to Delft to visit the Oude Kerk and to go round the town by canal. Before embarking at the Hook on S.S. Amsterdam we went to Rotterdam, so war-devastated in May 1940 but now re-built; visiting the Florinde, a magnificent flower show, and the like; and ascended the Euromast.

It was a delightful holiday and Kath and I liked Holland and her people very much: intelligent, clean, industrious, artistic and lively.

Shortly after our return, I drove to Chickerell Camp at Weymouth on attachment at annual camp to 43rd (Wessex) Divisional Signal Regiment, T.A.

commanded by Lt. Colonel A.L. Davies, T.D. Here I was put in charge of the training of recruits. This was a very good experience for me, because it gave me a new look at the T.A. and its signal regiment. Not only did I train recruits but I also lectured the officers in the presence of the army commander, General Sir Nigel Poett. And it was good to meet again General Sir William Scott, their Honorary Colonel, who had been Signal Officer-in-Chief; Brigadier "Slap" White who had become Chief Signal Officer, Southern Command; and my old P.S.I. Taffy Williams who was now in the 43rd. This attachment, in lieu of my own annual camp, I greatly enjoyed, learned much from it, and gained new friends.

Shortly after my return, Kath, Christina, Rosemary Cockerton and I paid another visit to the Lake District, quartering ourselves at Keswick visiting most of the lakes; Sawrey, where Beatrix Potter lived; and Hawkshead. Rosemary was a delight to us. We all dined at the George on the occasion of our 19th wedding anniversary.

I returned to work to find myself seconded back to the Department of Engineering for a term on the insistence of that great man, Harry Hodson.

Of that autumn, two things stand out in my mind: the death of Gilbert Harding of TV's 'What's My Line' fame, who had worked with Eric Cotton-Smith on intelligence in India during the war; and a splendid lecture 'The Making of an Army' by Field Marshal Viscount Slim of Burma, in the City Hall, Sheffield under the Basil Hicks bequest to the University.

I recollect how Slim dealt with the fear of the invincibility of the Japanese army. He made a practice of attacking Japanese platoons in battalion strength. Because some soldiers were deliberately catching malaria to avoid conflict, he sacked any commander in whose command malaria exceeded 5%, and he moved the malarial units up to the front. This stopped it! He recounted, too, how he was sitting on a hill in Burma with the American General "Vinegar Joe" Stilwell, watching the Chinese Army in retreat. Vinegar Joe leaned to him and said: "Well, General, I guess you and I aren't exactly cousins, but we have a common ancestor". "Who was that?" asked Slim. "Ethelred the Unready" replied Joe!

Slim was a great soldier. His lecture began punctually at 1930 hours and finished promptly at 2030 hours. It was he who, when Chief of the Imperial General staff appealing for recruits to the Territorial Army, described every Territorial as being "twice a citizen", which although perfectly true had not been appreciated before.

As a family, we entered the Christmas season with the appropriate festivities and so into the New Year of 1961.

1961

In March 1961, the Reverend Father Gerald Kelly, who had succeeded Father O'Dowd at Hassop, was succeeded by Father Roger Birks, a convert who had been a solicitor and in the Royal Navy, serving in a destroyer on D-Day.

On 18/19th March, my Chesterfield squadron provided the radio communications for the Rover Scouts' arduous 'Four Inns' Walk in the Peak District.

On Holy Saturday, 1st April, I drove to Madingley Hall, Cambridge, on a 'Liberal Studies in Technical Education' Course, attending the Easter Vigil liturgy in Cambridge. Easter Sunday was spent most pleasantly; we were taken round the Cambridge colleges. On the Monday I attended Holy Mass in Saint Edmund's Hall where the Rector, Canon Corboy, was most hospitable to me and a colleague from Edinburgh. I witnessed two Ethiopian priests celebrating Mass in the magnificent Coptic rite.

The next day all of us accompanied Professor Vyvian Ramsbottom, the assistant secretary of the Cambridge Extra-mural Board and a friend of Richard Grimwood-Taylor, to London for the inaugural meeting of the 'Association for Liberal Education'. I took the opportunity to visit the Thyssen exhibition in the National Gallery. In all it was a very useful course, during which time I was also able to visit Grantchester and the Fitzwilliam Museum, and Ely Cathedral on the way home.

In our military training strong emphasis was given to adventure-training. Exercise 'Alaric' was devoted to 22 miles of hard slog, mostly through bog, Leash Fen between the Baslow-Chesterfield and Baslow-Sheffield roads, in particular. We carried out two forays on Kinder Scout. Just before the first, our compasses had been withdrawn for calibration, and the result was dreadful: the mist descended on us and it was impossible to take a bearing. In my group of three we tried to move in a straight line, one moving, two stationary, until we heard what was like the thundering sound of a waterfall: it was a minute mountain stream which we were then able to follow. We eventually arrived in Edale via Crowdenbrook to find the main group missing. Sergeant-Major Elshaw at our Edale base had taken the precaution of alerting the Mountain Rescue Team. Later, that evening, the missing soldiers found their way by devious means to base. Never again, I swore, would I attempt Kinder Scout without a compass! We had learned our lesson. We became so proficient on Kinder Scout that I gave permission to the wardens to call us out to help them at any time.

We now had a new training major, Major Melville Gordon-Jones, a very efficient and conscientious soldier who had given splendid service in the Indian army. Unfortunately I could not get leave of absence from work in order to go to camp with my regiment, which had again gone to Washington in Co. Durham, but I visited them during the middle weekend for the guest night dinner and regimental parade, and wrote the signal instruction for their exercise.

As the regiment returned from annual camp, I drove to Warren Camp at Crowborough on 15th July 1961 on attachment to 52nd (Lowland) Signal Regiment T.A. as second-in-command to Lt. Colonel Hugh Lang, who gave me a very warm welcome. I was responsible for the pipe band and I drove with Major Ian Carmichael to Tunbridge Wells showground to arrange for the band to give a display there. I reconnoitred the training area in order to organise the regimental exercise. It fell to me to organise the regimental sports and I was grateful that they were blessed with good weather and great success. The Adjutant was Major Charles Stuart Galbraith with whom I established a strong friendship. Charles had served in the Cameronian Regiment before joining the Royal Signals. In his later years before retirement he held very responsible appointments at H.Q. N.A.T.O. In the course of the camp I met the splendid Honorary Colonel, Colonel Murray Niven, T.D., D.L.; Colonel "Jock" Linton of the Adjutant-General's Branch, later to be Brigadier as Chief Signal Officer, Scottish Command; and Brigadier Mackenzie, Secretary of Glasgow T.A.A.F.A. who had been General Urquhart's General Staff Officer I at the Battle of Arnhem. I became particularly friendly with Captain Alistair Inglis, a quietly-spoken Scottish lawyer who was a cousin of Hugh Lang. With him I visited Rudyard Kipling's home, Batemans, near Battle.

During the exercise, a Mr Day, an airline pilot, complained that the noise of the generators prevented his sleeping which was so essential to his occupation. The commanding officer and I entertained him and he proved most charming and two days later, he entertained Hugh and myself at his home. Thus the gentle word turneth away wrath!

I organised the trade boards, and also was able to help the C.O. in the matter of an accident. At the end of camp I bade farewell to the train party as they marched off to the swirl of the pipes! This attachment taught me many things in the matter of leadership. For Hugh Lang I developed the greatest admiration. Before we bade farewell to each other, he confided to me that I had been selected to succeed to the command of my own regiment.

Shortly after my return from annual camp Kath and I led a group of 24 International Summer School Society students to Diano Marina on the Ligurian coast of Northern Italy. We flew there from Gatwick to Nice, and thence by coach through Nice, Monte Carlo, Menton and San Remo, to the Hotel Villa Igea. Here there were great opportunities for swimming and visiting the beautiful mountain villages in the hinterland. On the coach which we used to drive into the Maritime Alps to take the chair lift to the Redentore (The Redeemer), 8,000 feet above sea level, I met none other than my former company commander, later to command 8 Army Signals, Lt. Colonel Harry Bett of Naples days, for whom I had the greatest admiration, and his wife. Later in our holiday, I spent a pleasant evening with them.

Amongst the towns and villages we visited were Diano Castello, Monesi, Cervo, Alassio, Albengo, Porto Maurizio, Imperia and San Remo. We also had a most memorable day visiting Genoa by train. There we visited the house of Christopher Columbus, the Church of the Annunziata, and the Palazzi Andrea Doria, Bianco and Rosso.

The group of students were very kind to Kath and me on the occasion of our 20th wedding anniversary.

Owing to mist in England, our plane was delayed nearly 24 hours and we were accommodated at the sumptuous Hotel Plaza, the best hotel in Nice. My diary records that it was almost a fiver a day!

The pilot, a Captain Skillman, a lecturer at Brooklands Technical College, flew only during his holidays; he very kindly drove Kath and me from Gatwick Airport to our friend Olga at Virginia Water.

Before resuming college, my squadron engaged in a training exercise on Kinder Scout and, in the heavy mist, I stumbled on the wreckage of an aeroplane. Throughout the autumn I worked hard in administering and training my squadron. I was required to write a letter to my commanding officer to the effect that I was willing to command the regiment. At the annual divisional exercise at Bestwood Lodge, Nottingham, headquarters of the 49th Division, I introduced myself to the divisional commander, Major-General Birkbeck, a very tall man who had served with the Airborne Forces; so tall and heavy that on occasion he suffered concussion on landing by parachute.

1962

After a white Christmas I fell ill with enteritis and, as usual, I returned to work before I was fit, and consequently fell ill again. Returning to work before I was recuperated has been one of the hallmarks of my life.

On 15/16th February a dreadful gale occurred. Sheffield was like a blitzed city: trees were down everywhere, blocking the roads and causing lengthy detours. Chatsworth lost 7000 trees!

About this time, the Assizes were held at Sheffield. I took as many classes as I could to observe the proceedings, and good it was for their education.

On 13th March, I was teaching my delightful domestic science students when one of the girls reported that the students' common room was on fire. Despite wearing my best suit I stampeded into the room, kicked the blazing settee to pieces, ripped down the curtains and used the fire extinguisher. Saving the situation did my best suit no good and I was rather distressed that I barely received a word of gratitude from the authorities; nor did I claim for my suit!

In early April, accompanied by Ron Eyley, a distinguished journalist, my squadron carried out another very tough exercise on Kinder Scout in the most appalling conditions of blizzard. The soldiers were magnificent and Ron Eyley gave us very good publicity, which helped greatly in the matter of recruitment.

On our return from a delightful holiday based on Virginia Water, involving Windsor Castle, Stoke Poges, where Thomas Gray wrote his famous 'Elegy in a Country Churchyard', the National Gallery and Sheridan's 'The School for Scandal', Kath and I returned home to find that our dear friend Miss Annie Holden, a splendid seamstress, had been found dead in her home. I was her executor and I executed her will on my own through the Office of Customs and Excise and thereby gained useful legal experience. Miss Holden, a dear friend of Kath's mother, was a very hard worker, very beautiful and very proud of having danced with the Duke of Devonshire and Mr Hoyle of Holme Hall.

On 6th June 1962, we had an election in West Derbyshire because our M.P. Sir Edward Wakefield had been appointed High Commissioner in Malta. The Conservative candidate was Aidan Crawley, and the Liberal candidate Colonel Ronald Gardner-Thorpe whom I greatly admired and who eventually became Lord Mayor of London. However, I was a Conservative well-versed in the Common Market, and since Aidan Crawley was putting up on a Common Market ticket it fell to me to go round before him in his electioneering, giving addresses on the Common Market. I will never forget 50 cows listening to me at Flagg!

At a pre-election meeting in the Bakewell Town Hall I presided, the chief speaker being the Right Honourable Christopher Soames, Minister of Food, Agriculture and Fisheries, and son-in-law of Churchill. In the audience reporting for the News of the World was Randolph Churchill, Winston's son. Afterwards in the Rutland Arms Hotel I had a drink with him, and Mr and Mrs Crawley and Christopher Chataway who, unfortunately for me, drank the drink bought for me by Randolph.

At the eve of the poll meeting in Lady Manners School, the gathering was addressed by the Right Honourable Lord Hailsham (Quintin Hogg) who was magnificent. Clearly he had enjoyed his dinner on the train: on arrival at the school he signed the visitors' book, drank half a bottle of champagne and gave a scintillating address. That night he gave four other addresses in West Derbyshire with half a bottle of champagne between each. I would dearly have loved to hear his last!

1962 was the year of the great Liberal revival, but Aidan Crawley on 6th June defeated Ronald Gardner-Thorpe by a narrow margin of some 1200 votes. In retrospect, I consider that Gardner-Thorpe deserved to win, although Crawley turned out to be a very good M.P.

In July Kath and I had the great pleasure of going to stay with Major and Mrs Peter Gilham at Chester in order to see the splendid Mystery Plays in the Cathedral Close.

Annual camp was held at Scarborough where we occupied Burniston Barracks. We trained and drilled very hard indeed because we were to be visited by our Colonel-in-Chief, H.R.H. Mary, Princess Royal, aunt of Queen Elizabeth. On the eve of her visit I fell ill with fever, but I was determined to be on parade, commanding my squadron the next day, and I dosed myself strongly with aspirin.

Her Royal Highness arrived at 1045 hours on Friday 27th July 1962, and after introductions and inspecting the Quarter Guard, was greeted on Parade by the Royal Salute. I escorted H.R.H. round the soldiers of my No.2 Squadron, and after the march past, round the Signal Centre. H.R.H. enjoyed a splendid lunch with the Master of Signals, Honorary Colonel, past commanders and civic dignitaries to the music of the military band outside the marquee. In the afternoon, H.R.H. attended our sports day and I sat with her for a few minutes discussing her home at Harewood. Her Lady-in-Waiting, Miss Gwynedd Lloyd, I found very charming. After the departure of H.R.H. we held a splendid guest night dinner at the Everley Hotel in Forge Valley with many past soldiers of the regiment.

In the course of the next week's training and trade boards we were visited by Major General Birkbeck, G.O.C. 49 Division.

On 25th August, Kath and I travelled to Paris through Sheffield United Tours, going by coach from Chesterfield to Lympne whence we flew in a Dakota to Beauvais, and then by coach to Paris, to the Hotel Bel Air in La Place de La Republique.

We visited the tomb of Napoleon; his son the King of Rome; his brother; and Marshal Foch, that great Colonel-in-Chief of the First World War. Thence we went by train to Chartres to see the beautiful stained glass windows in the lovely Gothic cathedral of Notre Dame.

At Versailles we visited the Palace and the delightful Le Hameau with Mr and Mrs Starr-Kine of the U.S.A. Diplomatic Service.

Another day we devoted to La Sainte Chapelle with its beautiful stained glass, La Conciergerie, the prison of Queen Marie Antoinette, Les Galleries Lafayette, Montmartre and Sacré Coeur, where we watched the artists at work.

On our 21st wedding anniversary on 30th August, we admired the beautiful Impressionist paintings, especially those of Van Gogh and Toulouse-Lautrec in the Jeu de Paume, in the delightful Tuileries Gardens. Thence we travelled to Fontainebleau for lunch and a wonderful tour of the Chateau.

On 31st August, the anniversary of Henry V's death, we visited the Chateau of Vincennes where he died. In contrast, that evening we went to Les Folies Bergères which was most enjoyable.

Amongst other places we visited were La Place des Vosges, where Cardinal Richelieu lived; the lovely little Carnavalet Museum; the wonderful Cluny Museum; Malmaison, the home of Napoleon and Josephine; the beautiful terraces of St. Germain en Laye; and the Elysee Palace, residence of President de Gaulle. It was a memorable holiday organised mostly by dearest Kath, and was remarkably cheap.

On the day of our return, Christina arrived from Penzance where she had spent her holiday with the Cockertons, she and Rosemary being great lifelong friends.

Christina had now finished her year in the sixth form at Lady Manners School, and on 10th September started a year's study at Chesterfield College of Art.

The international situation was very dangerous, and in the month of September we held a mobilisation exercise based at Bestwood Lodge, the H.Q. of 49 Division. Despite the underlying gravity of the situation, we made the best of it, and our canteen proved to be a great asset! This was followed by two supporting exercises on the next two weekends, and I had the great pleasure of meeting the Commander-in-Chief, General Sir Roderick McCleod. Over the weekend of 13-14th October, we held a squadron exercise involving firing on the Totley ranges, bivouacking at Edale and adventure training on Kinder Scout, finishing at the Snake Inn on the Snake Pass where we were awaited by our regimental medical officer, Major Desmond Stoker.

By now the Cuban Crisis was at its worst. The U.S.S.R. under Kruschev had stationed nuclear missiles on the island of Cuba and President Kennedy was threatening action against the U.S.S.R. The world was on the brink of nuclear war! Tom Wragg, having taken some of the Chatsworth paintings to the U.S.A., was in Washington at the time, and he said that you could have cut the atmosphere with a knife. Kath and I had gone to London to stay with Olga and to see Ibsen's 'Peer Gynt', which was wonderful. The next day we walked through Windsor Great Park and saw the Queen and Princess Anne, the Queen driving her shooting brake after riding, and I dwelt on the responsibility she must have been feeling. The next day, 28th October, Kruschev backed down and agreed to remove the missiles, thank God. It had been superb statesmanship on the part of Kennedy, and neither he nor Kruschev tried to humiliate the other in any way.

1963

The New Year opened with appalling winter weather. From 4th to 8th January I attended a Liberal Studies course at Lady Margaret Hall, Oxford, which I found very interesting and useful. I returned home to big snow and heavy frost. The Right Honourable Hugh Gaitskell and Cardinal Godfrey died within a few days of each other. The back-boiler at home froze overnight. Kath, unaware of this, lit a fire. Thank God, the boiler did not burst, but it developed a leak and had to be replaced. The harsh winter lasted well into March.

On 30/31st March, my squadron carried out a hard communication exercise involving the establishment of a radio beam from the summit of Kinder Scout to Sleaford in Lincolnshire. At the conclusion of the exercise, the 3-ton truck turned over on the return journey near Edale. Private Sherman of the W.R.A.C. suffered a broken pelvis and Signalman Chapman injured his arm. There were 15 soldiers in the truck and we were fortunate that the injuries were no worse. I paid several visits to Pte. Sherman, who was admitted to the Sheffield Royal Infirmary. She was a very plucky girl.

Annual camp was spent at Scarborough. I led the Chesterfield Convoy on Saturday 1st June 1963. I vividly remember that, two days later, that Great and Good Peasant become Pope, John XXIII, died amidst universal grief. He had indeed caused fresh air to blow throughout Christianity.

Our annual camp involved a recruiting day for the regulars, and I met my friend Lt. Colonel Jack Knowles, who joined up with me and later went down on the ill-fated Lancastria in June 1940, and was now in charge of recruiting.

Three days after the conclusion of annual camp, Cardinal Montini of Milan was elected Pope Paul VI.

On 29th June, as Tom Wragg and I were leaving Bakewell for the Royal Signals Association Reunion in Catterick, we saw President Kennedy land by helicopter at Chatsworth, where he was visiting his sister Kathleen's grave, the Duke and Duchess, and the Hungarian Solymossy sisters, who had earlier served his family. The practice of attending the Royal Signals Association Reunion I maintained until 1994.

A portrait of the author, 1963

Impression by Bos '63

Major Melville Gordon-Jones relinquished his appointment as training major to the regiment on 13th July 1963 and was succeeded by Major Terry Ross.

Our old friend John Gates, who had been our cipher officer in Italy and was now one of Her Majesty's Inspectors of Planning Applications, called and stayed with us during a visit to the Peak Park Planning Board, and we all had a delightful dinner at the Rutland Arms Hotel on 15th July.

Five days later Kath and I departed on a COSMOS tour of Austria, flying across the channel from Southend to Ostend and then proceeding by coach, bypassing Bruges and Brussels to Liége, thence over the Eiffel to Adenau where we stayed, then crossing the Mosel and Rhine at Koblenz and along the Autobahn via Ulm, Munich and Mittenwald to Seefeld where we stayed a week. During this time we explored the beautiful Austrian countryside; Innsbruck, so delightful a city; Salzburg with its strong Mozart connections; Schloss Linderhof, built by Ludwig II of Bavaria; and Oberammergau, where we refreshed ourselves at the Hotel Alois, owned by Anton Preising who had played Christ in the 1960 Passion Play and endorsed his photograph for us. Nearly 40 years later, in 2000, I met his grandson who played Judas magnificently in that years' splendid production of the Passion Play. On the return journey to the United Kingdom, Kath and I were able to explore Brussels where we stayed the night before flying across the Channel. Prior to our journey home, we visited Hampton Court and a West End theatre to see 'My Fair Lady'.

For the next five weeks I was at Chatsworth almost every day supervising the Old Masters' drawings exhibition in the theatre. During this time I met many very interesting people. The Duke and Duchess were kindness itself to me. Mary Dowager Duchess introduced me to the Poet Laureate, John Betjeman, and Lady Elizabeth Cavendish, her daughter. Assembled at Chatsworth for the wedding of Lady Emma Cavendish to the Honourable Tobias Tennant were Lady Diana Mosley, her sister Nancy Mitford, and their niece Constance Romilly, the daughter of Jessica Mitford, and it was good to be introduced to them. I watched the wedding on a beautiful day, 3rd September 1963, from the bedroom of old Mr Tom Wragg, father of my friend Tom who played the organ for the occasion in Edensor Church. I had a grandstand view! On another occasion I met Sir Bernard and Lady Lovell of the great Joddrell Bank telescope fame.

On 4th September, at a dinner at the Rutland Arms Hotel, we bade farewell and made a presentation to the Reverend Father Roger Birks who was leaving Hassop for Melbourne. Father Birks had served in the Royal Navy on D-Day, and before taking Holy Orders had practised law as a solicitor. Present on the occasion was a charming Maltese priest, Father Carmel Mifsud. He taught at St. Paul's School, Malta and had been choirmaster in the Co-Cathedral at St. John in Valletta.

In view of my forthcoming command of the regiment, I attended the Royal Signals Commanding Officers' Study Weekend at Catterick Camp, where I met many old friends and made a new friend in Major the Earl Kitchener (Henry) of Khartoum. During the autumn we continued to exercise in the provision of radio beam communications, from the summit of Kinder Scout to Sleaford.

At Divisional H.Q. in Nottingham I attended a fascinating study group on leadership and listened to splendid lectures by Professor Boswell of the Royal Military Academy and to the American and French Military Attachés. The exercise was called 'Bear Leadership', the Polar Bear being our 49th Divisional Emblem.

On Friday 22nd November, a day nobody then living will ever forget, President John F. Kennedy of the U.S.A. was assassinated in Dallas, Texas, to be succeeded immediately by Vice-President Johnson.

During half-term in October, Kath and I had a delightful little holiday in the Cotswolds, Blenheim, Oxford (Balliol College), Windsor Castle, Virginia Water and London, where we were joined by Christina, who on 19th September had departed from home to start her course at Hornsey College of Art.

At Christmastide we had the usual family gatherings and reunions. I always welcomed the advent of Uncle Hubert, who during World War I had been a captain in the 6th Battalion of the Sherwood Foresters Regiment and been awarded the Military Cross in August 1918 for conspicuous gallantry. We were very close, almost like brothers. He would have been glad to know that 35 years later I was to be appointed Honorary Colonel of the Derbyshire Cadet Battalion of the Worcester and Sherwood Foresters Regiment.

Chapter VII

In Command: 1964–1967

1964 opened with my having to do two men's work in college since one of my colleagues had moved. Despite the pressures of work, I took on the great responsibility of command of the 46th Signal Regiment, T.A. at midnight of Leap Day, at a regimental dinner held at the New Bath Hotel, Matlock. This was attended by my dear wife Kath and the Honorary Colonel, my dear friend Gerry Underwood, who gave me the sound advice to listen to all and make my own decisions, putting me in a mind of Pope John XXIII's dictum: "Hear all; see some; believe a few!" In the course of the evening I made presentations to the retiring commanding officer, Lt. Colonel A. Vic Emery, Major John Gibbs, Captain Amies Goldingham, Major Sam Turner and Captain John France. A few weeks earlier, No. 2 Chesterfield Squadron had made a presentation to me on my handing over command to Major Peter Revill. Unlike most commanding officers I never had the benefit of holding the office of second-in-command for some three years. I had, as it were, been flung in at the deep end, but I had clear ideas on what I wanted to do.

Had it not been for great sacrifice and patience on the part of Kath I could not have held my job in Sheffield and commanded a regiment spread over three counties. She was wonderful and I could never repay her. Kath was not very keen on being the Queen Bee, but she filled the office with great dignity and was loved and respected by all.

After attending the annual signals exercise at York, together with my second-in-command, Tom Wragg, and the training major, Terry Ross, who had hitherto commanded the signal squadron on Malta, I visited the Royal Signals School at Blandford to reconnoitre preparations for annual camp, based on the school. At Blandford I met my old regimental sergeant major of O.C.T.U. days, R.S.M. Gay who was working there as a clerk, and I was delighted that he remembered me. He was a great man of whom, as a cadet, you lived in fear and dread; but he produced good officers and was a splendid disciplinarian and parade organiser. We had the pleasure, too, of attending the annual lecture of the Royal Signals Institution on 'The laying of the Trans-Pacific Cable'.

Tom Wragg was a brilliant signals officer, and had been appointed M.B.E. for conspicuous service in North Africa, Sicily and Italy. I strongly wished to retain him as second-in-command despite the fact that he would be 50 years old on 17th October. I therefore visited my divisional commander, Major General C.M.M. Man, at Bestwood Lodge to plead for his retention. The general, for whom I had the greatest liking, respect and admiration, was very charming to me but had to say no, and rightly so.

In the course of my holidays I supervised, at Tom Wragg's request, the display of Old Master drawings in the theatre at Chatsworth: Leonardo de Vinci, Michelangelo, Rembrandt, Titian, Inigo Jones and so on. Here I had the pleasure of meeting many interesting people.

Annual camp at Blandford lasted from 18th July to 1st August. 337 (Nottingham) Squadron were not with us since they had been with their parent formation to Otterburn in early June. The camp was a great success, including a three-day exercise named 'Badger Chase' which was visited by General Man, who as always was very helpful in every respect.

Colonel A. Burrows, the commander of the famous 30 Signal Regiment, based at Blandford, took me round his regimental HQ. In the course of camp, we were visited by Brigadier Max Charlton, Chief Signal Officer Northern Command, and of course Gerry Underwood our Honorary Colonel, for whom we put on a splendid party on the morrow of our principal dinner night. Not far from Blandford is the Tank Museum at Bovington: this we visited, putting me in mind of my time with the 11th Armoured Division in 1941/2. I had the pleasure, too, of visiting T.E. Lawrence's cottage at Clouds Hill. Over the door in Greek was written 'Nothing Matters'. It had come to the ears of Brigadier Charlton that I was too anxious about many regimental matters and he gave me the splendid advice: A living C.O. is better than a dead C.O. All this illustrated the great care shown throughout the services.

Shortly after my return from annual camp, at Bakewell Show, I met my friend Colonel Gardner-Thorpe to whom I had taken a great liking at the 1962 by-election. Apart from being the Liberal prospective candidate he was also treasurer of the Liberal Party.

But the great event of the summer was the arrival at the Peacock Hotel, Rowsley, of my dear old friend Major Joe Waldron retired from the U.S. Signal Corps, his wife,

Trudy, and their charming little daughters, Debbie and Janet. Joe had contracted polio during the Korean War and I could not help feeling distressed at seeing him in a wheelchair. But he is a man of strong character and although so grievously disabled he did far more than many a completely able man. Kath and I took them round Haddon Hall; Chatsworth, where we were escorted by the housekeeper, Miss Solymossy; Robin Hood's stride; and Little John's grave at Hathersage for the sake of the children. Joe and Trudy were made particularly welcome by the Hudson family at the Wheatsheaf. And, of course, they all fell in love with Kath.

Thereafter, Kath and I enjoyed a delightful Belgian holiday, organised by Kath, based in Bruges and Dinant. Bruges is a delightful town and we made full use of its canals, attending the Festival of Canals one evening which showed the history of Bruges. We visited the Basilica of the Holy Blood, Saint Salvator, and the Church at Notre Dame with its beautiful Madonna and child sculpture by Michelangelo.

Ghent and Namur on the Meuse and the Sambre were fascinating. Thence we went to the fortress town of Dinant in the Meuse, which had suffered so severely in World War I and again in World War II in May 1944, when the German panzer divisions crossed the Meuse and made their remarkable dash to the Channel Ports, myself being on the receiving end at Calais.

At Annevoie we visited the Benedictine Abbey, Maredsous, where they brewed the most wonderful beer!

We took the train to the town of Han where we descended the River Lesse by flat-bottomed boat, getting drenched in a heavy thunderstorm.

En route back to Bruges we paid a visit to Brussels where we enjoyed visiting Notre Dame du Sablon, St. Michael's Cathedral, and the magnificent Gallerie des Belles Artres.

From Bruges we returned via Ostend and Dover, visiting Christina at Onslow Gardens. Christina and Olga joined us to visit Hampton Court, where we saw Lord Boothby who had a Grace and Favour apartment there.

In November, we lost our friend Lt. Colonel Victor Holland, who had actually escaped from Tobruk in 1942 by joining an Afrika Korps convoy. On 4th November he had had an examination of his prostate gland which he found not too unpleasant, but two days later he died in his Sheffield dentist's waiting room. His funeral in Bakewell Parish Church was well represented by the Royal Corps of Signals: Colonel Gerry Underwood, Colonel Richard Grimwood-Taylor, Major Tom Wragg and me; and Lt. Colonel Bob Glanville, Secretary of Derbyshire Territorial Army and Auxiliary Forces Association.

We held our annual divisional study period at H.Q. 49 Division where I had lunch on both days with General Chris Man. The divisional dinner was held in Cripps Hall at the University of Nottingham, the splendid band of the south Nottinghamshire Hussars providing music, culminating in the Post Horn Gallop.

Early in December, Kath's father "Garg" fell ill, at a time when I myself was ill. His condition deteriorated each day, and several times I had to attend him during the night. I think he had had a second stroke, for he was suffering from confusion and had lost his bearings. Mary and Bill joined us in sitting up with him during the night. On 11th December, his 90th birthday, he received many cards and presents and one special one from Haig House British Legion Club, which he had told me only a few days earlier had kept him alive. That night I had to put in an appearance at our regional ball in Nottingham. I got home about 3.00am and relieved Mary for a while. At about 12.30pm on Saturday 12th December, he died very peacefully. What a life! Trained by his father as a blacksmith in Bridge Street, he was one of two Bakewellians who volunteered for the Imperial Yeomanry to fight in the Boer War in South Arica.

For a time he acted as Lord Roberts' despatch rider. He was seriously concussed by a kick on the head from a horse and received a small pension to his dying day. On their return he and Mr Littlewood were given a rousing welcome, being drawn from the railway station in a carriage pulled by the townspeople. The town gave them a splendid dinner in a packed town hall. Later he married Sally Kay whose grandfather had established Kay's Boarding School for Young Gentlemen in what is now a complex of shops near the old market hall. They had three children: Jack, Mary and Kathleen. He bought a shop in Matlock Street which he turned into a flourishing boot and shoe business. Up Parsonage Croft, he built Thorncliffe for himself, but Kath was actually born at the shop on 8th September 1914 just after the declaration of the First World War.

Garg was a special constable, church warden, county court bailiff, chairman of the Bakewell Urban District Council and Justice of the Peace. Gone now were the clatter of his hooves over the South African Veldt. He had lived a good, but by no means easy, life. The church was full for his funeral, including my brother and sister-in-law, and the Royal British Legion provided his bearers, including our good friend "Jonah", Captain G.F. Jones. All this was a very sad blow for Kath; and then on 22nd December, Denise Lloyd, one of Kath's greatest friends, died from cancer in Addenbrooke's Hospital, Cambridge, leaving her husband, Desmond, and four children, Stephen, Phillipa, Peter and Robert, to whom Kath became virtually a second mother. Naturally, the family Christmas festivities were rather dimmed; and so 1964 came to an end.

1965

1965 opened with three more deaths: the poet T.S. Eliot on 4th January; my Aunt Nellie on 7th January; and Sir Winston Churchill on 15th January. I attended Auntie Nellie's funeral at the top chapel in Charlesworth and it was like a scene from Wuthering Heights! The wind was gale force; the rain hurled down; and she was placed into the family vault with her ancestors. She had always been very kind to me and latterly to Kath and Christina. I felt very sorry for Uncle George and I met many of my relations, some of whom I had not seen for 20 or 30 years. Sir Winston's funeral was, rightly so, a very elaborate affair. His coffin was borne on the Thames after the funeral service in St. Paul's, and the cranes by the dockland bowed to show the respect of the dockers. His body was conveyed to Bladon not far from Blenheim Palace where he was born, and the gravestone says just "Winston Churchill".

Some months later, on 8th April, a third Boer War veteran, Mr Arthur Groome, died. Mr Groome was a Freeman of the City of London, having been born in hearing distance of Bow Bells. He had fought, too, in World War I and was a tremendous stalwart of the British Legion and one of the founders of Haig House British Legion Club, Bakewell. In all, a very honourable man.

There died, too, on 28th March, my Colonel-in-Chief, H.R.H. the Princess Royal, who had been destined to visit the regiment on annual camp at Scarborough on 29th July. She was a princess of great respect.

The weather in the early months of 1965 was very cold with lots of snow and appalling driving conditions. Frequently I had to dig my car out of the snow.

As commanding officer I had to do much travelling, especially since the regiment was very much involved in all that might occur in the event of Nuclear War. As a consequence of this, I was closely involved with, amongst others, the Police Mobile Columns.

On 10th April at the Peveril Hotel, Dovedale, we "dined out" my second-in-command and great friend, Major Tom Wragg, M.B.E.; Major Clive Didcot, M.B.E.; and Lt. Colonel Desmond Stoker, my regimental medical officer. With their great experience, they were all huge losses to the regiment. My new second-in-command was Major James Lawson, and we immediately went to Northern Command H.Q. at York to visit the chief signal officer, Brigadier Peter Pentreath, with whose family we had luncheon at Strensall. Thence we went to Scarborough to make arrangements for annual camp, calling on the mayor's secretary and Mr Sedman of Messrs T. Lawton & Co. (Charles Lawton, the great actor, was of that family) in connection with our guest night. For the next few weeks I was kept very busy in regimental affairs covering the three counties of Derbyshire, Nottinghamshire and Leicestershire. Major General Chris Man, Brigadier Terry Spencer-Smith (commanding 148 Brigade), and Colonel Stedding (commanding 22 Engineer Group), were all very helpful to me.

In my civil career at Sheffield Polytechnic, I was delighted to be appointed lecturer in the humanities on 27th May, Ascension Day.

During June, Kath and I had a most enjoyable holiday in the West Country: Wells, Dunster, Porlock, Barnstaple, Clovelly, Tintagel, Polperro, Dartmoor (including Princeton Prison), Widdecombe, Glastonbury and Gloucester.

On 19th June, Kath and I were received at Chatsworth by the Duke and Duchess of Devonshire, and the Marquess of Hartington at the coming-of-age celebrations of the Marquess. It was a most delightful occasion: champagne, a wonderful buffet, fireworks and so on. Also in attendance were Lady Dorothy MacMillan, Mr Harold MacMillan, Lady Norwich (Diana Manners) and many more.

But on Friday 2nd July, I had a completely different experience! Kath and I, with Tom and Ida Wragg, Desmond and Marjorie Stokes, and Ronald and Paivia Knighton, attended a Royal British Legion Carnival dinner at the Wheatsheaf. After dinner, at the carnival dance in the town hall, when we were selecting the carnival queen, three men tried to enter without paying: John Craven, Robert Robinson and a man called Buxton. I courteously told them that they must either pay or go away. Craven said he would knock my f****** head off, assaulted me with a heavy chair and then they left. Craven and Robinson returned a little later. Tom Wragg and I confronted them in the entrance. Mrs Stoker called my name from upstairs, I looked away and then I received some thunderous blows from Craven: my upper denture was broken, my upper teeth were driven through my bottom lip, and both lips and throat were badly bruised as the result of a karate blow. When I recovered my wits I found Tom sitting on Robinson and then Tom, who had been grievously assaulted, suffered a stroke and was completely paralysed, losing his speech. By now the police had arrived and Robinson was taken into custody, Craven having fled. Tom was taken by ambulance to Chesterfield Royal Hospital and subsequently transferred to Sheffield Royal Infirmary. Whilst Robinson was being questioned in the police station by Sergeant Venables, a stone was thrown through the window, cutting the head of the Sergeant. Having concluded that these men came from Buxton, Inspector Frank Woodings and three constables went out to the police car to find all the tyres slashed! In another car, they took the top route to Buxton and encountered a drunken man, who turned out to be Craven. They had to draw their truncheons and use them to arrest him and take him to Buxton police station cells. In the course of this, both Inspector Woodings and Sergeant Harry Marshall received facial injuries. In the fullness of time the men were charged with causing grievous bodily harm to Tom and actual bodily harm to me in the local magistrates' court, and then remanded for the Quarter Sessions at, if my memory serves me right, Leicester. Here, on listening to the defending council, you might have thought that they were angels from Heaven, visiting earth! Craven was sentenced to five years imprisonment and Robinson, being underage, just probation. Robinson broke the terms of his probation a little later and was put away. On his release, Craven went in for burglary with an accomplice. Some disputes occurred and on Boxing Night a few years later outside the Eagle in Buxton his accomplice murdered him with a shotgun!

Before the magistrates' court hearing Craven and Robinson met me in the street, and waved at me as though I were a long-lost friend. In court Craven said he was sorry for assaulting "that old man". That was me and I was only 45 years old. Of that I took a dim view. Tom eventually recovered about 60 per cent of his mobility and speech; but his movements were much slower and his speech always slurred. The Criminal Injuries Compensation Board, eventually awarded £1750 to Tom and £103 to me.

Despite my injuries – ultimately necessitating some 25 visits to the dentist – the next morning, after visiting the doctor, I deposited Kath at Wellingborough and drove on to Larkhill to visit Major Bill Heaton and his squadron who were billeted at the School of Artillery, near Stonehenge, on exercises. The next day, I assisted at Mass in the Garrison Church, inspected the billets and so on and returned home, collecting Kath from Wellingborough.

After I made my statement to the police, Inspector Frank Woodings and I became lifelong friends. Rashly I took only two days off work and made daily visits to Tom in the Royal Infirmary.

I must here emphasise that Tom and I sustained our injuries in pursuit of our work for the Royal British Legion, from whom we received hardly any recognition! I had submitted a detailed report on the matter to General Man, because I did not want the services to be brought into disrepute, and the army immediately threw a protective screen round me.

Despite all this and a subsequent fever I went off to command my regiment in annual camp at Burniston Barracks, Scarborough on 24th July. When I gave my opening address to the troops, I had no idea that within four days the startling news of the reorganisation of the Territorial Army would hit us, and that I would have to readdress the regiment. The T.A. as we knew it was to be replaced by the T.A.V.R. (Territorial Army Volunteer Reserve) in three categories: T.A.V.R. I could be called out at any time for immediate action; T.A.V.R. II would be called out on embodiment; T.A.V.R. III was for home defence, a kind of Home Guard. The biggest cuts were in the artillery, cavalry or Royal Armoured Corps, and the infantry. Whereas every county had once had its infantry battalion and yeomanry regiment, there were now going to be tremendous amalgamations. Royal Signals, Royal Engineers and the like would still be of the highest importance. This was the plan of the very intelligent Secretary of State for Defence, the Right Honourable Denis Healey, who had a distinguished war record. I had to leave annual camp to attend conferences on the matter with Major General Man, my divisional commander, and Brigadier Pentreath, my Chief Signal Officer. Nonetheless, in the course of camp we carried out our exercise and were visited by the army commander, General Sir Geoffrey Musson K.C.B., C.B.E., D.S.O., who was deeply concerned about the recent attack on me in Bakewell, and Brigadier Spencer-Smith commanding 148 Brigade.

In the course of camp we had our regimental guest night with our Honorary Colonel, Gerry Underwood; Brigadier Pentreath; Colonel Betty Michell, assistant director of the Women's Royal Army Corps; Colonel Richard Grimwood-Taylor; past commanding officers Richard Pickford and Vic Emery; and Tom Wragg, recently paralysed, who succeeded in tying his shoe lace which was a real achievement. Brigadier Pentreath paid us the great compliment of saying that we were more like a family than a regiment. We had, too, a splendid regimental parade for the Honorary Colonel. Later he underwent a prostate operation in Manchester and Tom and I visited him when he was in an understandably emotional state.

Let me now leave military affairs. Kath was very keen on visiting Lourdes, more than I was. Accordingly, on 19th August we joined at Victoria Station our group of pilgrims, led by Father Gaffney, a Salesian priest, who proved to a splendid leader. Amongst the pilgrims was a Benedictine, Father Richardson; a Franciscan, Father Ford; and a delightful lady from New York, Miss Madge Bowe. We flew by BAC1-11 in 1¼ hours to Tarbes and arrived in Lourdes in time for lunch, and to attend the Blessing of the Sick, and the torchlight procession in the evening, and to visit the Grotto where Our Lady appeared many times to Bernadette Soubirous in 1858. All of these things deeply impressed us.

In the course of our pilgrimage I met a very charming and cultured young lady who told me that she had witnessed a miracle during the Blessing of the Sick; she was not the type of person given to falsehood or vivid imagination, and I believed her.

The village of Bartrès is very attractive. Here, Bernadette was fostered out as a very young girl to a farm which we visited. And it was a great experience to visit the marvellous caves with a great subterranean lake, at Bettharen, and to ascend by cable car (Telegraphique) the mountain called Bouét. We went into the Pyrenees to Pont D'Espagne, by way of a beautiful village called Lafayette. From Pont D'Espagne, Kath and I took the chairlift to way above the snow line and had an invigorating walk in the thin air.

It was a delightful pilgrimage and we held three very pleasant evening parties on the instigation of Madge Bowe who was suffering from cancer. Father Gaffney became a good friend of ours. Madge survived her cancer and became a lifelong friend.

Before the resumption of my teaching duties, Kath and I set out on her birthday, 8th September, for Keswick calling en route on Colonel Gerry Underwood, much recovered from his operation. The next day, having been round Derwentwater by launch, we drove on to Edinburgh to stay with the Malcolms. We visited the castle, Holyrood Palace, so reminiscent of Mary, Queen of Scots, Rizzio and Lord Darnley, and went down the Royal Mile with a festival guide. We had a delightful journey home via Jedburgh Abbey, Durham Cathedral and Bedale. The 300 miles seemed so little!

In mid-September at the divisional rifle meeting at Beckingham, I heard the dreadful news of the brain haemorrhage suffered by Topsy Man, the General's wife. The General had to make the very hard decision to assent to an operation regarded as being successful in only 50 per cent of cases. He began to dream that he was back in the Japanese P.O.W. Camp. Thank God, the operation was successful.

An old member of my regiment, Sergeant Archie Heaton, who went through the Dunkirk evacuation and after the war became a permanent staff instructor, a wonderful, friendly and very humble man, was buried on 28th September.

That autumn I did not enjoy good health, but despite this I maintained my academic work, with a few occasional days off when I was far too ill, and had a chest X-ray. I maintained all the duties and responsibilities of commanding the regiment, with so many altercations taking place owing to the reorganisation of the Territorial Army, consequent on the defence review of the Wilson government. It was a particular pleasure to have my old commanding officer of the Italian campaign, Inky Udell, at my officers' training weekend at the Peveril of the Peak in Dovedale.

The divisional study period 'Bear Reality' was conducted by Major General Chris Man, who introduced me to Air Vice-Marshall Lewis, commanding the Royal Air Force College at Cranwell, and Mr Gerry Reynolds, M.P. Under-Secretary of

State for the Army, who addressed us on the reorganisation. He was a good young man, highly regarded by the Duke of Norfolk, president of the council of T.A., but he worked far too hard as a result of which he died only a few months later. We held our dinner at the University of Nottingham in Sherwood Hall. Our chief guests were Mr Reynolds and Lt. General Sir Geoffrey Musson, Commander-in-Chief, Northern Command. The Band of the Sherwood Rangers played magnificently during dinner.

On 29th November, there was a very heavy snowstorm whilst I was in Sheffield and all the roads to Bakewell were blocked. I had to spend the night with Professor and Mrs Wilfred Saunders in Sheffield and the next day I came home by taking the train to Grindleford. On the thawing of the snow many floods occurred and Kath had to deal with heavy flooding whilst I was in Sheffield. It affected, too, our regimental ball held at the Royal Victoria Hotel, Nottingham, for floods at Derby prevented many people from attending.

On 15th December I attended the General's conference at Bestwood Lodge on the government's white paper on the reorganisation of the Territorial Army. The following day the white paper was approved in the Commons by a majority of one! For several weeks I was kept quite busy in visiting my squadrons and making provision for the new Territorial Army Volunteer Reserve. Despite this I found time to write an article on Hassop Church for the Derbyshire Life and Countryside Magazine, aided by my friend Tom Wragg who did the photographs, especially of the beautiful chasuble, reputed to have been embroidered by Queen Catherine of Aragon when she was visiting Haddon Hall with her first husband Prince Arthur. Whilst there, Prince Arthur disappeared one day and was found asleep by the cross at what is now Hassop Roundabout. Not long afterwards, he died at Ludlow Castle. At Hassop he had dreamed that the Angel of Death had come to summon him, and on his deathbed at Ludlow it is said that he cried: "Ah, the dream I had at Hassop!" That beautiful chasuble was later displayed in the Graves Art Gallery in Sheffield to help raise funds for Saint Luke's Hospice in Sheffield, the founder of which was Professor Eric Wilkes, now retired in Calver.

On Christmas Day, Kath entertained the entire family, Peggy Bramwell and Kathleen Noton, at Christmas dinner.

Three days later, I attended, at Saint Luke's, Glossop, the funeral of my old Latin mistress Miss Newton, who gave me so great a love for the Latin language and whom I so greatly admired. At her funeral I met two of my old masters, Mr Hall and Mr Brown, and several old schoolfriends.

On New Year's Eve, I had to take to my bed, as so often I had done that autumn.

Early in January I had the pleasure of receiving at the Chesterfield Squadron H.Q. Colonel Sheila A. Heaney, assistant director of the Women's Royal Army Corps. We became firm friends and met on subsequent military occasions, by which time Sheila had been promoted to Brigadier as Director of the W.R.A.C., an office which she filled with great distinction.

On a bitterly cold, very foggy Saturday 22nd January, my annual administrative inspection was carried out by Brigadier Alf Freeman M.C. He was suffering from 'flu, and both the R.S.M. and I were very unwell. All concerned including Alf's brother-in-law, Richard Grimwood-Taylor, the Brigadier's S.O. II Roy Ledder, and Terry Ross thoroughly deserved the luncheon to which I entertained them, at Grange Farm between Nottingham and Derby. We came out from the inspection with flying colours.

Major Sinclair of the Middlesex Yeomanry very kindly represented me at the funeral of the late signal officer-in-chief, Major General Swainson.

As a relief from matters military, it was a delight to attend with Tom Wragg a lecture on Turner given by Sir John Rothenstein at the Graves Art Gallery, Sheffield on 24th January.

By now I was from time to time being consulted by the Ministry of Defence on the matter of the positive vetting of officers who had served under my command. The vetting was indeed very thorough.

Kath always helped me whenever and wherever she could, and accompanied me to visit Brigadier "Bun" Bowey D.S.O., the secretary of Nottinghamshire T.A.A.F.A., a very distinguished soldier and great rugger player. We then visited Kath's dear sister Mary, recuperating from an operation in a Nottingham hospital, and of good cheer, despite the later gravity of her condition.

Just before the onset of Lent, the Derby Station Mess, i.e. the Royal Artillery and Royal Signals, held a splendid cocktail party. The champagne was excellent.

For my regimental officers' training weekend the theme I selected was security, and it was very well organised by Captain Chris Robinson. My friend Inky Udell and Valerie Lloyd-Williams of the Ministry of Defence were present. The Honorary Colonel could not attend because he was at the disposal of Guy Jackson's ashes; instead my principal guest was Miss Catherine Cockerton who had nursed me at Bakewell during the winter of 1940 when so many of us had been ill from a nasty 'flu and spinal meningitis. It was my 'thank you' to her. Kath came over with her, and Catherine clearly enjoyed the occasion. We bade farewell to major Terry and Mrs

Anne Ross who were leaving for 15 Signal Regiment in Aden, and Kath and I made a presentation to them. Owing to the changing nature of the reserve forces, at a Mess Meeting we resolved to form a Trust for the Regimental Silver.

Terry Ross as training major had been succeeded by Captain Don Turner as a very capable and splendid Adjutant.

At the Derbyshire T.A.A.F.A. meeting on 7th March we were addressed by General Sir Geoffrey Musson, the General Officer Commander-in-Chief, Northern Command, on the reserve forces reorganisation. The commands within the United Kingdom were not to last much longer, being reformed as districts commanded by major-generals. The military pace of my life was not gathering speed. On 19-20th March the chief signal officer Brigadier Freeman conducted Exercise Smoke Signal, based on the new form of radio communications. My Honorary Colonel Gerry Underwood was guest of honour at our dinner. There was also present Lady Elizabeth Barnett of TV's 'What's My Line?' fame. She was very charming, and it was so great a pity that in later life her health deteriorated and she was electrocuted when an electric fire fell into her bath.

From 25-27th March I was at Catterick Camp for the reserve army weekend training of General Peter Bradley, the signal officer-in-chief. Here I met my old friend Colonel Hugh Lang, and Brigadier C. Vincent-Smith, and I dined with Colonel S.I. Williams, commander of the Middlesex Yeomanry, and my friend Lt. Colonel John Johnston. The scenarios for the exercise were Borneo and Cyprus.

In mid-April, together with my second-in-command I went to Scarborough to reconnoitre exercise sites for our impending annual camp, and I was delighted to meet Lt. Colonel G.P. Scrope, commanding the 4/5 Green Howards, who asked me to audit his imprest account. Geoffrey, a great soldier, came from the famous Scrope family which featured in Shakespeare's historical plays on the Tudors.

On 21st April, Colonel Gerry Underwood kindly represented me at the memorial service for a great signaller, General Sir Leslie Phillips.

It was now clear that 64 Signal Regiment T.A. were to merge into 38 Signal Regiment (Volunteers) T.A.V.R., and their commanding officer-designate Major Ken Gill and his Training Major Hugh Rodgers visited my Adjutant and me at my own H.Q. to initiate the process, which involved a tremendous amount of hard work and planning.

There was a pleasant break from military matters during Whit week, when Kath and I drove to Olga's empty house at Egham-on-the-Hill and radiated therefrom every day. We visited Guildford Cathedral (so very light inside owing to the absence of stained glass), Petworth Village and Arundel Castle. It was a delight to take the river steamer from Windsor to Maidenhead and back, to visit the R.A.F. Memorial at Runnymede and to dine with Alan and Mary Mitchell at their old Windsor home. We paid my first visit to Canterbury via Westerham, home of Churchill and birthplace of General Wolfe of Montreal fame. So beautiful was Canterbury Cathedral that my breath stopped on entering the hallowed place, and to see the spot where St Thomas à Beckett was murdered. What a wonderful way it was to learn history! After visiting Hampton Court, we took a boat on the river and visited the Kennedy memorial at Runnymede. We returned home, calling on Hubert and Ida at Wellingborough, and were delighted to see Christina's erstwhile pony 'Penny' in her field near Ripley. She whinnied with joy!

In the meantime I again travelled round my squadron, lecturing on the reorganisation of the reserve forces and encouraging my soldiers to sign declarations of intent to join the new T.A.V.R. (Territorial and Auxiliary Forces Reserve). I found time to take Tom Wragg and John Gibbs to the Royal Signals Old Comrades Reunion at Catterick Camp where we were right royally entertained, meeting so many old comrades, watching the massed bands play the Retreat, enjoying a good dinner, going to church and holding the A.G.M. of the Association. It was good to see again Major General "Pete" Thullier and Major General Whistler.

On Saturday 23rd July 1966, the regiment travelled to Burniston Barracks, Scarborough, for our last annual camp as 46 Signal Regiment, and we worked, trained and played hard. I had with my regiment nine charming young ladies, police cadets from County Durham, and they made a splendid contribution to our training, their blue uniforms contrasting with our khaki. On our sports day we were visited by Brigadier Dame Mary Railton, Deputy Controller-Commandant of the W.R.A.C., a very distinguished lady; and Lt. Colonel Sheila Heaney. They stayed for our regimental guest night dinner, being joined by Brigadier Alf Freeman, Lt. Colonel Bob Glanville, Basil Fenwick and Tom Wragg.

Our three-day regimental exercise 'Julius Caesar' was held in appalling weather. General C.M.M. Man visited camp, I took him round the exercise sites in this dreadful weather and he instructed me to bring the troops in. He then did what only a Major-General may do: he ordered a rum ration. The general we filled with brandy!

During the last few days we hosted 41 Commando of the Royal Marines, and at my second dinner night I had as guests Captain Alan Christie R.M. and Superintendent Veitch and Inspector Cowie of the County Durham Police Cadet Force. On the penultimate day the 41st Commander put on a splendid display alongside the band of the Royal Marines, under their director of music Captain

Vivien Dunne, who was later knighted. In the evening I was their official guest and attended a delightful reception. The next morning, through the courtesy of Captain Christie, I had the pleasure of a trip in their helicopter, a memorable way in which to finish our final camp which, despite the weather, had gone so well.

Shortly after camp, I went to London to visit the Adjutant General's Department at Stanmore, whence I was driven by Inky Udell, to express my gratitude for all their help and to arrange postings for my permanent staff.

On Monday 22nd August, my great friend of the United States Signal Corps, the Korean War-paralysed Major Joe Waldron O.B.E., his wife, Trudy, and his young daughters Debbie and Janet, arrived at the Peacock, Rowsley. Kath and I dined with them, being joined by Tom Wragg after dinner. It was a wonderful reunion.

The next day I collected them and took them to the hunting tower at Chatsworth, where Mrs Allinson, who was practising archery, entertained us and took us through the tower, to Swiss Cottage, and thence to the Wheatsheaf in Bakewell where everybody was charmed by Joe. After lunch I took them to Edale, down the Winnatts Pass to the Peak Cavern in Castleton, then home to a splendid high tea put on by Kath; the children were amazed at our open coal fire. That evening I had to go to regimental headquarters at Derby, taking Joe and Tom Wragg with me. They dined at The Barbican, and joined us in the officers' mess afterwards. Joe had to be carried up the stairs in his wheelchair, and his first words on entering the Mess were: "I am at home". Needless to say he charmed the entire Mess!

What energy we had in those days! The very next day, 24th August, Kath and I drove to London and caught the Vanguard flight to Malta G.C., where we arrived at 0110 hours to be met by our friend Major Charles Galbraith, commanding 235 Signal Squadron on Malta. He drove us to the Hotel Plevna in Sliema, which had been booked for us by our travel agent, Woodcocks of Sheffield. The next evening we were collected by Captain Michael Adams, Charles's second-in-command, and his wife Sue to dine at Charles' H.Q. at Mtarfa, a high point of Malta. Present, too, was W.R.N.S. Officer Janet Campin, P.A. to the admiral, who had been taught by my cousin Aline Egan at her Brighton school. She later married Charles, Gerry Underwood and myself being wedding guests. It was a delightful evening.

I ought to mention that owing to 235 Signal Squadron's excellent communications I had had no need to delegate command of the regiment.

On the 26th we were visited by Father Carmel Mifsud whom we had met during his sojourn in Bakewell a few years earlier, and he very kindly on several occasions drove us about Malta. It was wonderful to visit the sights of Malta and so good for our history. We visited the beautiful co-cathedral of St. John in Valletta, named after the famous Grand Knight of Malta, La Vallette, who withstood the Turkish Siege of 1665, gaining victory on 8th September – the birthday of our Lady, and of Kath! We enjoyed its splendid Caravaggio painting of The Beheading of St. John the Baptist. Father Carmel, now a schoolmaster at St. Paul's Bay, had been choirmaster at St. John's. In the armoury, we saw the engine of Faith, one of the three Gloster Gladiators – the others being Hope and Charity – which had defended the island in the worst days of the war. I took the opportunity to visit the Malta College of Art, Science and Technology, now the University, where I was kindly received by the principal's secretary. I swam in Paradise Bay, where we met three poor lepers, two men and a woman, God bless them. Father Carmel then took us to the vast and beautiful Dome in Mosta, his hometown, where we met and had tea with his charming mother.

On 30th August, our silver wedding anniversary, we rose early to catch the ferry from Marfa to the island of Gozo, where we visited the Neolithic temple, Calypso's cave and the splendid Church of Our Lady of Ta Pinu, having lunched at the Duke of Edinburgh Hotel in Victoria. I had a delightful swim in the bay at Xlendi before returning by hydrofoil to Valletta. To our silver wedding dinner at the Pevna we had Charles and Jan, Mike and Sue, and Charles's Adjutant, Captain Janet Hill. It was all most enjoyable.

Father Carmel took us, too, by boat to the very beautiful Blue Grotto, and what wonderful colours we saw!

One morning, Charles gave me an excellent briefing on the role, organisation and administration of 235 Signal Squadron, and escorted me round the entire outstations for reception and transmission of signals, and the camp at Imtarfa. That afternoon, whilst swimming out to sea from the Pevna Lido, I saw a naval yacht and asked if I could board it for a rest. It was the Admiral's barge of the U.S. 6th Fleet. Captain Alexander, Commander Rigg, and Chaplain Sullivan invited me on board and were most kind to me, and returned me to Kath at the Lido. I had been swimming with four charming army schoolmistresses, one of whom had been at Acton Reynold's School with my former student, Susan Phillips of Sheffield, and Captain Alexander very kindly took them on board and took them to the island of Comino. The chaplain was most gracious to my dear Kath.

Thursday 7th September was the eve of La Vallette's victory over the Turks on 8th September 1665, and Kath and I had the great pleasure of seeing the Knights of St. John in procession, headed by Archbishop Sir Michael Gonzi after the celebration of the Requiem Mass for La Vallette, tomorrow being the National Day of Victory.

That afternoon, with the aid of Father Carmel, I bought a diamond ring for Kath.

Father Carmel met Charles Galbraith and his Adjutant, Janet Hill, before saying goodbye. Charles, Jan Campin, Janet, Mike and Sue Adams joined us for dinner. At midnight we sang happy birthday to dearest Kath – a great occasion – and we bade farewell to our friends of 235 Signal Squadron. At 0125 hours we left for the airport, and after a late departure we had a wonderful flight over Sicily, with a marvellous view of Mount Etna and glorious views of the snow-capped Mont Blanc and Lake Geneva, landing at 0880 hours, to be collected by Olga. After resting for an hour we drove home via Wellingborough, a lovely conclusion to a glorious holiday.

My Nottingham squadron, 337 Squadron, had been nominated to spend their annual camp under command of 1 Divisional H.Q. and Signal Regiment, B.A.O.R., for Exercise Eternal Triangle III. The Honorary Colonel Gerry Underwood and I were to visit them. The commanding officer of 1 Div Signal Regiment was my old friend from wartime days Lt. Colonel Roland Borthwick, which was all to the good. Accordingly, having got leave of absence from the polytechnic, I caught a very early train from Chesterfield on 23rd September to London, where I was met by Inky Udell and Valerie Lloyd-Williams who took me to Victoria where we had drinks. Thence I joined Gerry at Gatwick whence we flew to Hanover, to be met by Roly Borthwick who drove us in his staff car, through the Minden Gap to Lippstadt, in Westphalia, to the Hotel Drei Kronen. We dined with Roly and his second-in-command, Major John Sturge who became a Major-General, at A. Mess of 1 Divisional H.Q. in the Field. A most pleasant evening, and so to bed!

The next morning, Gerry and I wandered round the market in the church square of Lippstadt, a pleasant town, and had drinks in a beer-house. Here I practised the little German that I knew. Jokingly, I said *"Ich habe kein Geld"* – "I haven't any money" and every German in that beer-house put his hand into his pocket to pay! We stayed longer, and when we left I could speak far more German than I could when we entered!

After lunch, we were collected and taken to main division H.Q., where we were briefed in the signals command vehicle by Roly Borthwick. The exercise was a battle between Redland (II Brigade) and Blueland (7 Armoured Brigade plus 31 Panzer Brigade). We visited G. Operations of Intelligence, the Commander Royal Artillery and the Umpires. Gerry and I visited C. Mess, where we met a most charming Polish sergeant-major (ex-cavalry), and the divisional admin area. On our return to Lippstadt we were joined for dinner by Roly, John Francis (an ex-Adjutant of ours), John Sturge and Roy Ledder, commanding my 337 Squadron. It was a most pleasant occasion, and Gerry was very generous.

I went to Mass in the morning, with the hotel cook. The church was full and the sidesmen wore red robes. Gerry and I were then taken to the Möhnesee where we saw the Möhne Dam which had been breached by Wing-Commander Guy Gibson and his Dambusters, during the war. After returning to our hotel where we rested and had a walk, we were collected and taken to dinner at C. Mess, being joined by Roy Ledder and Alan Ripley amongst so many distinguished young officers. In the mess afterwards we had the pleasure of meeting the commander of the Special Air Services. And so back to the Drei Kronen where, to Gerry's delight, I sang Brahms' Cradle Song, together with Herr Ober and the manageress!

After a short walk by the River Lipp the next morning, we were taken by Roly's driver to main divisional H.Q. and escorted round the radio relay detachment and the communications centre. After lunch, we were introduced to Major-General R. (Dick) Ward, the divisional commander, who had succeeded Major-General Miles Fitzalan-Howard, later the Duke of Norfolk. From there, Major Kleineschmidt took us to visit a Panzer Battalion where we were warmly received by the Commander, and inspected their A25 tanks. We were greatly impressed by the German commander and his second-in-command. That night we dined at Rear Divisional H.Q. Mess in a school room with John Francis and others including the divisional chaplains, one of whom, Father Mike Holman, was most kind to us. After a splendid day, we were escorted home by John Sturge.

We were up betimes the next morning, and driven by L/Cpl. George to Hanover, whence we flew to Gatwick where I bade farewell to Gerry who had been so good to me. En route home via St. Pancras and Chesterfield, I called on Christina and Rosemary Cockerton in their flat in Kentish Town, which seemed full of Christina's painting canvases; they were very kind to me. Eventually, I reached home at 2am and prepared to resume work the same morning.

I soon contracted a nasty chest infection and had to take to my bed from time to time. Lecturing and military training and administration do not go well with chest infections. Gerry Underwood came up to our Glossop Signals reunion at the Rutland Arms Hotel, and returned again for the regimental ball held on the occasion of our training weekend at the Peveril of the Peak Hotel in Dovedale. We had a great guest list: Colonel Gerry Underwood; Major-General Chris Man, our Divisional Commander; Colonel Sir John and Lady Crompton-Ingerfield, Sir John being the Chairman of the Derbyshire T.A.A.F.A; Lt. Colonel and Mrs Bob Glanville, Bob being the Secretary of T.A.A.F.A.; Brigadier and Mrs R.J. Wilkins and their daughter, Amanda; Inky Udell and Valerie Lloyd-Williams; and Doctor John and Ruth Emerson, who kindly brought Kath. Kath and I received some 150 officers and guests. After dinner, I recounted Gerry's 50 years service to H.M. Armed Services from the day he joined the 4th Hussars in Dublin during the troubles of 1916 to the present, and I asked General Chris Man to present Gerry with a solid silver salver bearing 56 signatures of officers past and present. It was splendid to note the Honorary Colonel's obvious pleasure.

On Friday 21st October 1966, Kath and I drove via Derby to Coventry to stay with Bob and Madge Wilkins. We were greeted with the news of the dreadful disaster at Aberfan where a slipping slag heap had crushed the school, killing 120 children and 30 adults. The village had lost almost all its children.

On and off, my chest infection lasted for the rest of the year, in which I was so occupied arranging the amalgamation of my 46th Signal Regiment T.A. and 64th Signal Regiment T.A., headquartered at Manor Top, Sheffield, into the 38th Signal Regiment T.A.V.R. I was to raise, in addition, 930 (Regional) Signal Troop; and 922, 923, 931, 932, 933 (Sub-Regional) Signal Troops. Above this, I was responsible for the disbandment of my own regiment with effect from 31st March 1967.

49th Division was to cease to exist from the same date to become East Midlands Region.

General Man arranged the annual divisional study period at Bestwood Lodge, aptly called "Bear With-It". In the course of this I spoke with great conviction and sincerity in favour of a united Europe. The divisional dinner was held at the University of Nottingham. It was a great occasion, which Gerry attended. I had the pleasure of conversing with Lady Elizabeth Barnett, Honorary Colonel of the W.R.A.C.; Lt. General Sir Richard Goodwin, the Military Secretary; Lt. General Sir Geoffrey Musson, Commander-in-Chief, Northern Command; and the past divisional commanders, Major Generals Tony Birkbeck and Peter Glover. The Nottingham Hussars' Band played its heart out, feet stamped to the post-horn gallop and highly polished brass gleamed, all amongst the multi-coloured mess dress. But underneath it all there was a sense of melancholy, because this was really a 'wake': the last glorious fling of the 49th (West Riding) Division which had served so well in peace and both the World Wars.

I attended command boards on the reorganisation. I received Lt. Colonel John Francis who was nominated to command 38th Signal Regiment T.A.V.R. We came out well at our annual administrative inspection. I entertained on various occasions my permanent staff and did my best to find employment for those made redundant. I visited all my squadrons and detachments.

I made visits to London to pay my respects to the Ministry of Defence H.Q. Royal Signals, and H.Q. 49 Division where General Man very kindly spoke so highly of my command of the regiment.

In the midst of all this, my dear old friend "Jonah", Captain G.F. Jones, died on 9th December 1966, and I arranged his funeral which Kath and I attended, having brought Mrs Jones, at Chesterfield Crematorium. "Jonah" was a great officer and gentleman with a vast knowledge of electrical matters, a pioneer of the storage heaters, and a tremendous authority on grandfather clocks and waterwheels. He had borne up to all the vicissitudes of life with great courage.

Christina came home for her Christmas vacation. Christmas dinner at Mary's was a very jolly occasion and on Boxing Day we attended a delightful party at Chatsworth, given by Ilona and Elizabeth Solymossy, the Hungarian housekeepers who had once been employed by the Kennedy family and were well regarded by them. Present were Kath, Christina and myself; Tom and Ida Wragg and their son Tom; and Dennis and Mrs Fisher and their children Ian and Ingrid. Mary, Bill, Rosalind and Serena joined us for our New Year's Eve Party. And so into 1967.

1967

Early in January, I had the pleasure of meeting two of Tom Wragg's American friends: Parker B. Allen and Harold Hugo of the Meridian Graviere Company, Connnecticut, who printed the brochures for the Chatsworth exhibition in the U.S.A. We became firm friends and I was destined to meet Parker's son, and Harold's brother, Clarence. Parker, the owner of the company, was held in high esteem by his employees.

On 11th January our dear friend Gerry Underwood flew to Malta, under arrangements made by me with Charles Galbraith of 235 Signal Squadron, to avoid the rigours of the English winter, and so mitigate his asthma. He was well looked after by Charles and his squadron. Charles attended Gerry's funeral with me in 1973.

In the course of the regimental reorganisation I visited the Glossop detachment of the 64th Signal Regiment in the very place where Gerry had recruited me to the Royal Corps of Signals on 8th May 1939.

My sister-in-law Mary was now quite ill, the cause being cancer of the pancreas. She was operated on at the Sheffield Royal Hospital on 6th February, and Kath and I seized every opportunity to visit her. She returned home on the 21st much better, but the cancer was taking its toll.

For the next two months I was kept very busy in the matter of reorganisation. At the officers training weekend at the Peveril on 25-26th February, I had 98 officers, their ladies and guests at our final dinner. The guests included: Brigadier Pat Hobson D.S.O., General Secretary of the Royal Signals Association; John Francis and his wife

Jean; Peter and Alice Gilham; our neighbours, Ronald and Pairis Knighton; and Alderman Ernest Robinson of the great Chesterfield family with his wife. I made presentations on behalf of the Mess to our retiring officers and, in particular, to Captain Don Turner, my Adjutant, who had been a great a tower of strength to me since his appointment. The Honorary Colonel, Gerry, presented Kath with a most beautiful bouquet, and me with an inscribed silver entrée dish. He spoke with deep sincerity and emotion of my services to the regiment, particularly whilst in command.

I attended in York the final dinner of the W.R.A.C., Northern Command and the last Exercise Smoke Signal where I bade farewell to my friends of Northern Command, Brigadier Alf Freeman in particular. I made my way, again, to Bestwood Lodge to make my official farewell to Major General "Copper" Gordon-Finlayson, Colonel (A/Q) King, Lt. Colonel (GSOI) Tony Way, Grenadier Guards and his GII Major John Stead. That same day, 30th March, I visited my regimental headquarters and sent a farewell signal to Gerry Underwood in Malta. The next day, 31st March, I addressed all the permanent staff, military and civil in the canteen, and signed the disbandment orders, my final act. It was a sad day for us all, but it had been a great regiment in both war and peace. The sadness was alleviated by a greetings telegram from 38th Signal Regiment (Volunteers), the new regiment which I had done so much to raise.

A few days later I received a delightful letter of gratitude from Major General Peter Bradley, the Signal Officer-in-Chief, soon to be followed by a similar letter from General Sir Richard Goodwin, the Military Secretary, announcing that with effect from 1st April 1967 Her Majesty had promoted me Brevet Colonel which delighted Kath and me.

My days of active command were now finished, but my military life was by no means ended.

Chapter VIII

Holidays

Lourdes

From the accounts given in the chronological section of this biography, it will be clear that Kath and I were pioneers in Bakewell of taking overseas holidays. Kath was not only a great homebuilder but a splendid organiser of holidays of a special nature. It was on her instigation that we went on a pilgrimage to Lourdes in 1967. I had never felt greatly attracted to Lourdes, where in 1858 Bernadette Soubirous, a peasant girl, had had visions of the Blessed Virgin Mary and, against all odds, had stuck to her story so that eventually the church acknowledged the truth of her accounts. Bernadette, like the patron saint of France, another peasant, Saint Joan of Arc, one of the greatest leaders of all time, was a very positive person. When she was shown the beautiful sculpted statue of Our Lady of Lourdes she said: "That is not what the Lady was like, but I suppose that it will do!" I am glad that we went. We were both deeply impressed. There is no doubt that whilst only a few of the many who go seeking cures at Lourdes are cured, all return with a much stronger faith.

Rome, Florence & Venice

Kath's dear friend Muriel Cockerton and her distinguished lawyer husband Richard joined us for three holidays. The best of these was a trip to Rome, Florence and Venice in 1971. Richard was very proud that one of his ancestors, John Taylor, had been the publisher of the works of the great poet Keats, and I was delighted to take him to Keats' house at the bottom of the Spanish Steps in Rome, where Keats had lived with Shelley, and Keats had died in the arms of Joseph Severn, the painter. Richard gave to the Curatrix, Doctor Vera Cacciatore, a letter sent to his great-great-uncle about Keats's illness; the letter is now prominently displayed in the room where Keats died. Vera told us that one day a very old priest had visited the house and told her that John Severn had died in his arms. Vera had said "Father, let me take you into my arms" which he did. When Vera told me this, I said "Vera, let me take you into my arms", which she did; and I feel proud of that succession! It was a great occasion. Kath and I took Muriel and Richard to the graves of Keats and Shelley in the English cemetery near Saint Paul's outside the walls. On Keats's memorial stone is written: 'Here lies one whose name was writ in water'. Not far away is buried the heart of Shelley who had been drowned near Leghorn and whose epitaph is: 'Nothing of him that doth change, but suffers a sea change into something new and strange.'

Muriel and Richard were enthralled by the glories of the Eternal City and they were no less enthralled by the glories of that jewel of Europe, Florence, with its tremendous works of art in stone and on canvas and buildings. Kath and I took the opportunity to visit Gabriella de Benedictis and her mother, with whom we had stayed in 1960. They made us very welcome and recounted the horrors of the dreadful flood of November 1965.

From Florence we travelled by coach through the valley of the River Po to Venice. Despite the November rain, Muriel and Richard were deeply impressed by its glories. For all four of us it had been a most enjoyable tour.

Spain

The four of us flew into unknown territory, for us, to Madrid in November 1972. Here we saw old Madrid, and visited the Royal Palace with its priceless tapestries and the Prado where we saw the magnificent works of El Greco, Velázquez, Murillo and Goya. We went out, too, to the Valley of the Fallen with its beautiful basilica built by General Franco in memory of the million dead of the Spanish Civil War, 1936-9. Thence we went to the Escorial Palace and Pantheon of the Royal Dead, built by Philip II, husband of Queen Mary Tudor.

Toledo and Segovia, too, we found to be of the greatest interest.

I have a pleasant memory of meeting a charming Spanish gentleman, married to an English lady, who asked me if I would kindly give him the poppy I was wearing to take home to his wife. This I was only too delighted to do.

Provence

For the late autumn of 1973, the four of us flew to Provence, staying in Arles at the Hotel Nord Pinus where our great war heroes Peter Churchill and Odette had stayed during the war with the staff of the German town major! Madame remembered it all very clearly and showed us letters from Peter Churchill. Both Peter and Odette were later betrayed and captured and suffered dreadfully at the hands of the Gestapo, but survived to be married after the war.

From Arles which itself is so rich in Roman buildings including a splendid arena and marvellous museums, we were able to visit Les Antigues; St. Remy, including the hospital where Vincent Van Gogh was a voluntary patient after cutting off part of his ear; Fontaine de Vaucluse; Orange; Nimes; Aigues Mortes, its town and port built for the Crusaders; Les deux Stes Maries; and Avignon with its splendid Palais des Papes and Pont d'Avignon. Near Nimes, I had the thrill of walking across the famous Pont du Gard in company with some Foreign Legionnaires.

For me the great thing about Arles was its strong connection with Vincent Van Gogh, who shared his house for a short while with Gaugin the painter. It was inspiring to walk down les Alyscamps (the Elysian Fields) painted by Van Gogh, and to see his famous Pont de Van Gogh over the canal.

Richard had been entranced by the Museum of Christian Art. Of the three holidays we had spent together, this, he said, he had enjoyed most. I suspect it was actually Rome!

U.S.S.R.

In May 1972 we left on our most adventurous holiday so far, to the U.S.S.R., splendidly arranged by Kath through Far Horizons. Taken by Alan Mitchell from Olga Roberts to Gatwick we flew in an Aeroflot TU 104B to Leningrad in some 3½ hours. I had received my visa only four hours earlier at Gatwick and we underwent a most rigid passport, visa and customs inspection at Leningrad. To go on the venture I required the approval of our Ministry of Defence who needed to know where I was every day! We were greeted by Nina Vasilyana Khokholova who spoke perfect English and was thoroughly efficient. She belonged to Intourist but she may well have been a member of the K.G.B., too! She was to remain with us throughout our tour. In Leningrad (now reverted to St. Petersburg) we stayed at the good hotel Sovietskoya. Everywhere we went we were given priority over the Russians. The weather was perfect. I was very conscious of the terrible sufferings of Leningrad in its 900-day siege by the Germans.

We drove by the River Neva, visiting the S.S. Peter and Paul Fortress; the Winter Palace of the 1905 and 1917 Revolutions fame; the Finland Station where Lenin arrived in 1917; the Smolny Institution, the first seat of government under Lenin; St. Isaac's, Church of the Atonement, the scene of the assassination of Czar Alexander II in 1881; the Kirov Theatre; the Nevski Prospect; and the cruiser Aurora whose guns signalled the Revolution of 17th October 1917.

Further afield we went by hydrofoil to Petrodvorets (Peterhof) to the beautiful summer palace of Peter the Great with its wonderful fountains. We visited, too, the splendid Pavlosk Palace of the Czar Paul who was murdered there, with its most beautiful objets d'art. But the greatest of the Palaces was the Winter Palace or Hermitage on the banks of the Neva with its remarkable interior and magnificent collection. I was particularly impressed by the Rembrandts and the El Greco collection, especially SS. Peter and Paul.

Kath, with her great love for ballet, organised our attendance at the Mali Theatre to see Delibe's 'Corsair', so magnificently danced, and some choreographic miniatures on a second occasion.

After this, we took the 70 minutes flight to an airport about 35 miles from Moscow. On the coach to Moscow we passed the furthest point of the German advance, and arrived at the biggest hotel in Europe, the first-class Hotel Rossiya overlooking the beautiful Red Square. Unfortunately for us, President Nixon of the U.S.A. was holding talks with Brezhnev and Kosygin during our stay and so, for security reasons, we were not allowed to visit the Kremlin or the ballet at the Bolshoi Theatre. However, the local Intourist girl, Ludmilla Pavlovna, conducted us round Red Square, St. Basil's Catherdral, Maxim Gorky Street, the University and so on. The next morning we were taken by boat down the Moscau River to the extremity of the city, and returned by the underground railway which was so vast and clean and beautifully kept.

On our own, Kath and I went by trolleybus to the Borodino Panorama where we were put to the head of the queue by the policeman and assisted by a guide who spoke a little English. It was nearly as good as actually being there. The H.Qs of Napoleon and Kutuzov were clearly to be seen, and we saw, too, the famous painting of Napoleon in retreat from Moscow. On the trolley bus we were impressed by the kindness of the other passengers, especially a charming little schoolgirl who was so glad to practise her English. We also attended the famous Moscow circus.

Fifty miles east of Moscow we drove through forestland to Zagorsk, before the

Revolution called Sergiev after St. Sergius who founded the monastery there. Zagorsk was named after an assassinated Revolutionary. It is now the headquarters of the Russian Orthodox Church, a most attractive walled monastery with beautiful churches, especially that of The Assumption. Prayer is continued throughout the day; the worshippers were mostly elderly shawled peasant women who showed great devotion. I noticed that our Intourist guide did not enter the churches, but we were left with the strong impression that God was not dead in Russia!

Kath and I watched the hourly changing of the guard at the Lenin Mausoleum and visited Lenin's tomb inside. The respect paid to the dead Lenin, clearly visible in his glass case, is very great. It had a separate guard of honour, and we saw bridal couples leaving their wreaths there! The weather was still glorious, and it was good to sit in the park near to the Tomb of the Unknown Soldier.

After lunch that day, we drove to the airport to fly 1000 miles to Simferopol, where Kutuzov had lost his eye in battle against the Turks in the Crimea. Thence we had a long coach journey to Yalta and the Oreanda Hotel, right by the sea.

Here we were cared for by a very charming and beautiful Intourist guide, Alissa Ivanovna, whose father had been killed in the war, when she was only three months old. On the Sunday, Kath and I were conducted by a very kindly policeman to the Orthodox Church which was very crowded, hard to get into, and harder to get out of! No, religion was not dead in the Ukraine. Alissa led us on a sea trip westwards of Yalta where we had superb views of the Livadia Palace where the Yalta conference of 1945 took place between Stalin, Roosevelt and Churchill; the Swallow's Nest; the Alupka Palace and the Sanatorium Ukraina. Personally that evening I enjoyed a splendid concert given by the Symphony Orchestra of the Crimean Philharmonic Society, with works by Franck, Liszt, Gounod and Puccini.

Yalta is full of beautiful rose trees and lovely parks. Alissa took us to the Livadia Palace, the Alupka Palace where Churchill was accommodated, and the swallow's nest protruding over the cliffs.

We were invited to a most enjoyable wine-tasting at the wine hall, which included a very friendly group of East Germans. It fell to me who had fought in the Great Patriotic War, as the Second World War was known in the U.S.S.R., to make a brief speech, translated by Alissa, and I am glad to say that it went down well.

Before leaving Yalta for Odessa, I gave my Veldtschön shoes and a towel to the chambermaid for her husband; and Kath and I were deeply touched when she wept with gratitude. And so by air to Odessa where we were taken to the Hotel Odessa and given a suite of rooms!

Here we were conducted round the opera house, the beautiful square, the bathing resort, the monument to the Unknown Sailor, guarded by children changing every 15 minutes, and the Potemkin staircase of 1905 fame, when the crew of the Battleship Potemkin mutinied.

That evening, our last night, we had a banquet and dance and I had the pleasure of proposing the toasts to President Podgorny; the Queen; Melissa, our Yugoslav tour guide; and Nina Vasilyana Khokhlova, who I discovered was a friend of Sir Raymond Asquith, having helped him in a film production.

The next morning, very early, we returned to England, changing planes at Leningrad.

It had been a most interesting and historic holiday leaving us with the impression that the people of the U.S.S.R. who had suffered so terribly through so many wars were very kindly and largely God-fearing. How different from so many of the politicians!

Yugoslavia & Italy

In 1973 Kath and I enjoyed a memorable holiday in Yugoslavia, based at Dubrovnik.

We returned to Italy in 1975, staying at Minori on the Sorrento peninsula, where we revisited the convent at Vico Equense on which we were billeted in 1944, and the Isle of Capri. Then we proceeded to Rome which was very busy, it being Holy Year. There we visited Madre Maria Pasqualina Monti who had been so kind to me at Vico Equense, now the Mother General of her Order, founding and administering training colleges, schools, hospitals, orphanages and convents all over the world. She and Kath were delighted with each other. It was the first and last time that I saw her after 1946. We attended a general audience in St. Peter's Square given by Pope Paul VI who blessed the beautiful rosary given to Kath by Madre Maria. Another day we went by train to Assisi where, I am delighted to record, Kath received Holy Communion together with me at the Tomb of St. Francis.

Bulgaria

Our next major venture was to Bulgaria in 1976. We stayed for a few days near Varna where so many of our soldiers in the Crimean War suffered cholera. I have always bitterly regretted that we did not, as Kath wished so much to do, take a three-day boat trip down the Black Sea to Istanbul. We surely should have done so and I still feel guilty about it. Some 23 years later I did visit Istanbul and realised how much Kath would have liked it. We did, however, travel to the capital, Sofia; the Rila Monastery; Plovdio (the old Phillipopolis); and Nessebar. At this time Bulgaria was under Communist rule, and I felt very sorry for the peasants in particular, who deserved better.

The Holy Land

We paid our first visit to the Holy Land in May 1977, through Inter-Church Travel under the splendid leadership of the Reverend Bernard Bateson. It was a wonderful experience, to be repeated by Kath once and by me 13 times, after my becoming a tour leader for the Inter-Church Travel after retirement in 1980. The first few nights we spent at Tiberias on the hill overlooking the beautiful Sea of Galilee some 500 feet below sea level. From here we visited Cana of Galilee, the scene of Our Saviour's first miracle in turning water into wine to save embarrassment to the bridal couple, and the birthplace of Nathaniel called Bartholomew; Nazareth with its beautiful triple church of the Annunciation, and the Virgin's Well where Our Lady drew water; Mount Tabor with its magnificent Church of the Transfiguration; Capernaum which Our Lord made his base, with its splendid ancient synagogue and the remains of Saint Peter's House; Tabgha with its Mensa Christi (Table of Christ) Church, where the Risen Christ cooked breakfast for the apostles and ordered Peter to feed His lambs and His sheep – that is, us; the Church of the Multiplication of the loaves and fishes; and the octagonal Church of the Beatification on the Mount with its superb view of the sea.

We sailed across the Sea of Galilee to the kibbutz Ein Gev. Here we had lunch on fish like St. Peter and were taken round by Mrs Ben Joseph, a pioneer of the kibbutz with whom on subsequent visits I became very friendly. Before the return sailing, I had a most enjoyable swim in the sea.

We went further afield via the Bridge of the Daughters of Jacob over the Golan Heights, through the Druze village of Masada, and the volcanic lake at Birket Ram with its splendid view of snow-clad Mount Hebron to the ruins of Caesarea Philippi, where the River Jordan bursts from the hill-side and where Our Saviour announced that he would build his Church on Peter who recognised him as the Messiah, and Son of God.

Overlooking Tiberias is the Hill of the Horns of Hattin, where Saladin inflicted so great a defeat on the Crusaders.

We journeyed to Jerusalem by coach, via Megiddo, one of Solomon's fortresses, with such magnificent ruins and water tunnel – the scene of so many battles, including General Allenby's defeat of the Turks in 1918, and the site of Armageddon; and Caesarea Maritima with its Roman and Crusader ruins, scene of St. Paul's imprisonment under the Roman Governor Felix; to the Holy Land Hotel near the Herod Gate in East Jerusalem.

Here our programme was full. We visited the beautiful Crusader Church of Ste. Anne, traditional site of the birth of her daughter, the Blessed Virgin Mary, close to the Pool of Bethesda and the Sheep Gate where St. Stephen was stoned to death in the presence of Saul, later to be converted as Paul. We followed in the footsteps of Christ on the Way of the Cross along the Via Dolorosa to the Basilica of the Holy Sepulchre and the Resurrection. This great church shows the divisions in Christianity. It is divided between the Latin, the Greek Orthodox, the Armenians, the Copts on the roof, and the Anglicans who have the Chapel of Adam, immediately below Calvary. There is a tradition that the first Adam was buried under Calvary, the scene of the Crucifixion of the second Adam, Our Lord and Saviour.

Another day was devoted to the beautiful German Benedictine Church of the Dormition, or Assumption of Our Blessed Lady on Mount Zion, very close to the Upper Room, and the Church of St. Peter Gallicantu, built over the site of the Palace of Caiaphas where St. Peter so bitterly repented of his treachery when the cock crew. Gallicantu means "of the crowing of the cock". That afternoon, we visited Bethlehem, stopping at Rachel's Tomb; Rachel died giving birth to Benjamin and Jacob buried her by the roadside. We found it very emotional to enter Christendom's oldest church, the Basilica of the Nativity, wherein is the stable-cave where Jesus was born. Thence we went to the Shepherds' fields where the Angels appeared.

We had a wonderful day travelling via the Inn of the Good Samaritan to Jericho, and on to Masada, Herod's palace, standing on a hill like an aircraft carrier by the shores of the Dead Sea. Here the Zealots committed mass suicide in A.D.81 rather than surrender to the Roman Legion besieging the fortress. Today, Israeli soldiers take their oath that "Masada shall never fall again" here. After floating in the Dead Sea, we pressed on to Qumran where the Dead Sea Scrolls were found, and thence to the remains of the Old City of Jericho under the shadow of the Mount of Temptation where Our Lord fasted in the wilderness. On the return journey we stopped at Bethany where I went down into the tomb of Lazarus, and at Bethphage where Our Saviour mounted the donkey on Palm Sunday.

We drove, by St. Philip's Well where he baptised the Ethiopian, through the valley of Esheol to Hebron where Abraham, Sarah, Isaac, Rebecca and Leah are buried in a massive mausoleum, sacred to Jew, Christian and Moslem alike. On our return via the Mount of Olives, we visited the site of the Ascension and followed the Palm Sunday route past the Paternoster Church, where Our Saviour taught the disciples to pray; the Dominus Flevit Church, where He wept over Jerusalem; to the Church of All Nations in the Garden of Gethsemane, where He endured His dreadful agony and was betrayed.

Whilst in Jerusalem, Kath and I visited the British War Cemetery on Mount Scopus. We paid a call on the Mayor of Jerusalem, the famous Teddy Kollek, to whom we had been given letters of introduction by Sir Maurice Oldfield, Head of our Intelligence Service, and our friend Tom Wragg. Unfortunately Teddy was out of his office, but he wrote a charming letter of apology to Sir Maurice. Teddy was highly respected by Jew, Christian and Moslem.

Before concluding this wonderful pilgrimage, we visited the Wailing Wall, the Temple Mount with its splendid Dome of the Rock built over the rock where Abraham was going to sacrifice Isaac, and the scene of Mohammad's mystical journey to Heaven; we also visited the Mosque of El Aqusa.

And so home!

The U.S.A.

Our longest venture occurred in May 1979, when Kath and I were invited to stay with our old friends Joe and Trudy Waldron at their home in San Gabriel, California. We had a wonderful 11-hour flight in an Air New Zealand DC10 over Iceland, Greenland, the Great Lakes and the Rockies to Los Angeles where we were greeted in to the New World by Trudy and Joe in his wheelchair. And so to bed, very tired.

After a long sleep we were taken by our hosts to Disneyland which included 'New Orleans' and 'The Grand Canyon'. We were greatly impressed by America the Beautiful, and the sincerity, courtesy and patriotism of all. It is a charming mixture of the vulgar and the exquisite – and everything immaculate!

After another long sleep, Trudy took us to the exquisite San Gabriel Mission founded by the Spanish Franciscans about 1773, whence two Franciscans went to found El Pueblo de Nuestra Senora, La Reina de Los Angeles (the little settlement of Our Lady, Queen of the Angels!) – now the massive city of Los Angeles.

We journeyed into Northern California via Fort Tejon where we were escorted round by a charming ranger of Apache and Commanche descent. The fort gave an excellent impression of what life was like in the army just before the Civil War. We continued north to the small city of Exeter. From here, Janet, the younger daughter of the Waldrons, and her husband Brad, drove us in their Cadillac to the Sequoia National Park, above the snow level, where grow those immense California Redwoods. We saw the vast 'General Sherman' tree, 2500–3000 years old still alive with sufficient wood in it to build a town!

The next morning Joe drove us to Goshen Junction, famous from Steinbeck's 'Grapes of Wrath', to catch the Greyhound bus for San Francisco; it was an interesting journey via Merced and Oakland, and we stayed at Hotel California. During the night there were riots by the gay population outside the city hall, but they did not disturb our tired selves!

We enjoyed a coach tour round The Praesidio, the Dolores Mission, the Golden Gate Bridge and the Japanese Gardens. Before a pleasant al fresco lunch at Fisherman's Wharf we took a cruise of the Bay and were very impressed by the bridges and Alcatraz, the former prison where Al Capone was held. Then we had the personal pleasure of taking tea with Doctor John Ellis with whom I had gone on a tour of the European institutions, the E.E.C., N.A.T.O., S.H.A.P.E., the European Parliament and Council of Europe, in 1978. Both of us belong to T.E.A.M., the European Atlantic Movement.

We returned to San Gabriel on a long train journey via Amtrak from Oakland station to Glendale. It was a fascinating journey through the Mission Stations established by the Spanish Franciscans, the oil fields with their 'nodding donkeys' and the 'Lone Ranger' country. We established splendid relations with those in our carriage including a retired plastic surgeon from Santa Barbara who had worked with Sir Archibald McIndoe, the great pioneer in plastic surgery.

That evening, Joe and Trudy gave a great party in our honour.

A visit was arranged for us to the Disney Studios and we were given V.I.P. treatment. We saw a film being made in a Wild West town and met the owner of the voice of Mickey Mouse! What a wonderful man was Walt Disney. Thereafter, we visited Hollywood and Beverly Hills.

The highlight of our stay was a tour we made to the Grand Canyon for senior citizens and we were really spoiled by our American counterparts. We had breakfast at Barstow, lunch at Hobo Joe's in Needles and so reached the Grand Canyon via Ashfork, Kingman and Williams. The sun was beginning to set and the Canyon varied with the colours of the setting sun. It was wonderful and magnificent and made one cry out to Almighty God "Gloria in excelsis, Deo"!

We stayed at the Yavapai Lodge in an immense suite, and the next morning Kath and I were driven out to Grand Canyon Airfield, where we flew 140 air miles within the Grand Canyon in a Cessna plane holding eight including the pilot. It was a most marvellous experience which can hardly be described. This I owed to Kath who was determined that we should fly within the Canyon.

We then went on a guided tour of the Eastern rim of the Canyon, and the ruins at a Tusayan Indian village. Kath and I attended Mass and received Holy Communion with others at the aptly-named 'Shrine of the Ages'.

The next morning we visited Desert View and drove through the Painted Desert, stopping en route at Glen Canyon Dam, i.e. Lake Powell. We skirted Lake Powell into Utah and arrived at Bryce Canyon National Park for our first view of that remarkable canyon, and so to Ruby's Inn where we were given a splendid lecture by a park ranger after dinner. We were now in Mormon country and there was no alcohol. The following day, after a guided tour of Bryce Canyon from various viewpoints, we drove through the Red Canyon to Zion National Park for lunch at the beautiful Zion Lodge where I met a charming Mormon who had been a missionary in Loughborough. And so we resumed our journey through Arizona to Las Vegas to the Mint Hotel, whence we drove uptown to the Flamingo Hilton Hotel to dinner and a very special ice show called Razzle Dazzle! We returned via the Strip to the Mint where I won a few dollars; and so to bed in a superbly air-conditioned room, the outside temperature being 120°F!

In the morning, following breakfast at El Cortez, I won 15 more dollars over free drinks before we embarked for our return journey to Alhambra via Barstow Station and Pasadena. It had been a wonderful experience and Murray, our leader, said publicly what a particular pleasure it had been to have Kath and me with them. God bless them all!

I thought Las Vegas to be very big then, but when I revisited it in 2000 it was about three times as big.

One day, Kath, Trudy and I caught the train to San Diego, where we were joined by Trudy's brother Jack Mullen and lunched on the Ruby E. Lee, a paddle steamer. Jack then drove us to the Mexican border which we crossed on foot and then took a taxi to Tijuana, where Kath and Trudy looked round the shops whilst Jack and I drank Mexican beer. On our way back to San Gabriel, Trudy took us through the Chinatown district of Los Angeles.

On another day I was invited to give two lectures on the British educational system and international affairs at the Pasadena City College of the University of Southern California. I was made very welcome as Professor Leslie Wright by both staff and students who greatly admired my account and told me so. The college authorities were kind enough to write to Doctor Tolley at Sheffield City Polytechnic to say how greatly they had appreciated my two lectures. I am indeed proud to be a Professor of the University of Southern California!

Thereafter we went to Long Beach where Kath and I lunched on the Queen Mary and toured this tremendous ship. Thence we went to Port O'Call, the old fishing village near Long Beach, and in the early evening to the U.S. Navy Club, where we dined with Trudy and Joe and so many of the friends we had made during our stay.

The next day, our last, Kath and I returned to the San Gabriel Mission and after lunch were taken by Trudy and Joe to Los Angeles Airport, where we were booked in at British Airways by a girl of the Farmer family of Matlock. And so we flew home in a jumbo jet after a splendid holiday under the care of our dear friends.

Greece

In May 1980 Kath and I flew by night to Athens, where I had last been in 1946 but was now so much busier with traffic. After a good sleep, I took Kath to the top of Philopappos Hill to the beautiful chapel of Ayios Giorgios – St. George is very highly respected in the Orthodox Church.

We were given a splendid tour of Athens, notably the Acropolis, by a Greek guide and later we visited the Theseum and the Plaka.

Via Thebes we went across the Grecian plain, listening to the story of the luckless Oedipus who unwittingly killed his father and married his mother, and via Livadia to Delphi with its wonderful Temple of Apollo on the slopes of Mount Parnassus; Pythia was the priestess of the oracle whose prophesies were always interpreted in verse. In the museum we saw the beautiful Charioteer statue of about 475 B.C.

Another day was devoted to the beautiful monastery of Kaisariani in the lovely woods on the outskirts of Athens where both Plato and Socrates taught; and, after a scenic coach drive, to the Temple of Poseidon at Cape Sounion, rebuilt by Pericles in 500 B.C.

We headed on another occasion to the Peleponnese, crossing the Corinth Canal and visiting Ancient Corinth where St. Paul delivered some of his famous sermons; and thence to Epidaurus, the sanctuary of Asklepius, the God of medicine, with its magnificent theatre blessed with perfect acoustics. And so to Tolo, our second base, where dear Kath very unfortunately bruised her toe on the steps of the hotel: her toe never properly healed.

From Tolo we enjoyed a delightful cruise of the islands of Hydra and Spetses, together with many dolphins, so pleasant to watch.

On the way back to Athens Airport, we drove to Mycenae to visit the Lion Gate, and the Beehive Tomb of Agamemnon himself, and refreshed ourselves at the Corinth Canal Restaurant.

Crete, 1981

On Tuesday 5th May, through Inter-Church Travel, Kath and I flew from Manchester to Iraklion, landing at the airport which was merely an airstrip when I was based there from February-April 1946; this was my first return to Crete and it was all very nostalgic. Our leader was the Right Reverend Bishop Ronald Goodchild, retired Bishop of Kensington, to whom Kath and I took an immediate liking and I met several times thereafter at Inter-Church leaders' conferences. Ronnie was flying with the major group from London and Kath and I waited at the Astoria Hotel for his arrival. Thence we drove west to Chania to the Hotel Porto Veneziano in the picturesque harbour, along a splendid coastal road built under the European Recovery Programme or 'Marshall Plan' named after President Truman's Secretary of State.

After a good night's sleep we visited Chania and, in particular the Venizelos graves. Venizelos the younger I had encountered in 1946. It was a great pleasure to travel to the Akrotiri monasteries of Agia Triada (Holy Trinity), St. John the Hermit and our Lady of the Angels, being entertained to raki and Turkish delight at Agia Triada.

The next day we drove to Paleochora on the south-west coast. We stopped en route at Kandanos, a reborn village which had been destroyed by the Germans because of the killing of 25 soldiers by the Partisans during the occupation of 1941-45.

We visited, too, the Orthodox academy of Kolymbari just beyond Maleme Airfield where the German gliders landed in 1941 and where I landed amongst their wreckage in 1946. The Orthodox monks were very kind to us.

We departed from Chania for Matala Bay, stopping for yoghurt and honey en route, and having lunch at the lovely old town of Rethymnon, which we explored, including the old mosque, on the way.

After the Eucharist celebrated by the Bishop, myself acting as warden, we swam and after a delightful picnic lunch arranged by Kath, we visited Phaestos and the lovely convent and school of Kaliviani. Phaestos was a great Cretan city of about 2000 B.C. and is still fascinating. In the distance can be seen the cave where Zeus was born.

Another day, we made a hazardous journey over atrocious roads to Kali Limenes, the Bay of Fair Havens where St. Paul's ship sought shelter on his way to Rome, and where he appointed Titus as Bishop of Crete. Kath and I had a delightful lunch with Bishop Ronald in the local taverna, and then we returned in the same hazardous fashion, calling at the well-nigh deserted monastery of Odigitrias where I met a monk 100 years old!

Eventually we departed for Iraklion, called after the God Hercules, stopping en route at the excavated ancient city of Gortys, probably visited by St. Paul and the seat of St. Titus, first Bishop of Crete. The laws of Crete are carried on the walls of Gortys and there are the remains of a beautiful Byzantine church. We stopped, too, at Agia Varvara which I remember so well from war service in 1946. On arrival in Iraklion, having established ourselves in the splendid Astoria Hotel, Kath and I walked to the harbour through the Venetian fortress and visited the beautiful Venetian Loggia. Here we met the charming Catholic priest, Papos Petrus, whom I was to meet on many subsequent occasions.

The next morning we visited the ancient city of Knossos, excavated by Sir Arthur Evans, full of memories to me of Professor Hutchinson, one of Sir Arthur's young men who first took me round Knossos. In the course of our tour we heard the dreadful news of the assassination attempt on the Holy Father, John Paul II, the previous day, 13th May. The Archaelogical Museum in Iraklion, which is always so crowded, I found hard work.

On the 15th we drove to Elounda of TV's 'Who Pays the Ferryman?' fame, and went by boat to Spinalonga, the deserted former leper island – in 1946 it was still a leper island! Thence to Agios Nikolaos – a small village in my time there, but now a large seaside town patronised mostly by the British. Not far away is the lovely village of Kritsa with its beautiful very old, delightfully frescoed church of Panagia Kera, Our Blessed Lady, literally "The All-holy Lady". We returned by way of Neapolis, the birthplace of Pope Alexander IV.

We went further east to the entrance point of Crete via the old monastery of Toplou, to Vai where I swam. On the return journey we stopped for drinks in the delightful port of Sitia.

On the Sunday after the Bishop's Eucharist in the hotel, Kath and I attended the Liturgy in the Cathedral of Agios Titos, Timothy the Archbishop of Crete presiding. Here we venerated the head of St. Titus, contained in a beautiful reliquary just presented to the cathedral by the Vatican.

Before we returned home we visited the Historical Museum, which was the British Vice-Consulate in my day, and I had the pleasure of meeting the curator. On a private visit to Knossos we visited the Villa Ariadne and met Professor Hugh Warren near the taverna, where I had visited Professor Hutchinson and his mother. He confirmed that Hutchinson was dead, and that the villa, built by Sir Arthur Evans and used as a German H.Q. during the war, had been sold – virtually given away – to an Italian.

It had been a splendid holiday reviving so many memories.

Chapter IX

Home Affairs, My Academic Work, Local Government

Home Affairs

On the death of her father in December 1964, Kath inherited Rock House, the old family home on Buxton Road, Bakewell. It had been built for her Noton ancestors in, I believe, 1763, for Richard. His son Richard Junior built the second part north of the first, and his son John Noton knocked the two cottages into one. With it was a smallholding, and they brewed their own beer. John was succeeded by William, Kath's great-grandfather, and his daughter Lois (1857-1955) who married Joseph Howard (1844-1923), son of Ann Howard, on 7th August 1871 in the Congregational Church on Buxton Road. Lois gave birth to ten children of whom John, Kath's father, was the third and, the property being leasehold, he bought the freehold from the Duke of Rutland in the Duke's sale of 1921; at the same time, he bought the sheep-wash and adjacent land at the packhorse bridge. The house was still tenanted by John Lomas, coal-dealer, and on his retiring to Buckinghamshire, the house was empty. The original Rock House had in fact been built by the Duke of Rutland for the first Richard Noton in compensation for the enclosure of the common land on Monyash Road, and had been let to him at a nominal rent.

After great deliberation, Kath, Christina and I decided to sell Woodlands in Baslow Road and to modernise and move into Rock House, which we did on 29th September 1969. The feeling that it was the family home weighed greatly in our thoughts. It is a charming old cottage with a quarter-acre garden, very different from the large four-storey Woodlands. Kath was a great homebuilder and made it into a lovely home.

In December 1969 Christina flew to Medellín, second city of Colombia, to take up a teaching post in the Faculty of Arts in the university there. The students went on strike in 1970, the Colombian government temporarily closed the university and Christina had to take refuge in teaching art to North American children in Medellín. I do not think that this was much to her taste and we were overjoyed when she arrived home on St. Andrew's Day, 30th November 1970.

I recollect that these events occurred during the three years that Britain worked on British Standard Time (B.S.T.) i.e. permanent summertime, but it was not judged to be a success, particularly by the Scots!

My Academic Work

In 1966 Doctor George Tolley arrived from the Royal Air Force College, Cranwell, where he had been Senior Director of Studies under Air Vice-Marshal Lawson, to be the Principal of Sheffield City Polytechnic, the former College of Technology merged with the Training College for Teachers. Sheffield was amongst the first polytechnics to be created and it spread its wings wide to encompass many buildings, including Thornbridge Hall near Bakewell and Wentworth House, once the seat of Earl Fitzwilliam.

Whilst developing the new polytechnic, Doctor Tolley prepared for the Anglican priesthood and became a Non-Stipendiary Minister and later a Canon of Sheffield Cathedral.

His tremendous intelligence, wide vision and powers of organisation and administration were quickly felt to the benefit of both students and staff, in all of whom he took a deep personal interest. And he was strongly supported by his charming wife Joan.

I was transferred from the Department of Mechanical and Production Engineering to the new Department of Modern Studies, later the Department of History under the direction of another man of wide vision, John Salt, who had formerly lectured at Thornbridge Hall in the training of teachers. John appointed me as Treasurer and Administrator of the Department, and Secretary of the Examinations Board for the Honours Degree in Modern Studies. The principal lecturer in charge of this degree course was Michael Le Gillou who eventually joined the inspectorate, assisted by Doctor Geoffrey Taylor who, after working in Australia, became a master at Eton College, and Paul Nunn of great mountaineering fame who eventually tragically lost his life on K2 in the Himalayas. All these gave me tremendous encouragement, for I was a non-graduate, and I am deeply indebted to them. The degree embodied for the students an extramural project at the end of the second year, and I was appointed as the Extramural Project Organiser which involved hard delicate work in placing the students for a six-week extramural experience on which they were assessed. In the course of this work, I met many very interesting people in industry, and I was promoted to senior lecturer, for which I was most grateful.

Another of my colleagues whom I must mention was John Tyme who strove so hard to prevent the desecration of the countryside by motorways and the like. He did this at great personal cost. I am proud of him and he was taken to heart by my wife Kath and daughter Christina. John had been involved in the consequences of the blowing-up of the King David Hotel in Jerusalem by terrorists during his war service in Palestine.

At polytechnic level I became chairman of the staff association, having previously been treasurer, and so I was on friendly terms with so many members of staff. Many political jibes were made by the press against the polytechnics, but from my experience they were staffed by honourable, hardworking and dedicated men and women, academic and non-academic.

Shortly after the arrival of Doctor George Tolley, I was appointed to give history lectures to the annual England seminar of the staff members of the German iron and steel industry, and this widened to include tours of Eyam, Chatsworth, Haddon Hall and Bakewell, and to pot-holing and rock-climbing in the Castleton area, and in due time to a visit to the breweries. It involved civic dinners given by the Lord Mayor and the Master Cutler. All in all, I gained tremendous experience from these activities and made many lasting German friendships. On my retirement in 1980 the students took me to the German embassy, where I was afforded the greatest of hospitality. It resulted, too, in Manfred Rommel, the Bürgermeister of Stuttgart sending me a signed photograph of his famous father, Field Marshal Erwin Rommel of Afrika Korps fame. In 1958 I had been made an honorary member of the Heidelberg Branch of the Afrika Korps Association. These seminars lasted a month and I look back on them as being amongst my greatest achievements in my academic life.

In time the subjects of my lectures became predominantly communication, musical appreciation, military history and defence studies. I became a 'War and Peace' man! I am proud that all of the lectures succeeded in holding my students' attention. The musical lectures certainly bore fruit and I put all the composers in their historical context. In military history and defence studies I was able to draw on my own experiences and knowledge of the armed services.

At the request of the University of Sheffield I was appointed to the university's Military Education Committee as the polytechnic representative. On this committee

I served for 30 years, and for some 20 years represented the University at the Council of Military Education Committees of the Universities of the United Kingdom.

For a year I was seconded to the Department for Student Services under my friend Jim Robotham, an ex-Chindit, to find places for sandwich course students, and I made full use of my defence contacts to provide excellent experience for the students.

After my retirement in 1980, I continued to give lectures on military history for some three years on an expenses-paid basis. It is a great delight to me that so many of my students still remember and keep in touch with me over 30 years after my retirement.

And I am proud that the polytechnic is now the Sheffield Hallam University, largely through the inspiration of Canon George Tolley.

I must express my gratitude and admiration not only to him, but also to Douglas Thacker, and Air Marshal Sir John Rowlands G.C. who after his retirement from the R.A.F. as Head of Maintenance Command had been appointed as Assistant Principal at the polytechnic. Sir John, a very brave man, had been awarded the George Cross for bomb disposal work; I am proud of these existing friendships.

Local Government

In May 1972 I was elected to the Bakewell Urban District Council, of which my father-in-law John Howard had been chairman during part of the war. The U.D.C. had only one year's life left because in 1973 the entire local government of the country was being reformed. In May 1973, I was elected to the new West Derbyshire District Council, which took over the duties of Bakewell U.D.C., Bakewell Rural District Council, Matlock Urban District Council, Wirksworth Urban District Council, Ashbourne Urban District Council and Ashbourne Rural District Council, being based on the area of the Electoral Division of West Derbyshire. I put up as an independent and came second in the poll. At the same time I was elected to the new Bakewell Town Council which rejoiced in having a mayor!

We independents formed the biggest group in the W.D.D.C., largely thanks to the influence of Terry Wray M.B.E. whom I later succeeded as leader of the group. We were gentlemanly to the point of saintliness. When we appointed a chairman, we gave the vice-chairmanship to the Conservative group. We allowed them, also, to have a few chairmanships of committees where we took the vice-chairmanships. It all worked very well. My own metier was personnel and I became chairman of

The author's daughter, Christina, June 1995

the personnel sub-committee, a post which lasted throughout my council career. We had the great task of forming a W.D.D.C. staff. As chief executive we appointed Roy Bubbs whom I had taught for a year 1946/7, who had been clerk to the Bakewell Urban District Council. The other main posts we filled were director of administration: Graham Hodgkinson, town clerk at Glossop; treasurer: Alan Jackson, formerly treasurer of Bakewell R.D.C.; director of housing: Philip Bagshaw, Ashbourne U.D.C.; director of environmental services: Bert Maddocks, Matlock U.D.C.

At the end of 1973 I was appointed to the Peak Park Joint Planning Board on which I served until 1977. I had also been elected chairman of the West Derbyshire Conservation Committee, the work of which was very similar to that of the P.P.J.P.B. but on a much smaller scale. This post, too, I held throughout my council career.

I really did work hard in all my appointments, especially on the Peak Park Joint Planning Board, together with those giants Alderman Norman Gratton, Colonel Gerald Haythornthwaite, Mr Ivor Morton and Lord Vernon.

At the local government elections of 1977 I received an invitation to be sponsored by the Conservative group, which I accepted on the grounds that putting up as an independent is much harder, but I made it quite clear that I would never vote against my conscience or judgement and I was accepted on that basis. Again I came second in the polls, and did so again in 1980. In my role as chairman of personnel I helped many of the staff in the pursuit of qualifications, especially through Sheffield Polytechnic. My relations with councillors of all persuasions were excellent.

On the Bakewell Town Council I served some 20 years, being mayor of Bakewell 1978-9, the year of three Popes: Paul VI, John Paul I and John Paul II.

Christina married George Grima on 14th December 1978 during my mayoralty. George, an architect, was a collateral descendant of Pope Paul III, his mother being a Farnese. His father comes of a splendid Maltese family. His brother is Andrew Grima, the Queen's jeweller. The council dinner was held on 15th December: the theme was 'Christina' and I was delighted to spend the whole of my allowance on it!

We now came to the 1983 elections when I was absent leading a pilgrimage to the Holy Land. This was a great disadvantage because I was not helped very much by certain aspirants to the council and I failed by a few votes to be re-elected.

However, this was a blessing in disguise because it was all taking too much of my time, and was certainly not fair on my dear long-suffering wife Kath in this respect. That very same month of May I was delighted to be commissioned as deputy lieutenant for Derbyshire by my dear friend the Lord Lieutenant Colonel Peter Hilton, a triple M.C. and later to be knighted. Kath, Christina and I became great friends of his parents, Major-General and Mrs Richard Hilton. This appointment opened up new fields of endeavour for me.

Chapter X

Colonel G. (Gerry) J. Underwood, C.B.E., T.D., D.L.

Before the disbandment of 46th Signal Regiment T.A. and the raising of 38th Signal Regiment (V) I had secured the appointment of Gerry as Honorary Colonel of the new regiment, which he passed on to Colonel Richard Grimwood–Taylor a year later. Gerry was a bachelor living with his faithful house-keeper Annie in Shalden, near Alton in Hampshire. We had been friends since he recruited me in May 1938 and we had both attended Exercise 'External Triangle Three' in Germany during September 1966. We found each other to be good travelling companions. Gerry was basically a lonely man and it was indeed good of Kath to agree to my going on holiday with him for ten days or so, every year from 1968 until his death on 17th October 1973.

All his life, Gerry had been asthmatic with the result that he loved the power of his high-powered motorcars, latterly a Jaguar 420. And so it was that we set off for Austria in July 1968. At Dover, I met my old friend Captain Jack Jacques from wartime Italy, now Chief Customs & Excise Officer there, with the consequence that on the ferry, Gerry and I were invited to join the captain on the bridge. We sailed to Zeebrugge, and to our delight in our Bruges hotel 'Notre Dame' we were joined by Roland Borthwick, commanding 1st Divisional Signals in Germany.

By way of Aachen, Cologne, Bernkastel on the Mosel and Heidelberg we arrived at Salzburg, where we passed a very pleasant three days with delightful people. Thence we went to Saalbach via Bertchesgaden where we went by cable car very nearly to Hitler's Eagle's Nest with its superb views. On we continued to Velden where we visited Klagenfurt by lake steamer. Eventually we found our way to delightful Kitzbühel, which became a great favourite of ours. We loved to go to the bierkeller of the Hotel Goldener Greif to listen to the singing and zither-playing of the great Franz Karrer who became a good friend of ours. In the bierkeller, I made a point of addressing Gerry as Herr Burgomeister which brought us some great adulation.

We returned via Innsbruck and Oberammergau and the Rhine Valley where at Gurk we drank splendid wine, looking across to the famous Lorelei Rock. We continued to Ghent and Bruges where we went to lunch. A policeman found a parking space for and saluted Herr Burgomeister, and the waiter and waitress paid us particular attention and waved us off as a Burgomeister should be!

After arrival at the very early hour of 3.30 a.m. at Gerry's I had a good sleep, and after lunch collected dear Kath from her friends George and Sally Kim at Winchester. We spent the night with Gerry and returned to Bakewell. It had been a splendid holiday but it was good to be back home with Kath.

Kath and I supported Gerry as well as we could. Tom Wragg and I took him to the general meeting and annual reunion of the Royal Signals Association at Catterick Camp in June 1969, which he and we thoroughly enjoyed. He became a frequent guest at our home and was liked and respected by all grades of society in Bakewell.

On 21st July 1969, the day after Neil Armstrong and Buzz Aldrin landed on the moon, Gerry and I departed for Lake Garda. From Calais we drove through the World War I battlefields: St. Omer, Arras, St. Quentin, Bapaume, Le Sars where my father was so seriously wounded, over Vimy Ridge and through Gommecourt past numerous 1914-18 war cemeteries. We had lunch by the lakeside in Lucerne where, after one of the waitresses heard me calling Gerry "Herr Burgomeister", the entire staff turned out to wish us well "Auf wiedersehen, Herr Burgomeister!" They were delightful. Eventually we reached Torbole at the head of Lake Garda, where we had a great time for a few days. Unfortunately, Gerry ran over my right foot with his left front wheel whilst reversing. I was in great pain and the next morning attended the doctor's surgery, but it was closed because his son had just been killed on his motorcycle. I did not then worry about my foot, and it put itself right.

We returned home over the Brenner Pass into Austria and over the Arlberg Pass down to Lake Constance into Germany, through the Black Forest, into France, over the Rhine to Strasbourg, over the Vosges and back through the war-ravaged parts of France to Calais. Here I revisited scenes of the battle in 1940, which I found very hard, emotional and strange. And so to Dover and home.

Shortly afterwards, Gerry telephoned us with the sad news of the death of Brigadier R.J. Wilkins, who had been so splendid a secretary of the Derbyshire T.A.A.F. Association.

The Golden Jubilee of the Royal Corps of Signals occurred in June 1970, and

Gerry, Tom and I went to Salisbury Cathedral for the ceremonial parade and cathedral service, and thereafter to Blandford Camp for lunch.

This was the time when I was caring for the England seminar of the staff members of the German iron and steel industry, and we had staying with us for several weeks Horst Von Deusche who proved to be a charming house guest. Just after he left, I had the dreadful task of taking our dog Cindy, whom we had inherited from Denise Lloyd, to the vet to be put down. Gerry, who was staying with us, was most comforting to Kath and me.

Only a few days later, on 9th July, Colonel John Hunt of Holme Hall died. A fortnight earlier I had visited him with our German friends and I will never forget his words as we had a whisky together: "Leslie, this is no lasting city." Muriel Cockerton joined Kath and me at his funeral in Sheffield Cathedral.

Gerry and I motored back to Kitzbühel on 8th August 1970. The night before I had been having a drink with Harry Charlesworth, who had held a commission in the regiment, in the Wheatsheaf. His last words to me were: "Give my best wishes to Gerry Underwood". He was exhibiting his caravans at the Bakewell Show. During the night, probably in a state of coma due to diabetes, he was burned to death in his caravan, as I discovered on my return.

Gerry and I drove through the Ardennes, Bastogne, scene of the Battle of the Ardennes 1944/5, and Munich to Kitzbühel where we stayed at the Hotel Jagerwirt. We enjoyed the most delightful drives in the lovely country and enjoyed, too, our nightly visit to the Goldener Greif to listen to our friend Franz Karrer singing and playing his zither. We made many friends.

We returned via Zurich, St. Quentin and Bapaume.

It was always good to attend our Glossop and District Royal Signals reunion dinners with Gerry, usually in Bakewell, but thereafter in Glossop; and to attend the Sherwood Foresters' reunion dinner with many old friends in Chesterfield.

In July 1971 Gerry and I repeated the previous year's visit to Kitzbühel by the same routes. At the Hotel Jagerwirt we were given a great welcome, and an even greater welcome by Franz Karrer and other friends at the Goldener Greif. En route home we stayed at St. Quentin, and in the adjacent bistro we were well looked after by the barman who had been a prisoner of war and who remembered us from last year; we paid for no drinks!

In September 1971 Gerry, in the hope of mitigating the severity of his asthma, drove himself to Le Mont-Dore, a great health centre near Puy-de-Dôme not far from Clermont-Ferrand. Unfortunately, his health broke down and his doctor forbade him to drive home. On 11th September I received a telephone call from a charming Madame Massenet, who I believe was related to the composer, asking if I could fly out to drive Gerry home. Christina could have gone at once, but the medical staff decided it would be better if he stayed in the local town of Royat until I could fly out on the 17th. Woodcocks, the Sheffield travel agents, were wonderful. Christina and Kath drove me to Manchester Airport where I was met by their agent and flew by B.E.A. to Paris (Orly). Here again I was met and conducted across the airport to a small piston-engined plane which flew me to Clermont-Ferrand where I went by mini-bus to the Hotel Metropole in Royat. Here I found Gerry looking very sorry for himself and complaining of dysentery for the past five days. After I had commiserated with him, he asked me to pass his "breathing tablets", on which I read "Contre le Constipation". On my asking how long he had been taking these, he replied "Five days." I said, "Gerry, I think I can stop your dysentery. Your breathing tablets are laxatives!" He had got his tablets mixed up.

He very quickly recovered and was so well the next morning that he went back to driving his Jaguar!

We returned via Moulins, Nevers, up the valley of the Loire to Orleans, the scene of the burning of Ste. Joan of Arc where we stayed the night, and I attended Mass in its most beautiful cathedral. Thence we drove via Chartres, where we visited another exquisite cathedral, to Le Havre for the Southampton ferry, and Harfleur. On the night ferry we met Colonel and Mrs du Vivier, ex-Royal Signals. And so Gerry was safely returned home. For the remainder of his life he was so grateful for my going to his rescue.

On Christmas Eve he called with his sister, Ileene, so very different from Gerry but with all his charm. Between Kath, Christina, Ileene and me there was established a strong mutual love.

Through my visits to Gerry I had the great pleasure of becoming a friend of Sir Richard (Sam) and Lady Ursula Way, his neighbours. Sir Richard had been Permanent Under-Secretary of State at the War Office when John Profumo was War Minister. They were both very kind and interesting people.

In July 1972 Gerry and I flew to Munich to spend a few days in the lovely Austrian Tyrolean village of Saalbach. Gerry was far from well and his legs in particular were troubling him. But we hired a Volkswagen Beetle and on two evenings we drove through the Sturm Pass to Kitzbühel, where we were given a right royal welcome at the Goldener Greif by the proprietor Herr Harisch, Franz Karrer and the waitresses Dita and Rosemarie. Franz composed and sang a song in our honour to the tune of 'I Love To Go A-Wandering'.

On 5th October 1972, Austin Evitts and I travelled to London to the publication party given at the Anglo-Belgian Club in Belgrave Square of Airey Neave's book 'The Flames of Calais: A Soldier's Battle 1940' where we were the guests of Hodder and Stoughton Ltd, the publishers. We were received by Airey, who escaped from Colditz Castle after being taken prisoner at Calais in 1940. It was a most delightful occasion. The champagne flowed and I think that Austin and I drank more champagne than we had had water at Calais; nor did we suffer a hangover!

Amongst those we met at the party were: the Honourable Mrs MacDonald, Brigadier Nicholson's widow; General Sir Euan Miller who had commanded the 60th Rifles at Calais; Lt. Colonel Ellison-McCartney who commanded the Queen Victoria's Rifles; Lt. Colonel Reggie Goldney who commanded the Searchlight Regiment in which Airey served; Mr Hoskyns, the son of Lt. Colonel Chandos Hoskyns who commanded the London Rifle Brigade and received his death wound at Calais. Austin met many friends from his P.O.W. camp, and for me it was a particular pleasure to meet Airey's charming private secretary Miss Joy Robilliard.

It was a tremendous joy to meet again Lt. Commander Victor Brammall D.S.C. who had captained H.M.Y. Gulzar, and his second-in-command Lt. Commander Arthur Taylor. It was Victor who rescued me from Calais. I stayed in contact with Victor, who eventually died in sheltered accommodation at Newbury. He was a great man and deserved better of his country. I also became close to his son Paul, who most recently came to see me in Bakewell 75 years after his father saved my life.

During 1973 I visited Gerry on a few occasions and it was clear that his health was deteriorating. Nevertheless we flew to Munich on 22nd July to carry on to Kitzbühel, staying at the Hotel Maria Theresa. On only one occasion was Gerry fit for us to go to the Goldener Greif where again we received a tremendous welcome. Our courier in Kitzbühel was a retired Lt. Colonel Parachutist George Seal, who attended Gerry's funeral some three months later. The journey home was not easy. At Gatwick, Gerry was taken by van and wheelchair to the exit. Here, to the shame of our fellow countrymen, Gerry was helped by two Rhodesians and a girl from Borneo; they were splendid. On reaching Shalden, Gerry and I talked late into the night, and I returned home next day.

Again I visited him towards the end of September and it was quite clear that he was deteriorating, his legs in particular causing him trouble, but we spent an evening in a pleasant village pub near Jane Austen's home.

He paid his last visit to Kath and me at Rock House, walking in unceremoniously with his thumb stick, on his way to stay with Andrew Goodman for our annual reunion dinner at Glossop. That evening, 6th October 1973, Tom Wragg, Austin Evitts and I drove to Glossop where we rejoined Gerry. Although far from well he proposed the Loyal Toast and informed us all that he would be present at every reunion in the future; we knew that he meant "in spirit". He left reasonably early with Andrew Goodman and I was never to see him again. We met at Glossop in May 1939 and we parted there in 1973. I had my last telephone conversation with him the next night. A few days later he wrote to say that he was going into hospital. On the 15th he had his operation and the next morning received my last letter. On Wednesday 17th, Mrs Shelagh Jackson telephoned the very sad news of his death early that morning. I was very upset. That evening his sister Ileene telephoned me; she was very sweet and consoling. I resolved to keep my promise to Gerry to look after her to the best of my ability. At the weekend I drove down to The Old Forge to help Annie, Gerry's housekeeper, and Shelagh Jackson with the arrangements for his funeral. On Tuesday 23rd, I greeted the military and old friends at the church. Amongst the mourners were Brigadier Pat Hobson, Andrew Goodman, Robin Turner, Richard Pickford, Brigadiers Freddie Allen, Guise Tucker, McCormack and John Sturge representing the Signal Officer-in-Chief, and Lt. Colonel Charles Galbraith who brought a student Bandsman to sound the Last Post and Reveille. It fell to me to pronounce the Act of Homage.

It was a beautiful day and after the funeral, so well conducted by Hugh Crecy, I entertained old friends to whisky and tea in Gerry's beautiful drawing room.

Afterwards I revisited the grave to see the flowers and here I was joined by our dear friend Richard Grimwood-Taylor.

Thus passed my greatest friend: Recquiescat in Pace.

Chapter XI

Charitable Work, Matters Military

The European Atlantic Movement (T.E.A.M)

Considering the slaughter which the tribes of Europe have inflicted on themselves over thousands of years, but especially in the two World Wars of the 20th Century, it is no wonder that Winston Churchill in his great speech in Zurich in 1946, cried "Europe, Unite or Perish!" He converted me into a fervent European.

Shortly after the war, the Council of Europe was established in Strasbourg. Then, Germany and France decided to form the E.C.S.C., the European Coal and Steel Community as a means of ending the wars between Frank and Teton. They were joined by Italy and the Benelux countries. The U.K. was asked to join, but declined. Within a year, we became an associate member. The E.C.S.C. was so successful that the constituent nations decided to pool everything and formed the E.E.C., the European Economic Community, embraced by the Treaty of Rome. We were asked to join, but again declined, and formed the E.F.T.A., the European Free Trade Association, of some seven countries.

The E.E.C. flourished; the E.F.T.A. did not. Mr Harold MacMillan as Prime Minister tried to take us into the E.E.C. but the French President, Charles de Gaulle, realising how split the U.K. was over the matter, applied his veto. However, Mr Edward Heath as Prime Minister got us into the E.E.C. and this was ratified in a referendum held by Harold Wilson as Prime Minister. What a tragedy that we did not subscribe to the original Treaty of Rome!

In 1978 on Easter Monday, 27th March, I joined a party organised by T.E.A.M. at Victoria, London, and we set off by coach and ferry to the Hotel Bedford in Brussels. On the journey I established a lifelong friendship with Doctor John Ellis of the World Affairs Council, California, and Mr John Sewell, the chairman of

T.E.A.M. Our leader for this tour of the European institutions was Professor Alex McMinn of Liverpool. That night I was collected by my old friend Lt. Colonel Charles Galbraith of the N.A.T.O. staff and taken to his home for a delightful dinner with Jan and Captain Arthur Tallett of the United States Navy.

The next day we visited the H.Q. of N.A.T.O. and were well cared for by the U.K. ambassador to N.A.T.O., Sir John Killick, Air Marshal Sir Alistair Steadman and a splendid Italian nobleman, Signor Caracciolo of Neapolitan fame. With us on the tour was the Right Honourable John Taylor of the Ulster National Council who had been shot in the face by the I.R.A. A fine gentleman, he later rose to great heights in Ulster.

It was a tremendous pleasure to visit S.H.A.P.E., Supreme Headquarters Allied Powers in Europe, at Mons the next day. We were welcomed, briefed and cared for by Major General Harrod, and enjoyed the vin d'honneur and lunch in the officers' mess.

On the way back to Brussels we stopped at the field of Waterloo where I visited the Panorama and climbed the Monument. 62,000 soldiers had been slaughtered there on 18th June 1815. Choc sanglant! Des héros!

The next day was devoted to the H.Q. of the E.E.C. where we were given excellent lectures and briefings. After a very good lunch, I was asked to move the vote of thanks to the E.E.C. for their generosity. I quoted Churchill's cry at Zurich in 1946, and expressed our gratitude in Latin, the language of the last united Europe. I worked hard on that speech, which was well received, and I was gratified by the congratulations of the group. After further lectures at the E.E.C. next day, I found time to visit Le Musée Royaux des Beaux-Arts and the church of Notre Dame des Victoires.

On 1st April we continued to Strasbourg via Bastogne where we visited the American War Memorial to the 76,000 U.S. soldiers killed in the German Ardennes offensive, the Battle of the Bulge of December 1944 to February 1945.

The day after, Easter Sunday, most of the group accompanied me to the beautifully celebrated Easter Mass in the magnificent cathedral, the sermon being based on 'Le Christ crucifé et resuscité'. In the afternoon it was great to drive through the vineyards of Alsace to Riquewihr, a beautiful mountain wine village, returning to Strasbourg through Germany on the other side of the Rhine.

The next day was devoted to the Council of Europe H.Q. in Strasbourg. We were lectured on: 'The Council: its aims, function, and political role'; 'The European Convention on Human Rights'; and 'The Conservation of the Environment'. Our lectures continued the next morning and, after lunch, we continued our travels to Luxembourg.

Here we were briefed on the European Investment Bank and the European Parliament, which was to be established with a membership of 410 including 81 from the U.K. Thereafter I was able to receive Holy Communion in Luxembourg Cathedral. The next morning we were briefed on the European Court of Justice and after lunch proceeded to Bruges for our last evening on the continent. After dinner, I addressed the party and made presentations to Alex McMinn, his deputy Hilda Wright and Alan, our driver. And I so thoroughly enjoyed a drink of Trappist beer in the beautiful square thereafter.

Before leaving the next morning, I found time to visit Michelangelo's splendid Madonna and Child in the cathedral. It had been a wonderful study group and I had made good friends. And I was a stronger European!

In July 1979 I attended the international conference of T.E.A.M. at St. Edmund Hall, Oxford, lasting some six days. Here I met Doctor John Ellis and other friends from the 1978 tour. We had excellent lectures, amongst them: 'Can the West Survive?' by Lord Chalfont; 'Alternatives to International Violence' by Doctor Richard Mayne; 'The Changing Nature of the European Left' by Doctor Stephen Haseler; 'Educating Our Masters – the problems of Politicians' by Sir Geoffrey de Freitas; and 'The Threat from Without' by Admiral of the Fleet Lord Hill-Norton.

During the conference I was elected chairman of the group studying 'A Viable Defence Policy for a Democracy' with Derek Stubbings, a Derbyshire headmaster, as my rapporteur. He presented a splendid report at the end of the conference.

In the course of that week, we visited the Oxford colleges and Stratford-upon-Avon to see Donald Sinden in 'Othello'.

I had been greatly impressed by Admiral of the Fleet Lord Hill-Norton, whom some years afterwards I got to address the Sheffield Defence Studies Dining Club.

Ever since those days I have maintained my interest in the European Atlantic Movement and have subsequently joined the British Atlantic Council. The E.E.C. has now become the European Union with its own currency, the Euro, and it is my hope and prayer that the U.K. will not flag in its support of the E.U.

Inter-Church Travel Ltd

In May 1977, Kath and I had visited the Holy Land under the auspices of Inter-Church Travel Ltd, founded by Canon Arthur Peyton and a part of Thomas Cook Ltd, owned by the Midland Bank. We had greatly enjoyed the pilgrimage. And so it was that on my retirement in 1980 from the Sheffield City Polytechnic (thereafter Sheffield Hallam

University), I approached Inter-Church Travel. After an interview with the Honourable Geoffrey Browne, I was invited to become a leader of their pilgrimages and tours. The title was 'Spiritual Leader', and as a layman and member of a minority faith in the U.K. I felt a little troubled at accepting their invitation. However, I had no need to be. I cannot speak highly enough of the clergy: Church of England, Church in Wales, Church of Scotland, Methodists, Presbyterians, Baptists and Catholics with whom I have become close friends in Inter-Church. I was their only layman and one of the few Catholics.

Gournia, Crete, 9th October 1988

Up to 2002 I led 14 Holy Land pilgrimages, eight pilgrimages to Crete, two based on the Three Choirs Festival, two to Provence, one to Normandy, two to the Seven Churches of Asia, three to Malta, two to Cyprus, two to the Oberammergau Passion Play – 1990 and 2000 – and one to Croatia. On most occasions I have had ordained men and women in my flocks, but when I have not, I have undertaken the role of Chaplain and organised my own services. Not only have I made good friends amongst the Clergy, but also amongst my pilgrims who regularly keep in touch with me.

I must pay tribute to Canon Arthur Peyton, Canon Ronald Brownrigg who was Dean in Jerusalem for many years and has given well-nigh a life's service to Inter-Church, and the Reverend Peter Mallet, who after finishing as Chaplain General to the army succeeded Arthur Peyton. Many of the leaders have reached very high positions in their respective churches and all of them are blessed with splendid Christian ideals.

In 1983, on meeting my group of Holy Land pilgrims at Heathrow Airport I found amongst them Brigadier "Pip" Moran who had been second-in-command to Major-General Chris Man commanding 49 Division to which I provided the Signals element. "Pip" had been stationed in York and one might say that he was a direct descendent in military terms of Septimius Severus himself. He was one of the shining lights of the Duke of Wellington's regiment, a product of Stonyhurst and a very devout Catholic, and I am proud to number him amongst my friends.

On another occasion, at Eastertide in 1986, I left at 12 hours' notice to assume the leadership to the Holy Land of a group from Nottingham whose leader, the Reverend Richard More, had had to pull out owing to the illness of his mother. I was, so to speak, flung in at the deep end, but it was to prove one of the best pilgrimages I had led. It involved visiting the Caritas Hospital for Babies in Bethlehem, where I found that the Matron, the Reverend Sister Ipollita, was none other than the very beautiful nun whom Kath and I had met in the train from Rome to Ostia in 1978. A Swiss, she spoke beautiful English and explained that the hospital was necessary for babies born unfit in one way or another, owing to the habit amongst the Arabs of cousin marrying cousin. She was doing splendid work. Richard More is now a Canon and special adviser to the Bishop of Chelmsford and a great friend of mine.

In 1988 I was asked by Radio Sheffield at the instigation of Inter-Church to be one of the leaders of some 200 visiting the Holy Land in October. Amongst my 50 pilgrims were my great friends Canon George and Joan Tolley. The other 48 were mostly from the Barnsley and Wombwell districts, many of them Pentecostals, and I could not have wished for a better group. They were magnificent. We were under the Provost of Sheffield, my friend the Reverend Frank Curtis, who was chaplain to my Dunkirk Veterans Association in Sheffield. One of the other leaders, a Methodist, was the Reverend John Hudson, who remained a strong friend of mine. That, too, proved to be a memorable pilgrimage.

One of the most pleasant pilgrims I had was a delightful Jew married to a Christian, and in the synagogue at Capernaum I paid homage to him.

In the Holy Land I became very friendly with Joseph Aweidah and his family and staff who were the agents of Inter-Church. My favourite guide was Ishmael, a perfect gentleman, who unfortunately died after having his legs amputated owing to diabetes. I recollect that on one occasion, by the shores of the Dead Sea, the hottest spot on Earth, the coach had a puncture. The punctured tyre was replaced by the spare, to find that it was flat! Ishmael remarked "It is written, sir"! That taught me a great lesson in resignation! A new coach was sent out for us.

On more than one occasion when I returned home to my dear Kath, she remarked on the troubles in the Holy Land during my pilgrimages; but I knew very little about them. I got on equally with the Arab and Jew, especially the Russian Jews in Galilee. But the Arabs are so very welcoming and warm-hearted and they have so little. Every day I pray for peace with justice in the Holy Land.

My pilgrimages to Crete I found easy owing to my army experience there in 1946. Canon George and Joan Tolley went there with me again in 1993.

Never will I forget the Passion Plays of 1990 and 2000. They brought home so

Radio Sheffield group, Jerusalem, 18th October 1988

vividly the suffering and sacrifice of Our Lord and Saviour, Jesus Christ.

For Malta and Western Turkey I have developed a great affection, and I frequently return there in a private capacity through Saga, who took over Inter-Church Travel from Thomas Cook in 1988.

The annual conference of the Inter-Church Travel Leaders I have always thoroughly enjoyed. They are mostly not only spiritual leaders, but natural leaders, too. Particularly during the illness and death of my dear wife Kath, they gave me great support.

In 1998 I led a group consisting mostly of devout members of the Church of Scotland. In 1990, 1993 and 1997 I had the pleasure of leading the local Methodists there under the Reverend Albert Harbey and his wife, June. Albert and I always "hit it off" very well. He is a very devout Christian.

I must mention, too, the Reverend Doctor Jim Martin of the Church of Scotland, for so many years chairman of the Advisory Council of Inter-Church, who has been a strong pillar of support to me. A very ecumenically-minded man, he was a good friend of the late Cardinal Winning of Scotland.

The Most Venerable Order of The Hospital of Saint John of Jerusalem

In 1988 as a consequence of my many visits to Jerusalem I was asked by Colonel Sir Peter Hilton, Lord Lieutenant and President of the Derbyshire Council of the Order of St. John, to become the County Friend of the Eye Hospital of St. John of Jerusalem. I willingly accepted, and on my 1988 pilgrimage paid three visits to the hospital. I was delighted to find that the matron, Miss Pauline O'Donnel, had her home in Hope, Derbyshire, to which she planned to retire. She had served in the Queen Alexandra's Army Nursing Corps and was extremely competent. On my return from the splendid hospital, which exists for the faith and the service of mankind, I addressed the Derbyshire Council under the chairmanship of Mr Gilbert Hinckley and they agreed to covenant £1000 per year to the hospital, which they have done – and more – ever since. My visit had been worthwhile.

The hospitaller in London was Sir Stephen Miller, an eminent eye surgeon, and with the encouragement of Lady Miller I never failed to take something useful out to the hospital. I have paid eight visits to the hospital and I have attended the hospital symposium in London every year.

Unfortunately, Pauline O'Donnel contracted kidney disease and whilst on leave in Derbyshire had to be taken to the Royal Hallamshire Hospital in Sheffield where I visited her at Sir Stephen's behest, and where she died. Again at the request of Sir Stephen I represented him and the Order at her funeral in Pontefract in June 1990. She was a great woman and had founded the Sir Stephen Miller School for Nurses at the hospital. She was appointed a posthumous M.B.E. and I am glad to say that she knew it was on the way! At her funeral I met her sister, Jo Snell, who some four years later was to nurse my dear Kath devotedly in Newholme Hospital.

I have maintained the greatest interest in this splendid hospital in Jerusalem and propagated knowledge of it throughout Derbyshire.

On the recommendation of Sir Stephen I was invested as a Serving Brother of the Order and in 1999 I was invested as an Officer of the Order.

Gilbert Hinckley and I had the great pleasure of attending the farewell dinner to Sir Stephen at Fishmongers' Hall on his retirement in the fall of 1990, on the day that John Major succeeded Margaret Thatcher as Prime Minister. It was a magnificent occasion in that splendid hall with the orchestral section of the band of the Life Guards, amongst so many distinguished people. Queen Noor of Jordan, unable to attend, was represented by the Royal Jordanian Ambassador. After dinner, Gilbert inveigled me in going to Annabel's nightclub and that, indeed, was another experience.

The Derbyshire Council Meetings were occasionally attended by the Secretary General of the Order, and on two of these occasions Gilbert Hinckley very kindly had Colonel Sir Peter and Lady Hilton, others and me to dinner at his beautiful home. The late Patrick Drury-Lowe, a Knight of the Order, also very kindly had me to dinner at his home, Locko Park, when we were visited by the Lord Vestey, Lord Prior of the Order. Both Patrick and he had served in the Scots Guards. Lord Vestey's father, also Scots Guards, was killed in Italy on my birthday, 26th June 1944, in the fighting round Lake Trasimeno.

The annual symposium I have always found a tremendous pleasure to attend. Frequently members of staff from the hospital attend, and amongst the county representatives there are the most interesting people. The hospital is a direct descendant of that founded in Jerusalem when it fell to the Crusaders in July 1099.

The original Order, established by Pope Paschal II, continues in the Sovereign Order of the Knights of Malta. The British Order, the Most Venerable Order of the Hospital of St. John of Jerusalem, was re-established by Queen Victoria in 1882 and rapidly spread throughout the British Empire and Commonwealth.

The hospital has some 83 beds and carries out thousands of eye operations every year. It maintains a clinic in Gaza, and sends its outreach mobile clinics into the West Bank. It renders its services without regard to colour, class or creed and deserves the utmost support.

The Royal Signals Association

I joined the Royal Signals Association immediately after the War. The members of the unit, raised at Glossop in 1939, formed the Glossop & District Royal Signals Old Comrades Association, which was not a branch proper of the Royal Signals Association, but was affiliated to it and gave considerable financial support. Invariably the chairman of the association attended the O.C.A. dinners held annually in Bakewell until they changed to Glossop about 1970. Gerry Underwood remained president until his death in 1973.

At the annual general meeting of the R.S.A. in June 1972 I was elected vice-chairman of the central committee – that is, national vice-chairman. This appointment I held until 1984. I served under Major General David Price, Major General John Badcock and Major General Alastair Anderson. These were all splendid chairmen to whom the corps owed so much. John Badcock became Master of Signals. The secretary when I became vice-chairman was that wonderful man

Brigadier Pat Hobson D.S.O. Many felt that his decoration for action near Kohima in Burma should have been the V.C. He was succeeded by Lt. Colonel R.L. Murray, O.B.E., a brilliant administrator who was Secretary during most of my time.

My duties as vice-chairman entailed my going round the country to the annual dinners of the branches, spreading good cheer and commending them on their high state of morale. All of these branches used to attend the annual reunions and A.G.M. at Catterick Camp in June every year. They were great occasions and the various Royal Signal Regiments were generous to us in the extreme. The officers' and W.Os and sergeants' messes threw open their doors to us, and it was usually in the early hours of the morning that we got to bed. The camaraderie was magnificent.

On the Sunday morning there was held a splendid church parade followed by a march-past, the Master of Signals taking the salute. The honour of commanding the Royal Signals Association Contingent usually fell to me and invariably I had six generals under my command! Then would take place the A.G.M., followed by lunch, and demonstrations on the sports field involving the White Helmets, the motorcycle display team, and the Corps Parachutists.

In 1994, when the Signals left Catterick Garrison, these events were transferred to Blandford as the H.Q. of the corps.

My duties also involved attending the biannual meeting of the central committee. The November meeting always coincided with the laying of crosses in the Field of Remembrance outside Westminster Abbey, always attended by H.M. the Queen Mother, who stopped and spoke to many people.

Following the committee meeting we usually had lunch at the Royal Hospital, Chelsea, H.Q. of the Association, or at the Army and Navy Club in St. James's.

I had the pleasure of attending Her Majesty the Queen when she unveiled the Signals Golden Jubilee Memorial at Catterick Garrison in 1975. There were present, too, the great comedians Morecambe and Wise, who gave a splendid concert for the troops and received right royal treatment!

On my 62nd birthday, 26th June 1982, I had the pleasure, too, of being presented to our Colonel-in-Chief, H.R.H. the Princess Royal and of sitting with H.R.H. at lunch.

One of my greatest memories is of being the dinner guest of the Queen's Guard at St. James's Palace when the Royal Signals carried out public duties in 1972. My great friend Lt. Colonel Charles Galbraith and I were driven to the ambassador's entrance to the palace. It was a delightful occasion. I took snuff from a snuffbox made from one of the hooves of Marengo, Napoleon's charger at Waterloo.

Consequent on my vice-chairmanship I was appointed to the Corps Paintings and Silver Centre Pieces Committee. This met annually and we commissioned paintings of great events in the history of the corps, such as Pat Hobson's great bravery at Kohima, the Signals action at Pegasus Bridge on the eve of the invasion of Normandy, and the clandestine operations of the corps in the Falklands.

I was proud and privileged to do this work. Pat Hobson died a few years after retiring, and Ron Murray died on the golf course not long after his retirement. They were both great men.

The 1940 Dunkirk Veterans Association

On Sunday 5th November 1972 I commanded the massive parade of the 1940 Dunkirk Veterans Association from all over the north of England, gathered together by the Sheffield and District Branch for the dedication of their new standard in the cathedral in the presence of the national chairman, Major General Wade; the Lord Mayor and Lady Mayoress of Sheffield; the Master and Mistress Cutler; and the Mayors and Mayoresses of Barnsley, Doncaster and Rotherham. The service was conducted by the Provost, our Chaplain, the Reverend Ivan Neill. We marched from Somme Barracks to the cathedral, and after the service in the packed cathedral we marched back to Somme Barracks, past the Lord Mayor who took the salute by the town hall. I felt very proud, privileged and humble to command this parade of such splendid, selfless men who had endured so much warfare. Before the dismissal I complimented and congratulated all on their splendid turnout and bearing. Then we had delightful refreshments in the barracks. The driving force behind all this was the Honorary Secretary, Alwyn Ward, a most remarkable and artistic man, and an author. We became firm friends for the rest of his life and I then kept in touch with his widow, Norma.

This opened another chapter in my life. A year or so afterwards, the Sheffield and District Branch invited me to become their president, and so I remained until the demise of the association in June 2000. I am now president of the Sheffield and District Dunkirk Veterans, the National Association having finished.

My friends Major Tom Wragg and Colonel Richard Grimwood-Taylor joined my branch and on one occasion Richard took the salute at the annual parade and service with all his charm.

Every year until a few years ago we had a splendid parade and service in Sheffield Cathedral. Our chaplains were respectively Ivan Neill, who had been Chaplain-General to the Forces; Frank Curtis, the Provost; John Gladwyn, who became Bishop of Guildford; and lastly Michael Sadgrove, who had been Precentor of Coventry

At the Menin Gate in Ypres, Belgium, June 2000

Cathedral and then Dean of Durham. Of these splendid reverend gentlemen I cannot speak highly enough and I am sure that is the same for every member of the branch. They were not only great pastors but also great friends.

The Lords Lieutenant of South Yorkshire were all very good to us and almost invariably took the salute at our annual parades: Dr Robert Young, Colonel Sir Hugh Neill and the Earl of Scarborough. Of these we are all very proud.

There is a splendid spirit of comradeship in the D.V.A., and amongst its women's section to which my dear Kath belonged. The committees and officers were very dedicated. One of our chairmen was Don Ward who had the military medal. Following his retirement we had Albert Winter M.B.E.

Nearly every year the branch made a pilgrimage to Dunkirk and every year held a splendid annual dinner, once attended by Major General Carpenter as national chairman. My first pilgrimage with them was the last one in June 2000. The veterans from all over the world paraded in Dunkirk and were inspected by H.R.H. the Prince of Wales, the mayor of Dunkirk and high-ranking French officers. Then we marched past these famous people and in the afternoon attended a service in the military cemetery, which was taken by my dear friend Canon Christopher Samuels Q.H.C. of Chester, national Chaplain to the D.V.A., whose mother had been evacuated from Dunkirk as a military nurse. I had the great privilege and honour of laying the wreaths for the branch at Dunkirk and De Panne in Belgium. Here on a very wet day, the children had been given the day off school and as we marched through the town they lined the streets crying "thank you". And the mayor of De Panne entertained us all to wine in the town hall. Never will I forget the kindness of those French and Belgian people.

On the third day of the pilgrimage, before returning home, we journeyed down to Calais where I laid our wreath at the Royal Green Jackets 1940 War Memorial on the Western Mole; more of this later. Thence we journeyed to Ypres which deeply impressed me, for despite being battered to the ground in two World Wars, it has risen again in all its beauty. I visited the Cloth Hall containing the In Flanders Fields Museum, and the splendid Cathedral. My dear friend, Bernard Cotton, C.B.E., who was a parachutist, later Master Cutler of Sheffield and chairman of the North Eastern Development Corporation, a very remarkable and able man, unfortunately had a fall. Nevertheless we managed gradually and slowly to make our way to the Menin Gate for the service and sounding of the Last Post and Reveille. Instead of being on parade, we watched the parade, and that was a great experience.

Our numbers are falling, but still the spirit of Dunkirk lives on in our Sheffield and District Dunkirk Veterans.

Commmemorations Of Calais 1940 – The Royal Green Jackets

On the penultimate morning of our Dunkirk Pilgrimage in June 2000, the branch very kindly accompanied me to Calais where I laid our wreath on the Royal Green Jackets 1940 War Memorial. We had a march-past, and before laying the wreath I briefed the parade on the events of May 1940, when the Rifle Brigade, the 60th Rifles and the Queen Victoria's Rifles, together with the 3rd Royal Tank Regiment, 12 Wireless Section and about 1,000 Frenchmen, defended Calais to the last. Brigadier Claude Nicholson was given an hour to surrender. He spurned the offer, and four days of intense street fighting passed before the silence reigned over Calais which marked the end of a memorable resistance.

Only 42 survivors, of which I, naked and badly battered and bruised, was the last, were brought off by H.M.Y. Gulzar. The sacrifice of the combatants was not, however, in vain. Two German armoured divisions, the 1st and 10th Panzers, were prevented from turning against the British Expeditionary Force, who added another page to the glories of the Light Division. The time gained enabled the Gravelines water lines to be flooded and to be held by the French troops. Thus it was that the port of Dunkirk was kept open, as Churchill emphasised when he addressed a packed House of Commons on 4th June 1940.

Having laid the wreath, I led the Parade in reading the Lord's Prayer and the Act of Homage.

I found it overwhelmingly emotional and was deeply grateful when so many of our members said that they had found the occasion the most memorable of our pilgrimages. And I was delighted when a group of French ladies and gentlemen came to me and we discoursed in French about the matter. They were very charming people.

Through the kindness of Fred Breyer, honorary secretary of the Essex Branch of the K.R.R.C. (60th Rifles) Association, I was invited to join the 50th Anniversary of the Battle of Calais on Wednesday 23rd May 1990. I spent the previous night at Dover, and having breakfasted with His Honour Judge David Pitman, a trustee, and his charming wife Christina, I crossed on the ferry St. Christopher with Major General Alec Williams C.B., C.B.E., M.C., who had been Adjutant of the 2nd K.R.R.C. and escaped on the line of march with Major (later Major-General) Talbot, Brigadier Nicholson's Brigade Major whom I remember, and Lt. Miller Royal Signals. General Williams, suffering with arthritis, had an A.D.C. with him and I found them most charming. On the ferry, apart from the Royal Green Jackets, there were George and Arthur, Royal Signals, who had been part of the Line of Communications workers in Calais post office. They were both captured making their way to Dunkirk.

On arrival in Calais, Fred Breyer introduced himself and introduced me to Richard Frost, the very competent Hon. Secretary of the K.R.R.C. Association.

General Sir Peter Hudson, whom I already knew, introduced me to his wife Anne, daughter of the late Major Knollys commanding C. Company of the Rifle Brigade at Calais. I was able to describe some of the happenings to her and how and where her distinguished father had been taken prisoner.

At 1100 hours we assembled at the Royal Green Jackets Memorial on the Mole. We paraded at 1130 hours, I with the Queen Victoria's Rifles, under command of Tony Jabez-Smith. At 1152 hours General Sir Robert Pascoe and the French General Covet received the General Salute. Precisely at noon, H.R.H. the Duke of Gloucester received the Royal Salute and both British and French national anthems were played. H.R.H. then inspected the Parade and General Covet saluted each one of us individually. After a beautiful service and the laying of wreaths we marched past to tremendous clapping from the spectators. On parade were some 110 survivors of the battle. A guard of honour was provided by the Royal Green Jackets, the Royal Tank Regiment, the Royal Navy and French Marines; and berthed alongside the Mole was H.M.S. Alacrity.

I was delighted to have a conversation with Field Marshal the Lord Bramall, whom I had already met and had recently been installed as a Knight of the Garter.

We were then driven to the lovely town hall and entertained to champagne by the mayor, who made a speech of welcome in French, followed by the Duke of Gloucester who spoke in English; both were translated.

The waitresses in their beautiful Calaisienne costumes were the same lovely Calaisiennes who had been in attendance at the war memorial. Here in the town hall, I was introduced to ex-C.S.M. George Chapman of the Q.V.R., 85 years old, who had ordered me to hand over my rifle and to rest in the foxhole by the basin on 25th May 1940. And I met Sergeant David Redpath George L.R.B., a Chelsea Pensioner, who escaped with me on H.M.Y. Gulzar; and Mr Rolt, nephew of the gallant 2/Lieutenant A.P.R. Rolt of the London Rifle Brigade.

Thence I went with the officers of the 60th Rifles, the L.R.B. and the Q.V.Rs to a splendid luncheon at Le Channel, where I sat with "Beaker" Saunders and had the pleasure of meeting Lord Bill Deedes M.C. and discussing journalism with him.

After lunch we walked to La Place d'Armes for a massed band display by the Royal Green Jackets, the Royal Tank Regiment and the Light Infantry in the presence of H.R.H. etc. It was superb and all very emotional. Thence we were driven to the cemetery where I saw many of the graves including a sailor "known only to God". I think it might well have been that of the naval signaller who disappeared on the Thursday night of 23rd May 1940; or possibly that of our Signalman Brown of whom no trace had been found after the battle.

Having said goodbye to Fred and Hilda Breyer I found my own way to the R.F.A. "Sir Bedivere", where I had champagne with the R.G.J. Officers, the A.D.C. to General Williams, the Regimental Medical Officer and a Q.A. sister. The sunshine had been so brilliant that day that I had got sunstroke, and the R.M.O and the Q.A. sister advised me against dehydration. I said goodbye to Sir Peter and Lady Anne Hudson; F.M. the Lord Bramall; Major Hugh Bruce, late Royal Marines, and John Surtees, both of whom had been taken prisoner after fighting so valiantly; and a charming French colonel. And so back to the ferry whence from the stern I watched Calais fade away. On the ferry, apart from the splendid veterans and their families, I met Colonel and Mrs Goldsmith of the General Staff B.A.O.R.; he was a product of Ampleforth.

A glorious, memorable and poignant day. The next morning I watched the little ships leaving Dover for the Dunkirk anniversary and made my way home via the National Gallery. When I reached home I am not ashamed to write that I wept in Kath's arms. Kath told me that she still had the letter that I had written from Queen Alexandra's Hospital after my escape. And here it is – I found it after her death:

Letter written on Tuesday 28, May 1940

Sign. LWW 2586891

C. Ward
Queen Alexandra's Military Hospital
Millbank, S.W.1

My dear Kathleen,

By nothing short of a miracle I returned to England on Monday after a week of hellish experiences at Calais. Deo Gratias.

Just over a week ago 22 of us went to France, fully equipped in all things. Yesterday, three of us returned destitute of everything; I was naked except for a vest, pullover and blanket round me. It is a long story and I will tell some of it as briefly as possible.

Last week we arrived at Calais and were immediately bombed in the harbour. For a week we were bombed and shelled incessantly and the last three days we were in the lines with the infantry under machine gun fire, bombs and shells. A mere handful of English soldiers held out to the very last.

I will try to write things down in order, but it is hard to do so, Kath.

The Jerries started to attack Calais on Thursday night and that night I spent crouched under a tree to avoid the shells in Calais Park where our vehicles were stationed. Next morning we disabled all our vehicles in preparation for withdrawal and reorganised ourselves on the main dock where G.H.Q. was established. That night we spent on the Sand Ridges with Queen Victoria's Rifles – a splendid fighting regiment. On the Saturday we went through a terrific, hellish bombardment from aeroplanes, tanks, machine guns and snipers. I think my helmet stopped a machine gun bullet from an aeroplane. Jerry then dropped leaflets ordering us to surrender or suffer further. We then dug ourselves in round a lake to make a final stand and in doing this I dropped a very large stone on my foot. I never felt anything from this until I returned to England – I hadn't time – this is the cause of my brief stay in hospital. We kept watch round the lake throughout Saturday night and early Sunday morning, Jerry advanced on us. Under heavy fire we retreated to the French fort on the coast and from here some of us went on to the north pier. After a while the fort simply had to surrender and I saw our chaps running with hands raised on the Germans' orders. Poor fellows, they fought as long as they could!

Some of the men with us then threw their arms into the sea and went to give themselves up. Jerry then machine-gunned the pier but missed every one of us. I was then the only fellow left on the centre of the pier, another party being at the sea end and thinking it as impossible to escape, I decided to surrender. Having thrown my rifle, ammunitions and gas mask into the sea, I walked towards the jetty where Jerry was waiting. As I approached the pier end I deliberated with myself and at that moment two of our destroyers came into sight and began to shell Jerry. That second has perhaps altered my whole destiny for I decided then to risk getting to the sea end of the pier. As I ran from beam to beam beneath the pier trying to keep myself hidden I fell into the sea – high tide. Thank God I succeeded in grasping the pier beams when I came to the surface for it is very difficult to swim with heavy clothing and pack and bandolier on one's back! Finally I succeeded in reaching the party of 42 at the sea end of the pier and incidentally they thought I was German and had their weapons levelled on me. Since my clothes were wet through I discarded them and the others wrapped me in towels and greatcoat. And for many hours they clustered round me keeping me warm from the heat of their bodies. It was bitterly cold for everyone. One young officer hugged me like a mother for hours. I shall always remember these 42 men.

I must finish soon Kath, dear, but suffice it to say that after hanging on to the pier end for 12-14 hours we managed to signal with a torch to a naval boat and at 1.30am Monday morning were picked up while Jerry machine gunned the boat. Evidently, he never saw us for none of us were hit. If ever prayers were answered, dear, they were then! It is nothing less than a miracle that we are free and not prisoners or shot.

I was naked apart from a vest, pullover and blanket. All my money, personal possessions of high sentimental value including your photo and Gray's Elegy remain on Calais Pier head.

On arrival at Dover, went to Aldershot, telegraphed you, came to London hospital, foot X-rayed – O.K. – leave tomorrow for Saltburn.

3 out of 22 of our unit have come back! Pray that the others are alive and free. 2 I know are prisoners of war.

Hope to get leave soon.

Rifle Brigade, Tank Corps, and all fought to the bitter end and only 43 of the total of us have come back!

Must now close. Will tell more when I see you.

God bless you, darling,

Your loving friend,

Les xx

I paid another pilgrimage to Calais in May 1998, for the rededication of the Royal Green Jackets' War Memorial which had been removed to the Western Mole owing to the great alterations made to Calais harbour. I was taken over by my dear friends Fred and Hilda Breyer and Alan and Doreen Marchant. The Channel was like a mill pond! We stayed the night at the Hotel Tudor/Bristol.

At the Mole on the morning of 20th May I was warmly welcomed by Richard Frost, M.B.E., secretary of the K.R.R.C. Association; Major Ron Cassidy of the R.G.J. Museum, Colonel Ian McCausland, Regimental Secretary; George Boyden and Arthur Brown of II L. of C. Signals, whom I had met in 1990; and Dennis Stanniforth of Sheffield, a national serviceman of the 60th Rifles whom I had known for years, but not known our war connection! Through Richard Frost I had been made an honorary member of the K.R.R.C. Association, and later was made a discretionary member of the Royal Green Jackets Club in London.

After a beautiful service of rededication of the Royal Green Jackets' 1940 Memorial conducted by the Reverend R. Campbell Paget, an ex-R.G.J. officer, and the Very Reverend R.S. Wingfield Degby, Chaplain of the 1st Battalion the L.R.B. in 1940. Wreaths were laid by Lt. General Sir Christopher Wallace and Major General C.G.C. Vivyan, Colonels Commandant, and the mayor of Calais. The bands and bugles of the Light Division played and we marched past, 38 survivors of Calais first, followed by the association. Thereafter, I had a most delightful luncheon at the Hotel George V together with Campbell Paget, Lt. Colonel Michael Smith commanding the 4th (V) R.G.J. and his Training Major David Smith.

This was followed by a splendid musical programme and the Beating of the Retreat in La Place d'Armes, a bugler being on top of La Tour du Duc de Guise. I had the pleasure of speaking with F.M. the Lord Bramall K.G., General Sir Christopher Wallace and Brigadier Davies-Scourfield who had fought so valiantly in the battle. Thereafter we visited the Calais War Cemetery where I walked round the 1940 Graves. And so we returned to England and after staying the night with Fred and Hilda Breyer, who had been so kind to me, I returned home. As in 1990 it had been a very emotional occasion.

I am very proud of my strong association with the Royal Green Jackets.

Chapter XII

More Matters Military, My Honorary Degree

After the summer meeting of the University of Sheffield M.E.C. in 1977, I was approached by the University Registrar, Doctor Alexander Currie, O.B.E. and asked if I would accept nomination as the honorary colonel of the O.T.C. in succession to Colonel (Tim) C.E. Eley, who was approaching retirement, and had strongly recommended me to be his successor. I felt very proud to assent, for I had already through my membership of the M.E.C. formed a very high opinion of the O.T.C. Tim was the chairman of the M.E.C. when I joined in 1970 and had been succeeded by Professor Frank Benson, O.B.E., D.L. In December I was gazetted as honorary colonel, during the command of Lt. Colonel J.J. Quinnell who had succeeded Lt. Colonel Peter Bastock. I immediately went to H.Q. North East District in York to pay my respects to Major General Henry Woods, the G.O.C., whom I already knew, and we established a good relationship in the matter of my honorary colonelcy. I was the fourth honorary colonel in the succession of Colonel Sir Francis Stephenson; Doctor J.M. Whittaker, the University Vice-Chancellor; and Colonel C.E. Eley.

At a small dinner party, including Brigadier Anne Field, director of the Women's Royal Army Corps, the members of the M.E.C. and Officers of the Contingent, I was proud to speak very highly indeed of Tim, a great soldier, who had lost a leg shortly after D-Day in the invasion of Normandy. I was very fond, too, of his wife Kathleen. Poor Tim, who retired to the South Coast, barely survived his retirement by a year.

I took the duties and responsibilities of being honorary colonel very seriously indeed, and regarded it as my task to help the C.O. as much as possible without getting in the way! I made it my duty to get to know all the officers, W.Os, N.C.Os and cadets as well as I could, and I retain vivid memories of them all. With the chairman of the M.E.C., Professor Frank Benson, I established a particularly warm relationship which lasts until this day.

In 1978 John Quinnell was succeeded by Lt. Colonel John D. Ransom, a Royal Engineer like his two predecessors. That year, the Contingent held annual camp at Sennybridge, near Brecon, and Nesscliffe Camp near Shrewsbury. At the Sennybridge Battle Camp, the emphasis was very much on street-fighting and jungle-fighting. At Shrewsbury we held the Visitors' Dinner Night.

On my return from visiting the Contingent in camp, I travelled to the regular commission board at Westbury, where I was greeted by the Commandant, Major-General A.P.W. MacLellan, M.B.E., late Coldstream Guards, with whom I had the pleasure of dining. I was looked after by Lt. Colonel Ian Leslie of The Black Watch, and I was deeply impressed by the board's procedures. In the course of my three-day visit, I drove the careers officer from York University round Erlstoke Park, where I had attended the tactical school some 30 years earlier, and now an open prison; to Tilshead with memories of Exercise Surprise Packet in 1951; and to Stonehenge. The R.C.B. is an excellent and most fair board.

It was always a tremendous pleasure to attend the social functions of the O.T.C. which were mostly held at Endcliffe Hall, built by the famous steelmaker John Brown, with an eye to a visit by Queen Victoria which never took place! But it is a great building and has variously been the H.Q. of The Hallamshires, The Yorkshire Volunteers, and a field hospital.

In 1979 the annual camp of the O.T.C. was held at Chickerell, Weymouth, which I knew of old from the camp of the Royal Signals. Here we had the pleasure of a visit from the G.O.C., Major General Henry Woods. I have vivid memories of being taken out together with Lt. Colonel Ransom by the Infantry Platoon to the Smugglers Inn near Swanwick.

Immediately after my return from camp, I convened a meeting at the polytechnic of Flight Lieutenant Jane Dellow of the R.A.F. Presentation Team; Doctor Bernard Kingston, director of the university's careers service; and Ted Mears, careers officer of the polytechnic, to make arrangements for a joint visit of the R.A.F. Presentation Team to the university and polytechnic in 1980. This was held in the Polytechnic Hall, following a splendid lunch with our assistant principal, Air Marshall Sir John Rowlands, G.C. The team was under the command of Group Captain Clive Evans, assisted by Flight Lieutenants David Cyster and Jane Dellow. It was a tremendous success. Clive Evans told me that we had cooperated more than any other institution. Clive later commanded the R.A.F. station at Port Stanley following the South Atlantic War, and James' brother John became Sir John Dellow, commissioner of the Metropolitan Police.

For long it had been the policy of the Military Education Committee and of

North-East District to appoint a regular officer as contingent commander of the O.T.C. But early in 1980 the T.A.V.R. Association brought great pressure to bear on Professor Frank Benson and me to appoint a Territorial on the relinquishment of command by Lt. Colonel John Ransom. H.Q. North East District supported the T.A.V.R. and so it was that the Military Education Committee approved the appointment of Lt. Colonel Peter Mortimer of the Yorkshire Volunteers. Having a Territorial commander rather than a regular meant that we were entitled to a Regular Training Major, and accordingly Major Peter Matthews, an officer of great potential, was appointed. The contingent was now organised on an infantry battalion basis. About this time, too, Major Andrew Whitamore was appointed a company commander in the contingent. Andrew had been a regular company commander in the King's Own Shropshire Light Infantry, and on leaving the regular army had been appointed Clerk to the Company of Cutlers in Hallamshire. In both the O.T.C. and the Cutlers Company he was a tremendous pillar of support and I can never thank him enough for all the help he gave me in so many ways. It was a great tragedy that he died so relatively young in 1993.

In 1980 the O.T.C. held its annual camp at Knook near Warminster. As always I was well entertained by the officers and cadets. I inspected the training which was going very well. On the morrow of the splendid contingent dinner, my honorary colonel's parade was held and I addressed the Contingent, emphasising how proud I was of each and every member.

Also during 1980 the Military Education Committee was involved with the founding of the Sheffield Defence Studies Dining Club, with a nominal membership of 100 – around one-third academic, one-third military and one-third civic. Professor Benson, John Ransom, Lt. Colonel Keith Levick, myself and others worked hard on this, with the consequence that the inaugural dinner was held at Endcliffe Hall on 30th October 1980, and addressed by General Sir Hugh Beech, Master-General of the Ordinance, on 'Politics and the Soldier' in the presence of the Lord Lieutenant, Doctor Gerard Young. It was a resounding success, and the club has flourished ever since.

In March 1981 I bade my official farewell to John Ransom at Somme Barracks and shortly afterwards welcomed the new commandant, Peter Mortimer, who had great enthusiasm. That year we held annual camp at Penally near Tenby in South Wales. I had a very bad back and found it difficult getting into and out of the car. Consequently, I slept on a hard mattress on a table for relief from the pain. It was good to find amongst the visitors my old friends Colonel Derek Webster, D.S.O., and Brigadier Norman Butler, Chief Signal Officer, United Kingdom Land Forces.

Resplendent in full uniform, 1981

Amongst the guests at dinner was Herr Oberleutnant Helmut Schwarzaugle, commanding a Panzer regiment training nearby at Castle Martin, with whom I was delighted; we 'clicked' at once. After dinner, the permanent staff and cadets put on a fantastic cabaret based on Tchaikovsky's 'Swan Lake'. So good was it that they went the next night to Castle Martin to put it on for the Panzers! That evening I presented the shooting trophy commissioned by my signals friend Major General A. John Woodrow, M.B.E. who had been a cadet at Sheffield in 1936-9. John had recently retired as G.O.C. Wales. The next morning, my honorary colonel's parade was held and I made my usual inspection and gave an address. Before leaving, I said goodbye to Cadet Sue Roystrow who was going to the School of Signals. Sue, now back in civil life, married to an O.T.C. Officer, has remained a firm friend of mine. Owing to my back, the journey home was painful, but I broke the journey at Hay on Wye, calling on Ivy Hill, Colin's widow.

A few days after my return home, I attended the Admiralty Interview Board at H.M.S. Sultan, Gosport. With the Royal Navy's prowess in the selection of officers I was deeply impressed. At dinner I had the pleasure of sitting with the commandant, Rear Admiral J. Richard Hill, whose book, 'The Royal Navy Today and Tomorrow' was published that autumn.

On 8th August, as vice chairman of the Territorial And Volunteer Reserve Association for the East Midlands, I went in full uniform to Whittington Barracks, Lichfield, to inspect the passing-out parade of the 3rd W.F.R., 1st & 2nd Mercians, and 2nd Wessex and Wessex Yeomanry. The band was provided by the Junior Musicians from Lichfield. I inspected and addressed the parade and took the march-past, escorted by Lt. Colonel Anthony (Tony) L.O. Jerram, M.B.E. commanding 3rd W.F.R. and a very good commander indeed. I met several parents and lunched very well in the officers' mess. I was delighted to meet for the first time Major Michael Browne, W.F.R., who later rose to the rank of brigadier as the Senior Officer in T.A.V.R.A.

I was now always involved as honorary colonel to the T.A.V.R. Association of Yorkshire and Humberside, and I usually went with Colonel Ben Roper, my good friend in Bakewell. At the first meeting, addressed by General Sir Frank Kitson, Inspector-General of the T.A., I was very well received and cared for very kindly by the Marquess of Normanby, the president.

1981 finished its course in appalling weather of snow and frost, affecting travel and causing the cancellation of meetings. O.T.C. annual camp was held at Otterburn in early July 1982 and so I combined my visit with my attendance at Catterick Garrison for the A.G.M. and reunion of the Royal Signals Association, where I was re-elected national vice-chairman. Redesdale Camp, not far from Otterburn, is sited in most beautiful border country. I arrived from Catterick in time for a late lunch with Peter Mortimer; Peter Matthews, the training major; Stanley Burrell, the Adjutant; Professor Frank & Mrs Kay Benson; and Brigadier & Mrs Brendon McGuinness. Brendon, a product of the Jesuit School of Mount St. Mary's at Barlborough, was the new second-in-command of North-East District and eventually became General Officer Commanding Wales.

After supper, I donned combat kit and went on the artillery ranges in darkness to watch a night exercise, the Platoon in Defence. The next morning I addressed the contingent before the day's training and again inspected their training on the ranges. I then drove through beautiful scenery to Jedbugh in Scotland to visit the beautiful abbey.

As usual I was well looked after by the regimental sergeant major, the permanent staff and the cadets.

Before leaving I was delighted to find that 2/Lieutenant Fiona Gibson, on gaining a regular commission, was going to the Royal School of Signals.

Shortly after my return, because Peter Mortimer was relinquishing command in order to take a new job on promotion in the probationary service in Norfolk, I joined Professor Frank Benson in Sheffield to interview prospective commanding officers for the O.T.C: Major Richard Elliott (Yorkshire Volunteers), a Sheffield solicitor, and Brevet Lieutenant Colonel George Barton, Royal Army Ordnance Corps of Thirsk. On advice from North East District it fell to George Barton, who had great enthusiasm for the T.A.V.R.A., but Richard Elliott succeeded him and eventually became honorary colonel.

In August it fell to me to visit again Penally Camp as vice-chairman T.A.V.R. Association for the East Midlands to inspect the Derbyshire Army Cadet Force. I was delighted to be informed by the camp commandant that quite the most pleasant visit they had ever had was the University of Sheffield O.T.C. the previous year.

On 19th August, as honorary colonel of the O.T.C. I attended the funeral at Great Longstone of Colonel Sir Francis Stephenson who was the O.T.C's first honorary colonel. The second honorary colonel, Doctor Whittaker, was there too, and it was very pleasant to converse with him. The third, dear Tim Eley, was now dead, and I was the fourth.

On 4th December, my honorary colonelcy was extended to 26th June 1985, my 65th birthday, which was the limit; at this extension I was greatly gratified.

My last official duty in 1982 was to attend the council of the T.A.V.R. Association at the Royal Hospital, Chelsea, addressed after lunch by the Rt. Honourable John

Nott, Secretary of State for Defence, who casually remarked that the best thing in parliament was to be a back-bencher, preferably in opposition! It was good to converse with the president of the council, Major-General Lord Michael Fitzalan-Howard, who clearly remembered me from previous meetings. He shed great credit on his famous family.

On 1st February 1983, at the age of 90, Captain Joe R. Clarke, late King's Own Yorkshire Light Infantry died. Joe, a retired lecturer in physics at the University of Sheffield, gave sterling support to the Military Education Committee and the O.T.C. which he joined about 1912. Severely wounded and left for dead in the 1915 Battle of Ypres, he was reported "killed in action". The university flag was flown at half-mast and his obituary printed in the Sheffield Telegraph. But Joe had survived and rewrote his obituary. His head wound had received splendid surgical attention and a silver plate had been inserted. He left his skull to the university! To me he was always very kind, and he knew of my father, also a KOYLI Company Commander.

The constitution of the Military Education Committee was being altered early in the year, and at the request of the committee I visited the vice-chancellor, Professor Geoffrey Sims, to plead for the retention of Professor Frank Benson as chairman for a fourth year. Geoffrey received me most kindly and acceded to my request.

The 1983 annual camp was held at Barry Budden, north of Dundee. On 7th July, I arrived by train in time to meet Major-General "Dick" Gerrard-Wright, Director of Territorials, Volunteers & Cadets (D.T.V.C.) before his departure; a man who exuded leadership.

Lt. Colonel George Barton put on a pleasant private dinner in the evening for Colonel John Neale, Chairman of T.A.V.R.A., the Mistress Cutler and myself, amongst others. Next day I spent inspecting the training; the programme had to be altered owing to the sea fret and tides. That evening a splendid contingent dinner was held.

On the Saturday morning, following a church parade arranged by Lt. Colonel the Reverend Peter Bastock, a former C.O., I inspected my Honorary Colonel's Parade and before the march past I presented the Territorial Army Efficiency Medal to Staff Sergeant "Big Jim" Severn, a stalwart of the permanent staff.

En route home I visited the 38th Signal Regiment's cocktail party in Sheffield. What energy we had in those days!

On the glorious 12th August 1983, it fell to me to bid farewell to the O.T.C. training major, Major Peter Matthews, at a Contingent Dinner, and to welcome the new training major, Major David Higginbottom of the Parachute Regiment. Peter, a born leader, had been a very effective training major and he deserved to have reached greater heights in the army. David Higginbottom was a worthy replacement and we established a good rapport between ourselves.

Within a few days I went to London for a meeting of the T.A.V.R.A. Council, presided over by Lord Marshal Fitzalan-Howard and thence to St. James's Palace for the Cancer Research campaign conference, presided over by H.R.H. the Duke of Gloucester whose interest was so patent.

Through the T.A.V.R. I had established good relations with the East Midlands O.T.C., and in November I was collected by Cadet Andrew Gracias to give a lecture to the contingent on World War I.

In June of 1981, after three years as the vice-chairman of the Derbyshire committee of the T.A.V.R. Association for the East Midlands, I had been appointed chairman of the Derbyshire committee and vice-chairman of the association itself. My duties fell more or less into the last few years of my honorary colonelcy of the O.T.C.

One of my most pleasant duties was with the Lord Lieutenant to represent the association at a reception given by the chairman of Derbyshire County Council, on 16th September 1982, to commemorate the 75th anniversary of the Territorial Army. I responded to the chairman's welcome, paying particular tribute to B Squadron of the Derbyshire Yeomanry and C Company of the 5/6 Sherwood Foresters, both of which had been embodied in Bakewell in August 1914. The Yeomanry fought at Gallipoli and the Balkans; the Sherwood Foresters fought throughout the appalling slaughter on the Western Front.

In the association, in my time, we had Colonel Stephen Clark as secretary, and Brigadier Ian MacDonald as deputy, to be succeeded by Brigadier Peter Stevenson and Colonel Robin Drummond O.B.E. respectively. These were all brilliant administrators with tremendous military experience. The association meetings were held every six months or so, and were invariably addressed by such splendid generals as Sir Peter Hudson, Sir Michael Farndale, Sir Peter (later Lord) Inge, and Marshal of the R.A.F. Lord Cameron. Three of my subalterns rose to be chairmen of the Nottinghamshire Committee: Colonel Alan Hawksworth, Alan Ripley and Roger Merryweather. Alan Ripley who had commanded the East Midlands O.T.C. became honorary colonel thereof.

I greatly appreciated attending the council of T.A.V.R. Associations at the Royal Hospital, Chelsea, of which Major-General Lord Michael Fitzalan-Howard was President. These meetings enabled me to meet many old friends and to listen to statesmen like Sir John Nott and Lord Trefgarne.

My honorary colonelcy of the O.T.C. meant that I attended also the meetings of the T.A.V.R. Association for Yorkshire and Humberside with its wealth of members and speakers.

By June 1984 we had to put our mind to the appointment of the next commanding officer of the O.T.C. Professor Benson and I interviewed Major Richard Elliott of the Yorkshire Volunteers and were delighted to recommend him as being admirably suitable. That same day, 7th June, at the conclusion of the meeting of the Military Education Committee I moved a very cordial vote of thanks to Frank for his splendid service as chairman for some 12 years. I am indeed proud to number him amongst my best friends. Frank was to be succeeded by Professor George Clayton, a brilliant economist with a distinguished war record in the R.A.F.

In the same month, having had an operation on my right knee which made it impossible to wear my uniform, I went clad in dinner jacket to a dinner at the O.T.C. to bid farewell to Major Andrew Whittamore, company commander, and Major Stanley Burrows the quartermaster, and to address the officers and staff.

After attending the Chelsea meeting of the Council of T.A.V.R. Associations on 12th July I proceeded by train to Barnstaple to visit the O.T.C. in annual camp at Fremington. The next day I inspected the Contingent at my Honorary Colonel's Parade. That evening, the warrant officers and non-commissioned officers were entertained by the officers, and at midnight the Contingent embarked on a major exercise under Lt. Colonel George Barton.

On 29th October I went to a defence symposium at the R.A.F. College Cranwell as a representative of the University of Sheffield M.E.C. With me were Professor George Clayton; Professor Kenneth Royle, who had contributed so much to aircraft design during the war; Squadron Leader Colin Joyner commanding the Yorkshire Universities Air Squadron; and Doctor John Bennett. We listened to splendid lectures on 'The Threat', 'N.A.T.O. Strategy', 'The Way Forward' and 'Alternative Options for N.A.T.O.' We were taken round the fascinating college library, and I especially enjoyed the T.E. Lawrence (of Arabia) room. We had a splendid guest night with the R.A.F. staff band and its trumpeter. The next day there were various presentations on the R.A.F. College; Department of Air Warfare; Specialist Ground Training; the University Air Squadrons; Initial Officer Training; and the Cranwell Flying School. I felt very proud indeed of the R.A.F. The final day was marred by the assassination of Mrs Gandhi in India.

The O.T.C., two days later, put on a splendid dinner to bid farewell to Professor Frank Benson as chairman of the M.E.C.

In November at Chilwell, I attended my last meeting of the T.A.V.R. Association for the East Midlands, which was addressed by Air Marshal Gilbert, a product of the Yorkshire Universities Air Squadron. I felt very gratified when after dinner the chairman, Colonel Tom Forman-Hardy, paid a great tribute to me as vice-chairman of the East Midlands T.A.V.R. and chairman of its Derbyshire Committee – offices which I was soon to relinquish, although staying on as a member of Derbyshire.

Early in December I inspected, addressed and awarded cap badges to our first-year O.T.C. recruits. At Lady Manners School Speech Day, the speaker was the Duke of Devonshire, K.G., M.C., P.C., who told me that he was relinquishing the honorary colonelcy of the University of Manchester O.T.C. on his 65th birthday, 2nd January 1985, as I was to do for Sheffield on my 65th birthday, 26th June 1985.

On a very cold 20th March 1985, the O.T.C. dinner was held at Somme Barracks, when we dined out Lt. Colonel George Barton to whom I presented a decanter on behalf of the contingent. George had worked very hard with tremendous enthusiasm. He was succeeded by Lt. Colonel Richard J. Elliott, a Sheffield lawyer whose office was very close to Somme Barracks.

Two days later, on 22nd March, my dear friend Austin Evitts, who had commanded 12 Wireless Section at Calais in May 1940, died in Bakewell Cottage Hospital. He was a great, brave, Christian officer. The next day, I drove to Newark as the guest of honour of Lt. Colonel Nigel Cullen and the officers of the 3rd Battalion the Worcestershire and Sherwood Foresters Regiment, as a means of saying thank you to me for my efforts on their behalf.

On 6th June, the Military Education Committee meeting was held at R.A.F. Finningley where we were warmly received by the Yorkshire Universities Air Squadron distinguished commander, Squadron Leader Colin Joyner. The morning I spent in flight control. Following a very good R.A.F. luncheon, we held our meeting in the afternoon. When it was officially announced that I was to be succeeded as honorary colonel by Brigadier David Wilson, sometime military attaché in Moscow and now secretary of the Yorkshire and Humberside T.A.V.R. Association, both he and Professor George Clayton paid great compliments to me, which was very gratifying.

On Friday 21st, five days before my 65th birthday, I was collected and driven by Sergeant Clark to the O.T.C. for my farewell party. It was a wonderful evening – Colonel Derek and Mary Webster and Professor Frank and Kay Benson were there; Professor Clayton was away. Lt. Colonel Richard Elliott, in his address, spoke very kindly of me and presented me with a beautiful silver-topped inscribed crystal decanter which was later filled with whisky by the Adjutant. In my address I referred to Almighty God, Calais, Cassino and Crete and concluded with Isaiah Chapter 49, verse 15, having referred to my cadets, the splendid commanding officer I had left them with, the permanent staff and Clare and Mary, the civilian clerks. The contingent was at once my pride and my joy! I was seen off in grand style by the entire contingent at midnight. This was one of the most unforgettable occasions of my life! What splendid young people and permanent staff they were! The O.T.C. and the university reflected the greatest credit on each other.

At the request of the Lord Lieutenant for Derbyshire, on 11th July I attended a reception at County Hall Manchester, in aid of The Commonwealth Veterans Appeal made by H.R.H. the Duke of Edinburgh. I was received by Lord Michael Fitzalan-Howard, and presented by him to the Duke. It was a very pleasant occasion, its object being to raise money for the ex-service personnel of the old Commonwealth whose nations had achieved independence, but were not greatly interested in paying pensions to their ex-service personnel. Subsequently, at the request of the Lord Lieutenant I succeeded in raising a considerable sum of money in Derbyshire.

On 3rd September 1985, together with members of the Military Education Committee, we were driven a long journey of five hours to R.A.F. Coltishall, a very important Jaguar fighter station. Despite the ten hours of travel it was a most interesting and instructive visit and bolstered my very high opinion of the R.A.F.

A few weeks later the Sheffield Defence Studies Dining Club was addressed by General Sir Edward Burgess, the Deputy Supreme Commander Europe, greatly admired by the Rt. Honourable Dennis Healey, one of our great post-war Defence Secretaries.

The year ended on a very pleasant note for me when I heard on 9th December that the university's Senate and Council had agreed to confer the award of an honorary degree of Master of Arts on me.

At the A.G.M. of the Sheffield Defence Studies Dining Club held on 5th March 1986, I was unanimously elected chairman in succession to my dear friend Professor Frank Benson, and I held this post for some seven years. The first dinner at which I presided was held at Endcliffe Hall on 20th March, brilliantly addressed by Doctor William Wallace, deputy director at the Royal Institute of International Affairs, on European Defence Co-operation.

One of the greatest experiences of my life took place in the Firth Hall of the University of Sheffield on Friday 30th May 1986 when the Degree of Master of Arts Honoris Causa was conferred on me by the vice-chancellor, Professor Geoffrey Sims O.B.E., at the Higher Degree Congregation.

Kath and I took Dorothy Howard and Desmond Clifford-Lloyd with us. Kath and I were received by Doctor John Hawthorne, secretary of the Military Education Committee, and Miss Maureen Nelson. We were greeted by the vice-chancellor and Mrs Geoffrey Sims, and had sherry in the Registrar's office with our hosts Professor and Mrs Frank Benson.

The author receiving his honorary degree from the University of Sheffield, 30th May 1986

The procession consisted of the deputy marshal, Dr Robert Ashworth, myself and Dr Hawthorne as assistant marshal. After the vice-chancellor had declared the congregation open, I was led up to the platform where the public orator, Professor J.M. (Hamish) Ritchie, gave the oration about me and presented me for the degree. After much applause, the vice-chancellor very kindly admitted me! Then I took my seat next to the pro-vice-chancellor, Professor Galbraith, and near the Bishop of Hallam.

Then several other honorary degrees were conferred, including an M.Phil to Hugh Price of S.Anselm's School, whom I was delighted to congratulate on the platform. Thereafter, in his address, the vice-chancellor spoke very kindly of me. Thence we processed back to the Registrar's Office where I was congratulated by the Rektor of the Ruhr-Universität Bochum, Professor Dr Krut Ipsen, and the pro-chancellor, Mr Christopher Barker. Here, I was rejoined by dearest Kath and we went across to the upper rectory for supper; I met so many old friends. At our table we were joined by Professor Frank and Kay Benson; Professor Wilfred and Joan Saunders; Monsignor Moverley, Bishop of Hallam; and Mrs Pamela Sims. Kath, God bless her, was in great form.

Amongst my guests were Dr Marion Jepson; Canon George and Joan Tolley; Major Andrew Whitamore; Dorothy Howard; Desmond Lloyd; Dr Desmond and Marjorie Stoker; Ronald and Paivio Knighton; Squadron-Leader Colin Joyner; Lt. Colonel Richard Elliott; Miss K.L. Oglesby; Terry and Marion Thomas; Dr Gwyn Rowley; Professor Barry Dawson; Dr Terry & Elizabeth Rick; Dr and Mrs Giles Taylor; and Professor Robert Loynes.

John & Audrey Salt, Professor George Clayton (one of my sponsors), and Professor Tom and Monica Hanna could not attend.

It was a delightful party. From one and all Kath and I received nothing but the greatest kindness. Academically and professionally, it was the greatest night of my life.

Here is the oration:

Vice-Chancellor, Leslie William Wright has his roots here in this region, though on the other side of the hill by being born in Glossop. His was a generation fated to face the rigours of a Second Great War and it is not surprising therefore that by September 1939, as a 19-year-old lad, he had already enrolled in the Territorial Army Royal Signals Corps. In the following year he was with the British Expeditionary Force engaged in the defence of Calais and was captured by, but escaped from, the Tenth Panzer Division. With the Central Mediterranean Forces he experienced the Battle of Cassino, the gradual rolling back of the German army through Italy and the final defeat of Fascism. Vice-Chancellor, Leslie Wright treasures those wartime experiences, though one suspects that basically he is not a war-like man but rather simply a signaller, a grand communicator. By 1945 he was in Naples with the responsibility for the signals operation for the whole of southern Italy. This mass of communications he is said to have handled in a magisterial fashion, as befits a true Signals Master, and perhaps he was keener on his job by then because the signals he was receiving were heralds of the coming peace and not messages of continuing war. Peace indeed might have broken out sooner were it not for the fact that this brilliant young Signals Master is said to have received and lost top secret armistice terms from a certain quarter. There are many such legends about Leslie Wright still in circulation in Army circles. So he is also said to have been so overjoyed at the thought of peace that on V.J. night he drove a jeep straight down the hair-

raisingly steep steps for which the pedestrian passages of Naples are famous. He was, of course, only trying to raise his own hair, of which at that time he had more than he has now, and not anybody else's. There are other such tales from the daredevil past of Leslie Wright which are perhaps better kept for another occasion; the story behind a photograph still in existence of him dancing with a lifesize statue of Venus, the story of how he became a life-long member of the Friends of Abyssinia, and so on. Suffice it to say that this is the same man who returned from the wars to devote himself to education and service to the community. He joined the staff of the Sheffield College of Technology in 1949 and stayed with it after its merger to become Sheffield City Polytechnic, finally retiring as Senior Lecturer in the Department of History in 1980.

In the Polytechnic he generously put his very considerable administrative gifts at the disposal of staff and student alike, consistently insisting on what he graphically referred to as "the principle of simplicity" and regularly producing plans and procedures characterised by their clarity, respect for logic and meticulous detail. Here, indeed, was the military mind at its best, and the military personality too, for he always brought to every task a great zest and a deep-seated concern for the welfare of the troops - in this case the students. Much, though, as he loved them, students have to be examined and so it was he became the Examinations Officer. As such, Leslie Wright was customarily afforded the last word at the end of the deliberations of the Board and invariably he would wind matters up with an appropriate and pungent quotation. On one famous occasion even the gods seemed to approve his pertinent classical quotation for his words were accompanied by an enormous clap of thunder and a flash of lightning. Vice-Chancellor, I will not be surprised if something similar happens tonight.

The wisdom and infinite good sense of Leslie Wright were generously given to Bakewell Town Council, which he joined in 1973. He went on to become Mayor of Bakewell in 1978. Over the same period, he served on the West Derbyshire District Council and on the Peak Park Planning Board. It was a just and fitting reward for the respect in which he is generally held when he became Deputy Lieutenant of Derbyshire in 1983. The services of Leslie William Wright to the community at large have been great; he has also been a good friend to the University, of whose Military Education Committee he was for long a member. It was indeed a great source of pride to him when he became Honorary Colonel of the O.T.C.

Vice-Chancellor, I present to you Colonel Leslie William Wright, a man whom the Russian Guard at Lenin's tomb once mistook for Field Marshal Montgomery, but who is otherwise unmistakably a cultured man of peace, as eminently worthy to receive the degree of Master of Arts, honoris causa.

Amongst the great speakers during my tenure of office as chairman of the Defence Studies Dining Club were: the Rt. Hon. Michael Heseltine on the M.O.D. in retrospect, and I hit it off well with him; Field Marshal Sir John Stanisk on terrorism; General (later Field Marshal) Sir Martin Farndale on N.A.T.O.; Lord Mulley, sometime Secretary of State for Defence; His Excellency Baron Hermann von Richthofen, the German Ambassador, on European defence; and Admiral Sir John "Sandy" Woodward, Commander of the South Atlantic Task Force, on defence in general. These were all brilliant speakers and very charming guests. I cannot speak too highly of the delightful charm of the German ambassador, who shortly afterwards became ambassador to N.A.T.O; he is a supreme diplomat.

I felt very honoured when I was asked to give the Queen's Golden Jubilee Lecture on 'Calais, May 1940' on 24th October 2002. It was wonderful to be the guest of honour of my own club and I felt very gratified at the response my lecture received.

When I relinquished my honorary colonelcy of the O.T.C. I thought that was the end of firm military connections. But it was not. In 1988 I was appointed honorary colonel of the 5th (Derbyshire Cadet) Battalion of the Worcester and Sherwood Foresters Regiment and remained so until 1993 when at the age of 73 I handed over to Colonel Ken Hobbs.

As with the O.T.C. cadets, I found the army cadets to be splendid. They were brimming with enthusiasm, both girls and boys, and I greatly admired the permanent staff and the splendid A.C.F. Officers, Warrant Officers and N.C.O.s. As our reserve forces have been reduced the Army Cadet Force grows in importance and I regard them as the cream of our youth. During most of my honorary colonelcy, Colonel John Woodisse, an old friend of mine, was the commandant, and he eventually succeeded Ken Hobbs as honorary colonel. I feel very proud indeed of the A.C.F. movement, which shapes and develops the character and leadership potential of our young people.

Chapter XIII

Cancer Research U.K., North Derbyshire Community Health Council, 50th Anniversary of V.E. Day

Cancer Research U.K.

In October of 1978, when I was Mayor of Bakewell, I inaugurated at a meeting in the Rutland Arms Hotel, Bakewell of the Bakewell Local Committee of what is now known as Cancer Research U.K. Mrs Beryl Whitworth, a strong pillar of the Methodist Church in Bakewell, became my vice-chairman. In my time the committee raised some £200,000 at today's values in helping to eradicate the scourge of cancer.

From the East Midlands Organiser, Mrs Elizabeth Marlow, I received tremendous support. On a number of occasions I have met our patron, H.R.H. the Duke of Gloucester at our conference in London. H.R.H. is a most approachable man.

The committee still thrives and society owes them a great debt.

North Derbyshire Community Health Council

In 1980 I was appointed to the North Derbyshire CHC to represent the Royal British Legion and I remained on it for ten years. Its function was to represent the interests of the people in the matter of the National Health Service. For some two or three years I was vice-chairman to Mr Alan Jones, a retired headmaster and a splendid chairman. There was tremendous enthusiasm amongst the members who worked very hard. My main concern was care of the elderly and I felt that the geriatric services were very much the Cinderella of the services. Nonetheless, the

Council did great work at a minimum of cost. I was particularly glad to attend the meetings in Derby of the Family Practitioners' Committee which did great good.

50th Anniversary of V.E. Day

At the request of my friend Mr John Bather, H.M. Lord Lieutenant for Derbyshire, as Deputy Lieutenant I represented Derbyshire at the celebrations in London to commemorate V.E. Day 1945, on Sunday 7th May 1995.

A service of thanksgiving, reconciliation and hope was conducted in the magnificent Saint Paul's Cathedral. In my reserved seat under the Dome I sat next to a charming lady, Mrs Clare Russell, Deputy Lieutenant for Banffshire whose father had been page to King George VI at his coronation, and whose father-in-law had been the Second Sea Lord.

The cathedral was at its best, the service exquisite. Cardinal Basil Hume looked very distinguished and it was so good to see Field Marshals Lord Bramall and Sir Peter Inge, both of whom I spoke to later. The Queen and Queen Mother were so splendid, and there were 54 Heads of State present including Chancellor Helmut Kohl of Germany, Vice-President Al Gore of the U.S.A. and King Hussein of Jordan. Lord Bramall read the prologue, H.R.H. the Duke of Edinburgh read the lesson and Doctor George Carey, the Archbishop of Canterbury, preached.

After the service we were taken to Lancaster House where the string section of the band of the Royal Marines played most beautiful music. I had the pleasure of sitting with Mrs Clare Russell and Victor, Viscount Alanbrooke of Brookeborough, younger son of the wartime chief of staff Field Marshal Viscount Alanbrooke to whom we all owed so much. Lord Alanbrooke I found to be a most charming and modest man. After lunch I had a few words with F.M. the Lord Bramall K.G. whom I had last seen at Calais in 1990.

Thence we were taken by coach to the celebrations in Hyde Park. Here I was seated in the Royal Box with 60 or so heads of state; the Queen and the Royal Family; Lord Bramall; Sir Peter Inge; and General Wilkes, the Adjutant General. It was good to see together the Prince and Princess of Wales with the Princes William and Harry.

Sir Ian McKellen and Patricia Hodge gave readings invoking the spirit and bravery of wartime Britain. Young people from a theatre group performed a dance and song tribute to the fallen. All the heads of state were led by little girls to sign olive leaves and place flowers as symbols of peace and reconciliation. The ballet from 'Prince Igor' and the fourth movement of Beethoven's 9th Choral Symphony were performed.

After the performance I went to the veterans' tent for tea. Here I was presented by Nicholas Soames, grandson of Sir Winston Churchill, to H.R.H. the Prince Edward who enquired about my wartime service. Then I had a fairly long conversation with Nicholas Soames, recounting to him Churchill's meeting with Marshal Tito in Naples in 1944. I had the pleasure, too, of speaking with Michael Heseltine, Tony Blair, Paddy Ashdown, and a charming Russian naval veteran and his wife.

Tired, I wended my way to Marble Arch station, being photographed and smiled upon all the way down Park Lane. At Oxford Circus, a charming railway worker beamed on me, congratulated me on my medals and shook my hand.

Tired, I stayed the night at Olga's and returned home next day by way of Christina and George's to visit Kath in Newholme Hospital where, unfortunately, she had suffered a drawback in her recovery from her brain operation.

Chapter XIV

Kath, The Recent Years

Kath

Kath's robust health began to deteriorate a little in 1991 about the time of our golden wedding, which we celebrated at Christina's, and with a dinner at the Shakespeare Hotel in Stratford-upon-Avon. This was marred by the absence of Bob and Madge Wilkins, because that day Madge had been savaged by an Alsatian whilst collecting for her church. Nonetheless, Kath remained in good spirits and activity until the end of 1994.

Her birthday on 8th September 1994 we had celebrated in grand style by seeing 'Twelfth Night' at the Royal Shakespeare Theatre and holding her birthday dinner in the evening on the restaurant barge which plies down the river from Stratford-upon Avon through several locks and then returns. Bob and Madge joined us on the trip. It was absolutely delightful and Kath, in particular, enjoyed the spectacular floodlit views from the bows of the barge.

In the course of the next three months Kath tended to become unsteady on her feet and rather listless. To overcome this state for a few weeks she became a day patient at Newholme Hospital, and towards the end of the year Doctor Whittingham recommended that she should have a brain scan.

We went to Christina's for Christmastide, and Kath was very brave about everything and very appreciative of the great kindness we received from Christina and George, but nevertheless her condition deteriorated. We returned home on 29th December but owing to her rapidly worsening condition, I had to summon the doctor on New Year's Day 1995, and Kath was admitted to Newholme Hospital. Following a brain scan at Chesterfield Royal Hospital, Kath was transferred to the neurology department of Sheffield Royal Hallamshire Hospital, and on 27th March she underwent a serious operation by Mr Robert Battersby to relieve the pressure on her brain. The operation was a tremendous success in every way. Within a few days Kath was very nearly her normal bright self and I was able to take her out for drives and to visit old friends.

In early May at the request of the Lord Lieutenant I went to London to represent Derbyshire at the celebrations in Saint Paul's Cathedral and Hyde Park of the 50th anniversary of Victory in Europe. On my return I was distressed to find Kath was deteriorating. She was in fact the victim of the success of her operation; the pressure on her brain had been reduced too much. But she returned to her surgeon, Mr Battersby, who very simply increased the pressure and her condition consequently improved.

Unfortunately on 25th July 1995 she suffered a serious heart attack and was rushed to Chesterfield Royal Hospital, where she was given about two hours to live! But she proved them wrong and recovered. Her condition was so good that she attended at the request of Newholme Hospital a reception and meeting in the board room, where she was interviewed by an emissary from the Cabinet Office about conditions in the hospital, which later received the Prime Minister's commendation for efficiency. Thereafter her condition tended to fluctuate, and I myself had to go into hospital in January 1996. My younger brother Colin died on 28th June 1996, and together with Christina and George I went to his funeral in Oxfordshire. The day afterwards, Christina and I were summoned to return immediately to Newholme Hospital; Kath was very, very ill. She received the last rites of both the Anglican and Roman Churches and again improved somewhat. But it was clear that the end was nigh and about 0230 hours on 28th September she made her flight to Heaven. Fortunately, Christina and George were with me. We had been married 55 years!

The next few days kept us very busy in organising Kath's funeral and I cannot speak too highly of the loving help of Christina and George, and Kath's cousin Dorothy Howard. The Vicar, Edmund Urquhart, and Doctor Linda Ellsworth, were very helpful too.

Kath's funeral was held in the Parish Church at 1045 hours on the beautiful sunny morning of 3rd October 1996. Rosemary Cockerton and Dorothy Howard joined Christina, George and me at Rock House whence we followed the hearse to the church, which was full. Apart from immediate families and friends, there were present H.M. Lord Lieutenant John Bather; the Vice Lord-Lieutenant Martin Boissien the High Sheriff; Edward Wilkinson; Lady Winifred Hilton; Canon and Mrs George Tolley; a very strong representation from the University of Sheffield Military Education Committee; Colonel Richard Elliott representing the Officer Training

Corps; Colonel Ken Hobbs representing the Derbyshire Cadet Battalion of the Worcestershire and Sherwood Foresters Regiment and Richard Hunt representing the Hallamshire Regiment; and representatives from Probus, Cancer Research U.K., the Peacock Players (of which Kath was a founder-member). Newholme Hospital and so many more. Christina and I were deeply touched that Kath's goddaughter Philippa Lloyd, her niece Edwina Driscoll and her husband John, and Richard and Susan Hunt had travelled many miles to attend.

The funeral service was very beautiful, reverent and dignified, conducted by Edmund and Linda; the organ voluntaries were Elgar's Nimrod and Massenet's Intermezzo from Cavalleria Rusticana. And so to the

The author's wife, Kathleen Howard, circa 1943

cemetery where Kath is laid in a grave from which there is so beautiful a view. Donations to Riverside Ward, Newholme Hospital amounted to about £1,000.

Following the funeral we entertained the numerous mourners to food and drink at the Crispin Inn, Great Longstone. This was a good choice and the great friendship we received helped us very much in our grief.

All this reflected the greatest love and credit on dearest Kath who had done so much for so many, and been so loving and lovable a wife and mother. Recquiescat in Pace.

The Recent Years

Full well did I know the pain of loss after the death of Kath. But I was relieved that she was now free of the ills of this life and of all the burdens and restraints of being in hospital. As to myself it was now a matter of keeping as busy as possible.

Fortunately, Christina and George live only 90 miles away at Sherbourne, Warwickshire, so near to Stratford-upon-Avon, and I am a frequent visitor there. I cannot speak too highly of their kindness. My friends in Bakewell and Sheffield have been of great support to me, and I must mention in particular Kath's cousin Dorothy Howard and her friend Margaret Cadge.

In 1980 I assumed the office of secretary to the Campbell Blair Orphan Endowment Trust which helps orphaned children at Lady Manners School, and in 1993 I became chairman. The good work of the splendid trust kept me busy on many occasions.

Inter-Church Travel, too, decided to keep me busy. At their request in 1997 I led a pilgrimage to the Holy Land, including the Reverend Albert Harbey and many of his Methodist Congregation from Boston. In November I went on a Training Mission to Turkey to the Seven Churches of Asia, and in January 1998 to Malta. In 1998 I led a further pilgrimage to the Holy Land taking with me a large contingent from the Church of Scotland in the Motherwell district. That same year, I also led pilgrimages to Malta and in November to the Seven Churches of Asia (see Revelations Chapters 1 and 2). I led two more pilgrimages to Malta in 1999, and to the Oberammergau Passion Play in 2000. In 2001 I led two pilgrimages to Cyprus and in 2002 to Croatia, based at Makarska. On one of my Malta pilgrimages in 1998 it was a tremendous pleasure to have with me the Reverend Sam Davies who had been chaplain to the Gloucester Regiment in the Korean War; he was captured at the Battle of the Imjin River and had a dreadful time in the prisoner of war camp. His experiences are recounted in his book 'In Spite of Dungeons'. He and his dear wife Anne are great friends of mine. Sam and Anne joined me in a group I led to Menorca in April 2003. It was a delight to have them.

I was delighted in January 1997 when my Californian wartime friend Major Joe Waldron and his wife Trudy invited me to visit them in the spring. I flew from Heathrow to Los Angeles by Virgin Atlantic and I thoroughly enjoyed the 11-hour flight, the same that Kath and I had flown in 1979, over Scotland, Iceland, Greenland, the Canadian Great Lakes, the Grand Canyon and Las Vegas. At Los Angeles I was collected by Carlos, Joe's son-in-law, and taken to his home in Pasadena where I stayed the night with Debbie and Carlos and Jennifer and Scott. The next day, Joe and Trudy drove over to join us for lunch and then I returned with them to Air Force Village West, on March Airfield near to Riverside. The village is a retirement complex for officers from the U.S. Navy, Army and Air Corps and was founded by the great American airman, General Curtis Le May. Here I was given a delightful reception and dinner by Claire and Bob Ehms, who had suffered in the attack on

Pearl Harbour on 7th December 1941, and Claire's half-sister Lt. Colonel (Retired) Pauline Sutton of the U.S. Nursing Service. In August 1999 Pauline spent three days in Bakewell and was greatly liked by my friends.

The next day, Joe organised for me a public reception and dinner in the headquarters mess. We toasted the President and the Queen, and I addressed the assembled company in the best diplomatic form, and made many friends, especially Lt. General Jack Wright who had had a dreadful time as a prisoner of war of the Japanese, and thereafter rose to be a Divisional Commander and Director of Infantry of the U.S. Army. On retirement he became President of the Scouts Association of the U.S.A. I have an inscribed copy of his book: 'Captured on Corregidor: Diary of an American P.O.W. in World War II'. I have, too, the account of Yvonne de Ridder Files, who in her early 20s joined the Belgian Resistance, was betrayed and sentenced to death by hanging. Fortunately Antwerp was liberated by my old division, the 11th Armoured Division, three days before her execution was due. Yvonne's book is 'The Quest for Freedom: Belgian Resistance in World War II' and is inscribed "To Leslie Wright: One who shared the sacrifice of battle, the joys of victory, and savours the rewards of survival. It was delightful meeting you. Yvonne Files 1st April 1997".

I made many friends in Air Force Village West and I had the pleasure of returning there in 1998 and 2000. One great memory of 1998 is of being taken by General Jack Wright to the Ramona festival in Temecula. 'Ramona' is but a novel of the 19th Century but it did more to improve the plight of the Indians than any legislation. My visits to Joe and his friends have done me a great deal of good and I am grateful for and proud of the many friends I now have in Air Force Village West.

Epilogue

Notes for the address given to the Sheffield & District Defence Studies Dining Club in the form of The Queen's Golden Jubilee Lecture on Calais May 1940 by Colonel Leslie Wright, T.D. D.L. on 24th October 2002.

Mr Chairman, My Lord Lieutenant, Mr Vice-Chancellor Emeritus, Your Honours, Mr Chairman of the Sheffield & District Dunkirk Veterans, Ladies and Gentlemen,

I feel greatly honoured at being asked to give this address on the Eve of the Anniversary of the Battle of Agincourt, and of the Charge of the Light Brigade at Balaclava and the 50th anniversary of the Battle of El Alamein. But Agincourt, Balaclava and Alamein notwithstanding, I must confess that I feel rather like a retired Anglican vicar friend of mine who dreamed that he was giving a sermon, wakened up and found that he was!

However, here is the Prologue of my address:

<u>The Royal Americans</u>

On 4th June 1940, the Right Honourable Winston Churchill was describing to a packed House of Commons how the British First Army had been saved from annihilation at Dunkirk by a powerful German armoured force in close pursuit: "I have said this armoured scythe stroke almost reached Dunkirk – almost, but not quite. Boulogne and Calais were the scenes of desperate fighting. The Guards defended Boulogne for a while and were withdrawn by orders from this country.

The Rifle Brigade, the 60th Rifles, and the Queen Victoria's Rifles, with a battalion of British tanks and about 1000 Frenchmen, in all about 4000 strong, defended Calais to the last. The British Brigadier was given an hour to surrender. He spurned the offer, and four days of intense street fighting passed before the silence reigned over Calais which marked the end of a memorable resistance.

Only 30 survivors were brought off by the Navy, and we do not know the fate of their comrades. Their sacrifice was not, however, in vain. At least two armoured divisions which otherwise would have been turned against the British Expeditionary Force had to be sent for to overcome Calais. They have added another page to the glories of the Light Division. The time gained enabled the Gravelines water-lines to be flooded and to be held by the French troops. Thus it was that the port of Dunkirk was kept open."

At the ratification of the Treaty of Versailles in 1920 that great and gallant French soldier, Marshal Foch, said: "Ce n'est pas La Paix: c'est L'Armistice de Vingt Ans." "It is not Peace: it is Armistice for 20 years"!

Owing to the isolationism of the U.S.A., the ineptitude of the League of Nations, and the weakness of the Democracies he was proved right when Hitler invaded Poland on 1st September 1939, and we declared war, closely followed by France and our Dominions on 3rd September 1939.

Until April 1940, when Hitler invaded Norway and Denmark, there had been little land warfare. In April, my own regiment, 4 Corps Signals, moved south with the expectation of going to Norway. But Norway fell, before the regiment could get there.

On 10th May 1940, Winston Churchill succeeded the dying Neville Chamberlain as Prime Minister. He recorded that despite the gravity of the responsibility he had undertaken, he felt as though a great burden had been taken from his shoulders, for no-one could blame him, a voice crying in the wilderness for some years past, for the perilous situation of the country. That same day, the Germany Army in one of the most successful military operations of all time attacked in the West. Rotterdam was destroyed in one morning and the German Infantry Divisions powered through Holland and Belgium towards the Channel coast. Meanwhile, the elite Armoured or Panzer Divisions, under their great commanders Guderian, Von Kleist, Rommel, Schaal and others, swept through the heavily wooded hills of the Ardennes, supposedly impassable to tanks, crossed the River Meuse and made with all speed for the Channel ports of Boulogne, Calais and Dunkirk.

Clearly the Allied Armies and the British Expeditionary Force under the command of Lord Gort which had hurriedly been moved up into North France and Belgium were in mortal danger owing to the brilliance of the German attacks.

On Monday 20th May 1940, my own No. 12 Wireless Section was detached from N.W.E.F. Signals and drove through the night to Dover, where it was revealed to us by our Commander, Lt. Austin Evitts, who had come straight from the War Office and was still wearing service dress, that we were to establish a wireless net between Dover, Boulogne, Calais and Dunkirk, under command of the Royal Navy to provide communications for the evacuation of the B.E.F. of some 400,000 men! The sets were netted there and then, the control set went up into Dover Castle for Admiral Ramsay, and we sailed to Calais, receiving great cheers from soldiers coming from the opposite direction.

On arrival in Calais, where the docks were an inferno, our ship, the Autocarrier, was immediately bombed and had to leave at once without unloading our equipment, leaving us high and dry, in battle order only, on the docks. We marched to La Clinique, the H.Q. of the Senior Officer, Colonel Holland, had a meal of bully beef and hard biscuits and, despite the incessant bombing, slept for a few hours on the concrete floor.

In the course of the next two days an improvised brigade under the commend of Brigadier Claude Nicholson 16/17 Lancers, made up of those famous Regiments now known as the Royal Green Jackets, that is the Queen Victoria Rifles, 2nd Battalion the 60th Rifles, 1st Battalion the Rifle Brigade and the 3rd Royal Tank Regiment landed in appalling logistical circumstances. The Q.V.R., a T.A. Battalion, had at very short notice to be gathered from the cinemas, the N.A.A.F.I. and the like to be entrained for Dover, and were not allowed to bring their motorcycles or vehicles. Being a mobile battalion, they were armed largely with pistols, which are relatively useless weapons, and they were seriously depleted in personnel since they were trying to raise an additional battalion. Those two magnificent regular battalions the 2nd K.R.R.C. and 1st R.B. with their splendid relations between all ranks and magnificent battle drill were likewise embarked in a logistical confusion. The 3rd R.T.R. were split between two ships, personnel on one, tanks – with empty fuel tanks and weapons in mineral jelly – on another ship. If either had been sunk, the 3rd R.T.R. would have been useless. All these units were disastrously short of ammunition. The Q.V.R. was commanded by Lt. Colonel Ellison McCartney, Bursar of Queen Mary's College; the 60th Rifles by Lt. Colonel Euan Miller, later to be knighted as a Lt. General; the 2nd R.B. by Lt. Colonel Chandos Hoskyns who was killed; and the 3 R.T.R. by Lt. Colonel Keller.

Our wireless sets arrived on the Thursday afternoon, 23rd May, together with the 60th Rifles and the R.B. We immediately made contact with Dover, and established the Calais set in a copse near to a cemetery. The earlier part of that day I had spent my time in trying to police a horde of refugees who were gathering in the docks area. It was a pitiful sight. Men and women, old and young, children, babies at their mother's breasts, families with their entire belongings loaded on handcarts and perambulators – all of these crowded the dock area and hampered the military. And then the German bombers started the day's bombing and they could not distinguish between the refugees and the military.

It was good to be in a signals role again. Because we were using naval cipher there was attached to us a R.N. signaller and we were under orders not to use clear language in any circumstances.

Boulogne had now fallen; the road to Dunkirk was cut. Everything rested on the Calais terminal. Those of us who were not needed at the set returned into Calais to harbour in Le Parc St. Pierre, near the Hotel de Ville or town hall. That night all hell broke loose. We were attacked by the 1st Panzer Division, closely followed by the 10th Panzer Division, reinforced by tremendous corps artillery, and squadrons of dive-bombers in addition to each divisional squadron. The 3rd R.T.R. were using this as a harbour area, and they suffered many casualties. Still can I hear their calls for the M.O.

Poor Brigadier Nicholson, who had established his H.Q. in La Clinique too, received conflicting orders compared with which the order to the Light Brigade to charge at Balaclava was a pearl of wisdom! He was ordered to retake Boulogne; to head in the opposite direction to St. Omer; and to get 500,000 rations through to Dunkirk.

After that appalling night a temporary truce came about. Rightly or wrongly – wrongly I believe – we were to immobilise all vehicles except wireless and anti-aircraft ones. In the meantime, our set returned from its position to the west. Those manning it had suffered a tremendous bombardment with ill effects on the neighbouring graveyard. The naval signaller had left the set for purposes of nature, never to return. There was no means now of coding or decoding messages. We all made our way to Nicholson's H.Q. The Germans were now occupying a railway bridge, Pont Jourdain, with a complete field of fire down the Boulevarde to our H.Q. La Clinique. For a time I had the task of running between two sets through their field of fire, and it was decidedly unhealthy. At about the same time, not far from me, Lt. Airey Neave, later to escape from Colditz and to be assassinated in the House of Commons car park by the I.N.L.A., received a severe chest wound. He was with the remains of his Searchlight Battalion from the west of Calais.

At about 1500 hours, Nicholson, whose force was outnumbered 10-1 and outweaponed 100-1, decided to evacuate La Clinique and re-establish his H.Q. in the docks to which we retired in a splendidly controlled manner, with great speed. Nicholson now decided to leave a rear H.Q. here and to establish his main H.Q. in the massive citadel, built by that great military engineer Vauban, and he took with him our O.C. and the Calais terminal set. The rest of us became riflemen under the command of the Q.V.R. and of necessity we became swift learners.

Nicholson's defence of Calais rested on the outer perimeter running by and large round the 12 Bastions, also constructed by Vauban against the English. These were now falling and the defence rested on the inner perimeter running largely round the old town and the canal system.

I was allocated to a defence point near Bastion 2 adjacent to the Bassin des Chasses up the railway line, where I received nasty battle injuries to my arms and hands. We were ordered to wear our gas capes, too. But we were under the impression that we were to be evacuated at 0800 hours the next morning, which gave some hope in the unpleasant circumstances. Let me here pay tribute to the officers and all ranks of the rifle regiments. They were splendid; the way they volunteered for fighting patrols greatly impressed me. It was a cold night and as the hours passed it became clear that there was to be no evacuation. At about 0800 hours we were retired to the shambles of the Gare Maritime, under constant bombardment, where in the basement the cooks had prepared a glorious stew, the only real food I had in nearly seven days. There was there, too, a M.O. working on the wounded; he was tottering on his feet and of course was to be taken P.O.W. with his wounded, including Airey Neave.

At 1100 hours there was a ceasefire when André Gerschel, mayor of Calais, escorted by a German emissary, pleaded with Nicholson to surrender for the sake of Calais. The answer was no. Gerschel, a Jew, was later to die in a concentration camp. At 1500 hours, there was another ceasefire when a Lt. Hoffman entered the citadel under a white flag, demanding surrender. Nicholson wrote: "The answer is no. It is the British soldier's duty to fight, as it is the German's. If you want Calais, you must fight for it!"

The battle recommenced with great fury. I was now positioned on the western shore of the Bassin des Chasses when a biplane came and dropped leaflets on us, written in French and English, ordering us to lay down our arms and march to the northern end of the town to surrender. One of our Bren-gunners fired at the biplane which returned fire and hit my helmet in a part where it was thick, so the bullet ricocheted over my shoulder. There was now incessant bombing, shelling, machine gun and small arms fire, and in the course of the bombing whilst digging a foxhole with my helmet, a large boulder dropped on my right foot, crushing it. But I soon forgot about it. Some marines came over the skyline. The Germans had spies in the lighthouse and the town hall clock tower, and the marines suffered many casualties. The Germans were using tracer fire and Very signals as darkness descended. About midnight I said I could see the enemy mounting a machine gun in the roof of a factory. A kindly R.S.M. ordered me to hand my rifle to a Q.V.R. rifleman without one, and to have a rest in the foxhole. I took the last drink from my water bottle and went to sleep.

When I wakened up at sunrise, I found that four of us were left on our own. I had no rifle so I spent time extracting the cartridges from a Bren-gun magazine and putting them into rifle clips for the other three. For about 1½ hours we fought our private battle. Then a chance came to crawl beside a sewage pipe bordering the lake. We found an abandoned car, jumped in, and drove through the tunnel under Bastion 1 to the Bastion de l'Estran, defended by the L.R.B. Here a heavily pregnant French Jewess gave me a rifle and asked if I could get her and her husband to England! Later I saw her taken prisoner. With a few others I was ordered to take the wounded to a little boat which had entered the harbour by the Eastern jetty; the skipper was drunk, otherwise he would never have come in. This we did. The wounded included Major Hamilton-Russell, shortly to die. The little boat escaped, well below the Plimsoll Line.

Now I saw the German soldiers surround the Bastion de l'Estran. A white handkerchief went up on a rifle barrel, the gates were opened, and our soldiers, together with the pregnant French Jewess and her husband, emerged with their hands over their heads.

By now the enemy occupied the western jetty and pier, but the tide was low and so we had protection against their fire in the piles under the eastern pier. But as the tide rose, so did we, becoming sitting targets. Our small group now began to surrender. Now I was only 19, very impressionable, wanting to reach my 20th birthday, and I believed that they were shooting the prisoners, so I stuck it out on my own for about 45 minutes, when a tremendous sense of helplessness overcame me. I threw the bolt of my rifle one way into the sea and the rest the other way, and for some unknown reason my respirator, and proceeded to the mole to surrender to troops who were patently fresh. Just as I was about to shake hands with them, two destroyers came into action and I changed my mind. Without bothering to say auf wiedersehen, I did a quick about-turn and dashed spasmodically from pile to pile, and where part of the pier had been destroyed by mortar fire, I fell into the sea, and after that not a shot was fired at me. It is the only time in my life that I have swum in clothing and it is hard work. I succeeded in clambering back into the piles and despite my crushed foot, ran to the pier end, where to my joy, I saw about 40 men with rifles and pistols pointed. Good, I thought, they are giving me covering fire.

But they were not. The sea water had turned my khaki grey and I looked every inch a German death or glory boy. I was recognised by Driver Bond of my section just in time.

They took my clothing off me because I was suffering badly from exposure. Naked, I was kept warm by the others, one R.A. 2/Lt I vividly remember. As time went by, the tide fell and the Germans were stationed beneath us. When darkness fell, although the whole of Calais was aflame, we climbed a ladder into the port room, where a captain of marines had lit a fire, blacked out the windows, and made coffee. I was given the task with another of signalling out to sea "SOS we are British". After a while the captain ordered that I should be wrapped in a blanket and put under a table. At about 0200 hours on the morning of 27th May, I was roused by a cry "They are here!" Thinking it was the Germans, I felt distressed at being taken prisoner in a naked condition. But it was H.M.Y. Gulzar which had tied up at the jetty, been shot at and was making her escape. As we shouted and flashed torches the captain cried, "I cannot stop, I will turn round and you will have to jump for it." It was a steep jump. I was the last to jump, and found then that I could not walk. The boat was hit but none of us was hurt and many hours afterwards we reached Dover, 43 of us. I was carried off, the crew having given me trousers and a vest, the captain of marines shook each of us by the hand, and that night I finished up in Queen Alexandra's Military Hospital, Millbank, London.

Why were these splendid battalions sacrificed? There is no doubt that by engaging the attention of two crack Panzer divisions for the four days of the Flames of Calais, they had contributed greatly to the successful evacuation of some 340,000 British, French and Belgian troops under command of those great captains of war whose names became household: Alanbrooke, Alexander and Montgomery. "To create heroic legends, successful and heroic objectives are necessary, and what better one can there be than to sacrifice oneself so that others can escape?"

On that defeated but defiant army that escaped from Dunkirk were built the armies that, with the R.N., the R.A.F., the Merchant Navy and the people at home working a three-shift day, seven-day week, fought through all the vicissitudes of war in the Western Desert, Greece and Crete, North Africa, Sicily, the Italian Peninsula, Persia and Iraq, the jungles of Burma, and the invasion of Normandy. They were to be joined on 22nd June 1941 by the U.S.S.R., which suffered such appalling casualties, and by the U.S.A. with all its tremendous resources, after Pearl Harbour on 7th December 1941.

Eventually peace came to Europe on 8th May 1945, and in the Far East, following the dropping of the atomic bombs in Hiroshima and Nagasaki on 15th August 1945.

But I must tell you that the cost of the Second World War was more than 40 million killed, more than 25 million from the former Soviet Union, 6½ million in Germany, 6 million in Poland, and 2½ million in Japan. The British deaths were some 360,000, including 67,000 civilians.

But before I conclude, let me take you back into the citadel at Calais on the afternoon of Sunday 26th May. Lt. Austin Evitts, commanding 12 Wireless Section, led the first ten men out of the fortress of the citadel to surrender to the German 10th Panzer Division. The German Commander accused the British of having used "dum-dum" bullets, contrary to the laws and usages of war; but they turned out to be French bullets of poor quality. He also threatened to shoot 10 British soldiers for every German soldier killed if the Royal Navy did not stop their shelling. It was a bit difficult!

The survivors of the battle marched into captivity for five years. Early in the march, four prisoners escaped and managed to steal a boat in which they set sail for England, eventually being rescued by the Royal Navy. Two of them eventually became Major-General Williams and Major-General Talbot.

The late Airey Neave, after escaping and being recaptured, was eventually the first prisoner to escape from Colditz and reach England. After the war, Austin Evitts and I helped him with his book 'The Flames of Calais'. We attended the publication party in 1972 and drank more champagne than we had had water to drink during the battle! Here I met again Lt. Commander Victor Brammall, D.S.C. commander of H.M.Y. Gulzar, who rescued me and with whom I kept in contact for the remainder of his life. A heroic man, he died in sheltered accommodation in Hungerford.

In contrast to the treatment meted out to the prisoners in the citadel, let me tell you of my late friend John Penman, who as a 2nd Lieutenant commanding a platoon of the Argyll and Sutherland Highlanders held up the 7th Panzer Division at Saint Valery for 1½ hours a little after the Calais action. On being taken prisoner, he was hauled before the German commander, who spoke reasonably good English. This is what he said smilingly to John: "You are a very brave but very foolish young man, to try and hold up my division on your own!" His name was Erwin Rommel, that great and good German soldier who later commanded the Afrika Korps and as the Field Marshal commanding the German Forces in Western Europe was forced to commit suicide, following the attempted assassination of Hitler on 20th July 1944.

Here, ladies and gentlemen, I must conclude with the words of Airey Neave: "When next you cross the Channel to Calais and see the extended harbour, and the new buildings in Calais Nord and look at the exquisite beauty of La Place d'Armes where such bitter fighting took place, spare a thought, I pray you, for those who fought and died in the Flames of Calais."

Colonel Leslie W. Wright, aged 95,
laying the commemorative wreath at
the 75th anniversary of Calais, 2015

BELOW: The author with Paul Brammall (left), son of the captain of the H.M.Y Gulzar, the ship which rescued Leslie from Calais, at the latter's home in Bakewell, 5th October 2015